D1117618

GLOBAL CLIMATE CHANGE AND LIFE ON EARTH

Contributors

Dean Abrahamson, Hubert H. Humphrey Institute of Public Affairs, University of Minnesota, Minneapolis, Minnesota.

Jan Beyea, National Audubon Society, New York, New York.

James S. Clark, New York State Museum, Albany, New York.

Edward R. Cook, Tree-Ring Laboratory, Lamont-Doherty Geological Observatory, Palisades, New York.

Daniel J. Dudek, Environmental Defense Fund, New York, New York.

Paul R. Ehrlich, Bing Professor of Population Studies, Stanford University, Stanford, California.

John T. Hayes, Department of Geography and Planning, State University of New York, Albany, New York.

Richard A. Houghton, Woods Hole Research Center, Woods Hole, Massachusetts.

Laurence S. Kalkstein, Center for Climatic Research, University of Delaware, Delaware.

Stephen P. Leatherman, Laboratory for Coastal Research, University of Maryland, College Park, Maryland.

Robert T. Lester, National Audubon Society, New York, New York.

Janice Longstreth, Clement Associates, Fairfax, Virginia.

J. Peter Myers, National Audubon Society, New York, New York.

Robert L. Peters, World Wildlife Fund, Washington, D.C.

David W. Steadman, New York State Museum, Albany, New York.

Martin E. Sullivan, New York State Museum, Albany, New York.

Richard T. Wetherald, Geophysical Fluid Dynamics Laboratory/NDAA, Princeton University, Princeton, New Jersey.

Richard L. Wyman, Edmund Niles Huyck Preserve and Biological Research Station, Rensselaerville, New York.

Marilyn F. Walters-Wyman, Edmund Niles Huyck Preserve and Biological Research Station, Rensselaerville, New York.

GLOBAL CLIMATE CHANGE AND LIFE ON EARTH

RICHARD L. WYMAN

EDITOR

Foreword by PAUL R. EHRLICH

ROUTLEDGE, CHAPMAN AND HALL
NEW YORK LONDON

NORTHWEST MISSOURI STATE
UNIVERSITY LIBRARY
MARYVILLE, MO 64468

Published in 1991 by

Chapman and Hall
An imprint of Routledge, Chapman and Hall, Inc.
29 West 35 Street
New York, NY 10001

Published in Great Britain by

Chapman and Hall
2-6 Boundary Row
London SE1 8HN

Copyright © 1991 by Routledge, Chapman and Hall, Inc.
"Foreword: Facing up to Climate Change" Copyright 1991 by Paul R. Ehrlich.

Printed in the United States of America

All rights reserved. No part of this book may be reprinted or reproduced or utilized in any form
or by an electronic, mechanical or other means, now known or hereafter invented, including
photocopying and recording, or in any information storage or retrieval system, without
permission in writing from the publishers.

Library of Congress Cataloging in Publication Data

Global climate change and life on earth / edited by Richard L. Wyman.
    p. cm.
    Based on presentations at a conference held at the New York State
Museum, Albany, April 24–25, 1989.
    Includes bibliographical references and index.
    ISBN 0–412–02811–5. —ISBN 0–412–02821–2 pb
    1. Global temperature changes—Environmental aspects—Congresses.
2. Climatic changes—Environmental aspects—United States-
-Congresses. 3. Biological diversity conservation—United States-
-Congresses. 4. Global warming—Environmental aspects—Congresses.
5. Greenhouse effect. Atmospheric—Environmental aspects—United
States—Congresses. 6. Energy policy—United States—Congresses.
I. Wyman, Richard L.
QH545.T4G56 1991
574.5'222—dc20   90–8965
                                                     CIP

British Library Cataloguing in Publication Data
Global climate change and life on earth.
    1. Climate. Change. Effects. Humans
    I. Wyman, Richard L.
    551.6

ISBN 0-412-02811-5

574.5222
G56g

Does the educated citizen know he is only a cog in an ecological mechanism? That if he will work with that mechanism his mental wealth, and his material wealth, can expand indefinitely? But, that if he refuses to work with it, it will ultimately grind him to dust? If education does not teach us these things, then what is education for?

Aldo Leopold, *A Sand County Almanac*

Table of Contents

Foreword:
Facing up to Climate Change

Paul R. Ehrlich

Climates have always changed in response to changes in the Earth's orbit, variations in the tilt of its axis, volcanic activity, the drifting of continents, and so forth. It isn't climatic change itself that threatens humanity today, it is the potential *rate* of the change. Scientists are concerned that patterns of temperature and rainfall may be altered by global warming much too rapidly for human societies and especially for agricultural systems to adjust (Schneider 1989). They also worry that rising sea levels, caused by thermal expansion of the warmed ocean waters and the melting of glaciers and ice caps, will threaten the growing proportion of humanity that lives (and often farms) close to the oceans.

This concern is especially high because humanity is now having difficulty feeding 5.3 billion people (e.g. Brown 1989) and the population is now expanding by approximately 95 million each year. In 1990, the additional people to be fed are equivalent to the combined populations of Great Britain, Ireland, Iceland, Belgium, Denmark, Norway, Sweden, and Finland. Overpopulation and population growth are critical, not only in determining the possible effects of climate change, but also in altering climate (as several authors in this volume have noted).

It is probably best to think of population's role in terms of the standard (if oversimplified) $I = PAT$ equation (Ehrlich and Ehrlich 1990). The equation simply states that the impact (I) of a population on the environment results from the multiplicative relationship of the number of people in the population (P), their per-capita affluence (A) or consumption, and the environmental damage done by the technologies (T) employed to supply each unit of consumption.

The equation is oversimplified because, of course, the various factors are not independent of one another. For example, as P increases, T also normally increases, since the most accessible resources are consumed first, and so those supplied to each additional person must be mined from poorer ores, pumped from deeper deposits, transported further, and so on.

Nonetheless, $I = PAT$ tells us a great deal about environmental impacts,

Paul R. Ehrlich is Professor of Biological Sciences and Bing Professor of Population Studies at Stanford University. His latest book, coauthored with his wife Anne, is *The Population Explosion*, Simon and Schuster, New York, 1990.

including climate change. Per-capita consumption of commercial energy in a nation is a standard statistic that can be used as a surrogate for the AT portion of the equation for that nation. A great deal of what human beings do to destroy the environment involves the use of commercial energy—from bulldozing tropical forests and transporting beef grown on the resulting pastures to mining, manufacturing, factory farming, road building, condominium construction, and finding, extracting, transporting, and refining fossil fuels. The connection of energy use to climate change is obvious and direct because of the fossil-fuel contribution to the CO_2 and methane burdens of the atmosphere. Another important set of greenhouse gases, chloroflourocarbons (CFCs), are manufactured using commercial energy.

Considering per-capita use of commercial energy to equal AT, the impacts of various nations can be compared. For example, the United States, with 250 million people, uses about 280 GigaJoules (GJ) of commercial energy per capita annually, whereas India, with 835 million, uses 8 GJ (WRI 1988). The United States' impact is thus $250 \times 280 = 70{,}000$ and India's is $835 \times 8 = 6{,}680$; the United States' environmental impact is thus 70,000/6680 or over 10 times that of India, even though India's population is more than 3 times as large. In discussion of climate change, this disproportionate impact of rich countries is widely recognized in the oft-quoted fact that some 75% of the CO_2 injected into the atmosphere by fossil-fuel burning comes from rich countries.

One should not, on this basis, conclude that threats to the global environment are only based in rich nations. Poor nations play a significant role in the CO_2 and methane buildups through their destruction of tropical forests (rich nations, of course, play a substantial role in this destruction as well). Furthermore, the potential for gigantic global impacts as poor nations struggle to develop is tremendous.

For instance, should India or China choose to use its vast supplies of coal to develop, either one could easily increase its CO_2 injection more than could be compensated for by the United States' ending all use of coal (which now supplies 23.5% of its energy) and not substituting other carbon-releasing fuels for it. This would be true even if India and China only increased their per capita energy use to tiny fractions of the United States' (7 and 14%, respectively), and both had great success in controlling their population size. The basic reason, of course, is that both nations' populations are already gigantic; and even under very optimistic assumptions, India's is doomed to approach 2 billion before growth could be halted by birth control. The P multiplier in those nations' $I = PAT$ equations thus enormously inflates even relatively small increases in AT.

In the area of climate change, humanity is faced with a most complex and difficult situation. Increased concentrations of greenhouse gases are almost certainly going to lead to a warming of the planet, but the degree and rate of that warming and its climatic (and sea level) consequences remain hotly debated. Furthermore, changes in sea level and climate might well have disastrous consequences for terrestrial and aquatic natural ecosystems and for agricultural ecosystems. Although most people at least sense that rapid climate change could greatly injure agricultural systems, they are less aware of the potential for disaster in systems not directly managed by people.

Natural ecosystems supply humanity with an array of indispensable and irreplaceable services that support the human economy. One of them, the maintenance of an appropriate mix of gases in the atmosphere, is already faltering (that is what led to this book). Other services include the generation and preservation of soils, disposal of wastes, cycling of nutrients, control of the vast majority of crop pests, pollination of many crops, provision of forest products and food from the sea, and maintenance of a vast "genetic library" from which humanity has already withdrawn the very basis of civilization and which is the potential source of new materials for genetic engineering.

The impacts of changing climate on the plants, microorganisms, and other animals of the planet are discussed in an excellent series of papers in this volume. To the degree that other life forms are unable to migrate, acclimate, or evolve in response to rapid climate change, the essential services of ecosystems (of which organisms are working parts) will be compromised. Declining ecosystem services will add to the difficulties imposed on agricultural systems, which normally depend on natural systems for water, genetic variability, pest control, and so on.

What should we do about all this? Many of the steps that should be taken to slow global warming are discussed in detail in this volume, so I will just make some general observations. First, it is critical to prevent a lack of scientific certainty from becoming an excuse for inaction. Even a small chance of rapid anthropogenic climate change warrants taking precautionary measures, especially since there are other good reasons for curbing the emissions of CO_2, CFCs, and other greenhouse gases.

To put the certainty issue in perspective, however, suppose that the chance of climatic change being 100 times as rapid as the fastest changes at the end of the last ice age were only 10%. Since the possible consequences of that include the deaths of many hundreds of millions of people, possibly leading to widespread social breakdowns (Ehrlich et al. 1989, Daily and Ehrlich 1990), action is clearly called for. After all, if you knew there was a 10% chance that the airliner you were about to board would crash, you surely would switch carriers or stay home. Society makes strenuous efforts to insure against much less likely events (such as DC–10 crashes) which have trivial consequences compared to those of planet-wide rapid climatic changes.

Second, insurance against rapid climate change would carry more benefits than costs (although mechanisms would have to be set in place to assure that both were shared equitably). Major efforts to increase energy efficiency, to develop solar-hydrogen technologies, and reforestation, for instance, would be extremely desirable *even if climates were locked into the relatively favorable mode of 1930–1970*. Energy efficiency and solar hydrogen would decrease the environmental damage caused by mining, abate acid deposition and many forms of directly toxic air pollution, and could greatly limit the direct and indirect environmental damage done by automobiles. A gradually imposed gasoline tax of, say, \$3.00 per gallon in the United States would soon lead to smaller, lighter, more efficient cars, less highway and shopping-mall building, a trend toward more and better mass transit, and living near workplaces. Automobile commuting could gradually be taxed out of existence in many areas, and some of the enormous revenues collected could be used to provide alternative means (van pools, light rail systems) for lower income people to get to work.

Reforestation would also be extremely valuable in its own right. It would reduce floods, droughts, and soil erosion, provide a sustainable flow of timber and other forest resources, increase recreational opportunities, and help preserve biodiversity.

Perhaps the most important step in slowing global warming is controlling the size of the human population. It is obvious that, if the P factor in the $I = PAT$ equation continues to grow, any efforts to lower the A and T factors will eventually be overwhelmed.

This is the most important step because demographic momentum assures a substantial lag time between the start of any humane program to limit human numbers and the achievement of substantial results. The main bright spot in the picture is that the age structure of populations in rich nations is such that the momentum of growth is small (indeed a few are already at zero population growth (ZPG—or are even gradually declining in size). Thus the main culprits in adding greenhouse gases to the atmosphere are in the best positions to quickly achieve needed population *shrinkage*.

With enlightened political leadership, the population of the worst offender, the United States, could begin shrinking within a decade or so. Since *The Population Bomb* was written in 1968, roughly 45 million Americans have been added to the world's population. In terms of commercial energy use, that was the equivalent of *6 billion* Bangladeshis! Needless to say, reducing the American population to a level sustainable in the long term would be a major benefit, not just to United States citizens, but to the world. Global populations can only be supported now by exhausting "capital"—fossil fuels, high-grade mineral ores, and, most critically, rich agricultural soils, ice-age groundwater, and biodiversity. Overpopulation is a driving force behind climate change; we can only hope that this change does not produce a cruel solution to the problem of overpopulation.

Finally, let me mention what may be the most enduring and pernicious myth of the 20th century—the notion that perpetual economic growth is both possible and desirable. The former is clearly not true as long as material consumption is part of the growth. Only in poor nations is growth of the physical economy now clearly desirable, and, even in these nations, it must not be growth of the sort exhibited by today's overdeveloped nations. Countries like the United States should be striving for *shrinkage* of the classic indicators of growth; the nation should undergo a period of sustainable development in which the quality of life grows while the gross national product (GNP) shrinks (as would happen if it became possible for everyone to walk or bike to work). The notion dancing in the heads of some economists that a five- or tenfold increase in economic activity will be required by the middle of the next century to provide all human beings with a decent standard of living is merely an indicator of their culture-bound views of "decent" and their ignorance of what Earth's life-support systems will tolerate.

I now pass you on to my colleague's contributions in *Global Climate Change and Life on Earth*. They will expand your appreciation of one perilous element in the human predicament. I hope this book will provide incentive not only to learn more about the climate, but also to pay more attention to the health of both ecosystems and social systems. I believe that humanity now faces unprecedented challenges, for which we already have more than enough scientific information to start taking appropriate steps. After all, is it really worth waiting a few years to see whether the chance of ending civilization within a generation increases from 10 to 20%?

The real action is going to be social and political; and meeting unprecedented challenges will require unprecedented cooperation. To accomplish that, we are going to have to overcome racism, sexism, religious prejudice, gross economic inequity, and xenophobia. Recent events in Eastern Europe have provided a small start on the latter and have demonstrated once again that human social systems can change with extreme rapidity. The appearance of Mikhail Gorbachev has shown that superpower leadership does not have to be forever Reaganoid, that a person with a genuine global view can reach the top. Intelligence, compassion, and new-mindedness (Ornstein and Ehrlich 1989) are all out there. The question now is whether we can rally them in time to avoid climatic or other catastrophe.

References

Brown, L. 1989. Feeding six billion. *WorldWatch* 2:32–40.

Daily, G., and P. Ehrlich. 1990. An exploratory model of the impact of rapid climate change on the world food situation. Proc. Royal Soc. London B, 241, pp. 232–244.

Ehrlich, P., G. Daily, A. Ehrlich, P. Matson, and P. Vitousek. 1989. Global change and carrying capacity: implications for life on Earth. *Global Change and Our Common Future: Papers from a Forum*, R. S. DeFries and T. F. Malone (eds.), pp. 19–27. National Academy Press, Washington, DC.

Ehrlich, P. and A. Ehrlich. 1990. *The Population Explosion*. Simon and Schuster, New York.

Ornstein, R. and P. Ehrlich. 1989. *New World/New Mind*. Doubleday, New York.

Schneider, S. 1989. *Global Warming*, Sierra Club Books, San Francisco.

WRI (World Resources Institute). 1988. *World Resources 1988–89*. Basic Books, New York.

Preface

This book is based on presentations given by the authors at the conference entitled "Global Climate Change and Life on Earth: Evidence, Predictions, and Policy" held at the New York State Museum, in Albany, on April 24 and 25, 1989. My goal in organizing that conference and in editing this book is to inform as many people as possible about what we are doing to our planet. It is written to be comprehensible to the general audience and to college and university students alike, whether they are science majors or not. The main theme is the consequence for life of the greenhouse effect and global climate change. However, it would be absurd to write about climate change as if other forms of environmental degradation were not also occurring. Therefore we integrate information on climate change with information on overpopulation, air pollution, ozone depletion, species extinction, and habitat destruction. The result is a comprehensive treatment of perhaps the greatest threat facing life on earth since the extinction of the dinosaurs.

Sir Crispin Tickell, Ambassador to the United Nations from Great Britain, during a presentation on "Climate Change and Global Politics" at the New York State Museum, offered an analogy that may be useful for putting the issue of climate change into perspective. He called the analogy, "The case of the boiled frog." He said, "If you were unkind enough to put a frog into boiling water, he would jump out if able to do so. If you were to put him into cool water and then gradually heat the water, you would end up with frog soup." In many ways, this analogy serves to illustrate how humans perceive and respond to environmental problems. We do not usually react to things that take more than two or three human generations to occur, and we can not grasp great distances such as those measured in light years. However, for the first time in the history of civilization changes are taking place rapidly, and thanks to the mass communication media, we can see all over the world. Our perception can now begin to grasp global environmental problems because both time and space have shrunk.

The time period from 1970 to 1990, were the 20 years when humans finally began to understand what was happening to their environment. Change is not new. Humans have been changing the natural environment since the end of the last glaciation (some 8 to 10 thousand years ago). Since then we have been creating strains on the environment, but we could not see or understand them. Several civilizations have collapsed apparently because of accumulating environmental degradation. As Sir Crispin put it, "The frogs were being boiled, but they were being boiled pretty slowly."

The Industrial Revolution strained natural systems to a greater degree than those of prehistory. People once believed that natural systems were indefinitely tolerant. No matter what we did to them, they would repair themselves. Now we know that this is not so. There is an important distinction to be made between industrialization in temperate and tropical countries. In temperate ones, for the most part, there was sufficient water, fuel, and natural resources to sustain the Industrial Revolution for the time being. The Industrial Revolution in temperate societies were of necessity preceded by the Agricultural Revolution so that large populations could be sustained. In the tropical countries, water is scarce or only available seasonally, natural resources, such as fertile soils, are absent or in short supply, and as a result those countries have never had an agricultural revolution. Much of the developing world lies in the tropical region. Today, people of developing countries believe that if they try hard enough they can have the same kind of industrialized society as in the United States and Western Europe. Sir Crispin calls this "a profound illusion."

There are three kinds of environmental problems we face today that may be distinguished by scale: acid rain, ozone depletion, and global climate change. Acid rain (more precisely acid deposition) is a local, waste disposal problem that with good will and scientific effort can be solved locally. Ozone depletion is a global problem but with a narrow cause. Again, scientists and politicians should be able to solve the problem with local solutions. Climate change, however, is a global problem with global dimensions and requires a global response.

In the chapters that follow, we present descriptions of what global climate change is and what may result from environmental changes that may be associated with climate change. The first four authors present what we consider to be the evidence for climate change. Richard Wetherald's chapter discusses the main tool developed to allow for a detailed understanding of the control of the planet's climate system. General circulation models (GCMs) began as rather simple models to provide gross views of the important interrelationships among greenhouse gases, radiative cooling and heating, and climate. As the models matured, they incorporated more and more realistic assumptions and feedbacks. Nonetheless, we are still a long way from models that can tell us accurately what climate will be like with a doubling of the concentration of atmospheric greenhouse gases over the next several decades. Wetherald's chapter ends with a call for more work that will hopefully produce results that will put to rest much of the current debate over rates and extent of projected climate changes. John Hayes reviews the GCM modeling results regarding impacts on hydrology. He assesses the uncertainties of predictions and discusses recent studies that evaluate regional hydrological impacts and vulnerability of water-supply systems. He also supplies a rather surprising view of the expectations of water-resource managers and how these expectations are reflected in water-resource planning. Water-resource managers are not prepared to cope with large-scale changes in the distribution of available water, and they appear to be making little effort to prepare themselves.

Richard Houghton then provides an update on the sources of carbon dioxide and other greenhouse gases. His own contribution to the field has been the realization that the destruction of tropical wet and dry forests and burning of the wood adds approximately one-fifth of the total greenhouse gases emitted to the atmosphere. One way to ameliorate some of the effects of industrialization and stabilize the concentration of greenhouse gases in the atmosphere is reforestation. Houghton reveals the dimension of the work ahead. We need to reforest an area approximately one-third the size of the today's world cropland. Edward Cook concludes this section with a look at the history of climate change as revealed in tree rings. He allows us to see that climate changes have occurred in the past and that the effects have differed between temperate and boreal forests. The changes in boreal forest growth appear to be a response to changes in surface air temperature. The variability of tree-ring growth apparently associated with variable climate conditions makes it difficult to use tree-ring growth as an indicator of climate change, because it may take several decades for the trees to record significant climate change in their rings. Thus by the time the trees can give us a warning, the changes will already be here.

The second set of chapters uses information provided by the GCMs to predict what the consequences may be for life on earth. James Clark looks at basic ecosystem processes to determine how sensitive they are to changing climate conditions. He shows that nonlinear ecosystem responses make difficult the prediction of precisely how these processes will respond to climate change. One effect appears certain. When precipitation declines and evapotranspiration increases in continental interiors, the frequency of wildfires will increase. Also decomposition processes appear to be the most sensitive indicators of changing climatic conditions in temperate forests. Robert Peters details what may happen to biological diversity as the climate changes. Animals and plants are not likely to respond as entire communities, but species will move with changing climatic conditions independently of one another. New mixtures of species may expose prey to new predators and disease organisms to new hosts. He suggests that reserves established to protect communities may fail because the plants and animals will move out of the reserve boundaries following the moving climate conditions. The current role played by reserves must be enlarged and reserve planners and managers must become prepared to deal with climate change. Robert Lester and Peter Myers examine consequences of climate change for migratory wildlife. Migratory patterns of Serengeti ungulates are contrasted with those of migratory shorebirds. Migrating animals depend on food sources being available enroute, however the timing of the migration may be triggered by different environmental cues than those that trigger bursts in food production. Climate change may desynchronize the timing of migration and food production, food that is needed to complete the migration and for reproduction. Migratory animals present a challenge to conservation because they often cross national borders, thus requiring international cooperation. Next, I describe how climate change, acid deposition, and habitat fragmentation may interact synergistically to reduce or eliminate amphibian communities. Amphibians may be the best indicators of climate change because of their physiology, distribution, and life-history characteristics. The most abundant terrestrial vertebrate in northeastern North America is already being adversely affected by changing environmental conditions.

David Steadman shows how human occupation of islands and continents has coincided with loss of large numbers of species. Now three to four species of plants and animals become extinct each day. Some scientists believe that the combined consequences of habitat destruction and climate change doom as many as half of the species on earth to extinction by the year 2030. We are striving to preserve the other half. Stephen Leatherman examines how projected increases in sea level threatens low lying population centers and coastal wetlands. Continued sea level rise due to melting polar ice sheets and the thermal expansion of the sea pose threats to a significant portion of the world's population living within coastal zones, and he believes the prospect for coastal wetlands is bleak. A thoughtful look at changes in agriculture and economics likely to accompany climate change is provided by Daniel Dudek. Diverse interrelationships exist among agriculture, the environment, and the economy, and an understanding of secondary effects is crucial to a full appreciation of the consequences of climate change.

The last set of chapters deals with the direct impacts of climate change on human beings and on policy responses that are needed to stabilize the concentration of greenhouse gases in the atmosphere. Janice Longstreth and Laurence Kalkstein provide two views of how climate change may affect human health and mortality patterns, respectively. In developed countries, Longstreth sees the greatest impact in respiratory diseases as both global warming and ozone depletion will increase air pollution levels. In developing nations, impacts on public health cascade as climate change reduces agricultural productivity, which in turn increases malnutrition and susceptibility to infectious diseases. Kalkstein models the effects of global warming on mortality and finds that weather-induced summer mortality may result in 7200 deaths for the 15 cities included in the model. Jan Beyea presents a scary 400-year forecast, reminding us that climate change is not going to stop when we reach a doubling of the atmospheric concentration of greenhouse gases. He then begins a rational exposition of the energy options we have available. This is important reading for policymakers.

Dean Abrahamson gave the keynote address at the conference. He summarizes the predictions and uncertainties of the GCMs and makes the plea that swift action be taken. The final chapter was written by several participants and organizers after the conference in an attempt to end the book with some thoughts and analyses about what it is we need to do now. I hope by reading this chapter it will be clear what one can do as an individual to make a difference. It is time to get started. The frog is in the water, and the water is heating up.

Richard L. Wyman
Rensselaerville, New York
November, 1990

Acknowledgments

This book results from a conference held at the New York State Museum in Albany, New York and was inspired by the conference on the Consequences of the Greenhouse Effect for Biological Diversity that was sponsored by the World Wildlife Fund and held at the National Zoological Park. I thank the organizers of that conference for renewing in me a desire to inform people about what is happening to our planet.

This conference would not have been possible without the support and commitment of the Edmund Niles Huyck Preserve and New York State Museum. I thank my Board of Directors for giving me the freedom to pursue such things and Marty Sullivan for his trust that we *could* do something.

I am especially thankful to the speakers· who freely volunteered to make presentations and then turn them into chapters for this book.

There are so many other people to thank. My wife has been an inspiration and a constructive critic. I also thank all those friends, colleagues, students, and volunteers who have helped me search meter square quadrats of leaf litter for the most abundant terrestrial vertebrate in northeastern North America. Together we can make a difference.

Dan Blinkley, John Pastor, and H. H. Shugart provided valuable insight and constructive criticisms for which I am grateful. I am also pleased to be able to thank the staff of Routledge, Chapman and Hall, especially Gregory Payne, for support, encouragement, and advice during the production of the book. Cheryl Elkins retyped and helped edit much of the work for which I am grateful. Lastly I thank the late Jeannette Jancola for her assistance and spirit.

1

Changes of Temperature and Hydrology Caused by an Increase of Atmospheric Carbon Dioxide as Predicted by General Circulation Models

Richard T. Wetherald

Introduction

During the summer of 1988, one of the worst droughts in history occurred across most of the North American continent. During the subsequent winter, in the eastern United States, particularly in the mountainous watershed regions along the Appalachian range, very little snow fell. Regardless of what caused these phenomena, they serve as graphic examples of what can happen if our climate changes significantly from what we have become accustomed. In particular, the summer of 1988 has sparked a great deal of discussion on the greenhouse effect and whether or not it is beginning.

The Climate Dynamics Group of the Geophysical Fluid Dynamics Laboratory of NOAA, headed by Dr. Syukuro Manabe, began researching the greenhouse effect in the late 1960s and early 1970s. During this period, the data on atmospheric carbon dioxide (CO_2) of Keeling et al. (1989) working at the Mauna Loa Observatory in Hawaii and Antarctica indicated that concentrations of CO_2 were, indeed, increasing at a fairly consistent rate. The foundation for a transition of greenhouse theory from science fiction to science fact had been laid.

Model Description

Atmospheric scientists developed general circulation models (GCMs) to study the climatic consequences of increased CO_2. In simple terms, a GCM is a complex mathematical model composed of a system of partial differential equations derived from the basic laws of physics and fluid motion. These equations describe the dynamic, thermodynamic, radiational, and hydrologic processes of the atmosphere. A schematic representation of a GCM is illustrated by Fig. 1.1 where the

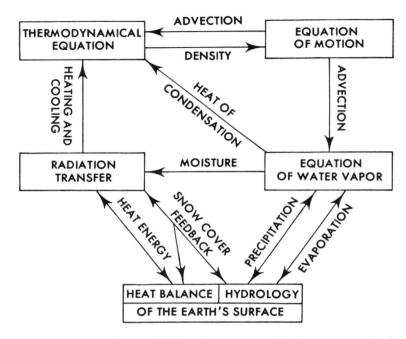

Fig. 1.1. Block diagram depicting the structure and major components of a general circulation model.

large rectangles denote the main components of the model and the arrows joining one rectangle to another denote the interactions that take place between each component. The equations represented by this block diagram are too complex to be solved analytically, so they must be converted into an arithmetic form that is suitable for computation by a digital computer. We run the model by dividing the entire three-dimensional atmosphere into a systematic series of "boxes" to which the basic equations must be applied and evaluated. In each box, the motion of the air, heat transfer, radiation, precipitation, and surface hydrology are calculated, as well as the interactions of these processes among each of the boxes. A sample grid system for this purpose is illustrated by Fig. 1.2.

The model is run with current CO_2 concentrations until it reaches a steady state. This run is the "control" or present-day climate experiment. The above procedure is repeated assuming twice as much CO_2 with no other change. After both experiments have been completed, the computed "climates" obtained are averaged over a long enough period to remove the natural variation present in each climate simulation (usually 10 model years). Finally, we compare the two climates to determine the changes caused by CO_2 doubling. A diagram illustrating this procedure is given in Fig. 1.3.

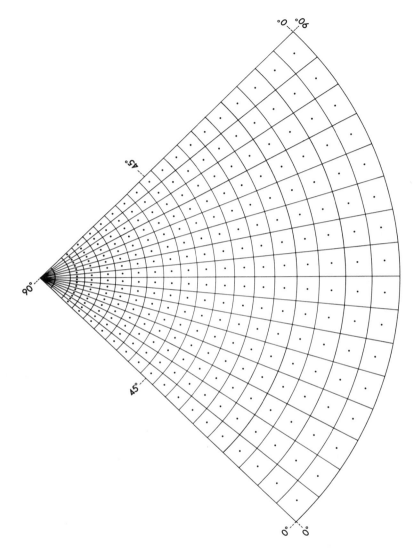

Fig. 1.2. A diagram of a sample grid system typically used in performing general circulation experiments.

Early Experiments

The initial experiments used a GCM with a simplified land–sea distribution, namely half land and half sea, to conserve computer time and to better understand the feedback mechanisms caused by the increase of atmospheric CO_2. The ocean

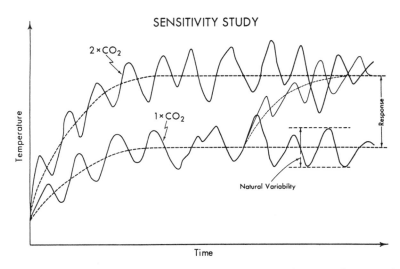

Fig. 1.3. A schematic diagram depicting the method used in conducting general circulation experiments. In general, two computer runs (integrations) are performed, one for the normal-CO_2 (standard) experiment and the other for a higher concentration of atmospheric CO_2 (usually a doubling of CO_2).

was considered to be either a "swamp ocean" or a thermally conducting layer without active ocean currents. Also, surface hydrology was incorporated into the model in a simplistic way namely, a 15-cm deep soil moisture "bucket" which may be filled by rainfall or snowmelt and depleted by evaporation. Runoff occurs as any excess water in the bucket over the 15-cm capacity.

Figure 1.4 shows the CO_2-induced latitude-time differences of the surface air temperature and soil moisture obtained by a simplified GCM that incorporated seasonal variation of solar radiation. The top portion shows that the change of surface air temperature is relatively small in low latitudes and much larger and more variable in higher latitudes. The relatively large polar warming is at a maximum in winter and early spring and at a minimum during summer and early fall. The relatively strong warming during the winter and early spring resulted from the poleward retreat of highly reflective sea ice and continental snow cover. This allows more absorption of solar radiation and release of oceanic heat by the surface during these seasons.

The bottom portion of Fig. 1.4 shows an enhanced continental dryness, which is centered around 35° latitude during the winter but shifts poleward until it becomes centered at approximately 45° latitude during summer. In general, the magnitude of this increased dryness over the continent is greatest in middle latitudes during summer. This summer dryness pattern was found to be caused by two factors:

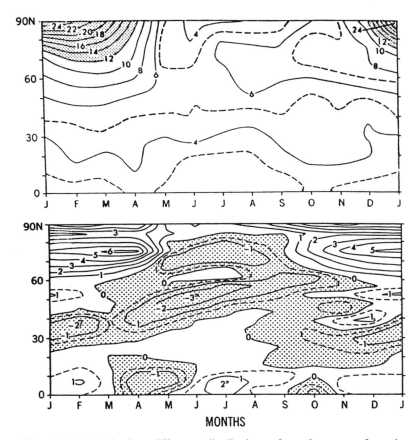

Fig. 1.4. Latitude–time difference distributions of zonal mean surface air temperature in degrees centigrade (top portion) and soil moisture in centimeters (bottom portion) caused by a doubling of carbon dioxide. Soil moisture differences are averaged over the idealized continent only. Here, the geography is assumed to be half land and half ocean. Source is Wetherald and Manabe (1981).

1. An earlier disappearance of snow cover during late winter, which causes an earlier beginning of relatively large evaporation from the soil. Because snow cover reflects a large fraction of insolation, its disappearance increases the absorption of solar energy by the land surface that is used as latent heat for evaporation. Thus, the end of the spring snowmelt marks the beginning of summer soil drying. In the high-CO_2 experiment, the period of snowmelt ends earlier, bringing an earlier start of the spring to summer reduction of soil moisture.

2. Changes in the middle-latitude precipitation pattern caused by a poleward shift of the middle-latitude rainbelt, a region associated with large-scale cyclonic disturbances. In the high-CO_2 atmosphere, warm moisture-rich air penetrates

further north than in the normal-CO_2 atmosphere. This is caused by a greater transport of moisture from lower to higher latitudes. Thus, precipitation increases significantly in the northern half of the rainbelt, whereas it decreases in the southern half. Because the rainbelt moves northward from winter to summer, a middle-latitude location lies in the northern half of the rainbelt in winter and in its southern half in summer. Therefore, at middle latitudes, the CO_2-induced change of precipitation becomes negative in early summer, contributing to a reduction of soil moisture.

These two mechanisms are illustrated by Fig. 1.5, which shows the latitude–time distribution of the continental snow cover for both the normal-CO_2 and high-CO_2 experiments and the latitude–time distribution of total precipitation amount for the normal-CO_2 experiment. The upper and middle portions of Fig. 1.5 indicate that, not only is there less snow depth, but snow cover is less extensive in the high-CO_2 case as compared with the normal-CO_2 case in middle latitudes. This implies that there is less snowmelt runoff during the spring season there. The snow cover also appears later in fall and disappears earlier in spring.

In the lower portion of Fig. 1.5, the mean position of the middle-latitude rainbelt for the high-CO_2 experiment (dashed line) is located poleward of its mean position in the normal-CO_2 experiment (solid line). Such a redistribution of the precipitation pattern results in wetter conditions to the north and dryer conditions to the south of the rainbelt in middle latitudes during the summer season.

The summer reduction of soil moisture does not continue throughout the winter season. In response to the increase of atmospheric CO_2, soil wetness increases during the winter season over extensive continental regions of middle and high latitudes (the lower portion of Fig. 1.4). In middle latitudes, this increase of soil moisture is mainly due to the increase of precipitation in the northern half of the middle-latitude rainbelt. Although total precipitation increases in middle and higher latitudes, a larger fraction of the total precipitation occurs as rainfall rather than snowfall, which causes the soil to become wetter. The lower portion of Fig. 1.4 also indicates that soil wetness is reduced during winter at 25° to 40° latitude. The reduced rainfall in the southern half of the middle-latitude rainbelt is, again, responsible for this enhanced dryness in these latitudes.

As shown in Fig. 1.6, both rainfall and evaporation increase during the winter months. However, as the spring season approaches, rainfall decreases rapidly and actually changes sign, whereas evaporation continues to increase. During summer, there is a decrease of rainfall, which continues until early fall. Evaporation during summer also decreases because there is no longer enough soil moisture to evaporate at the higher rate. These seasonal changes in rainfall and evaporation are consistent with the summertime soil dryness due to earlier removal of snow cover and the poleward shift of the middle-latitude rainbelt. Changes of snowmelt and runoff indicate earlier melting of snow cover and an earlier runoff period during spring.

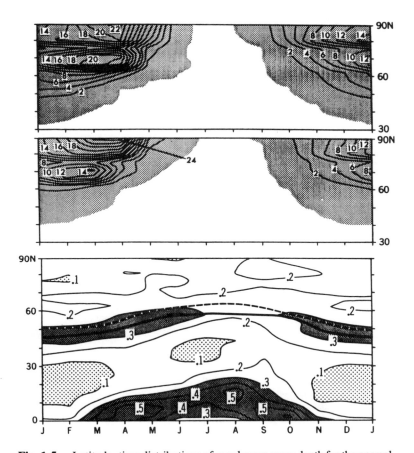

Fig. 1.5. Latitude–time distributions of zonal mean snow depth for the normal-CO_2 experiment in centimeters (top panel), zonal mean snow depth for the higher CO_2 experiment in centimeters (middle panel) and zonal mean precipitation in centimeters per day for the normal-CO_2 experiment (bottom panel) over the idealized continent. The positions of the middle-latitude rainbelts are depicted by a solid line for the normal-CO_2 experiment and a dashed line for the higher CO_2 experiment. Data from Wetherald and Manabe (1981) and Manabe et al. (1981).

More Recent Experiments

In more recent experiments, the GCM included a simplified scheme of cloud prediction and realistic geography. In general, the patterns of zonal mean temperature and soil moisture differences obtained from this more realistic model are qualitatively similar to those obtained from the earlier model (Fig. 1.7). The

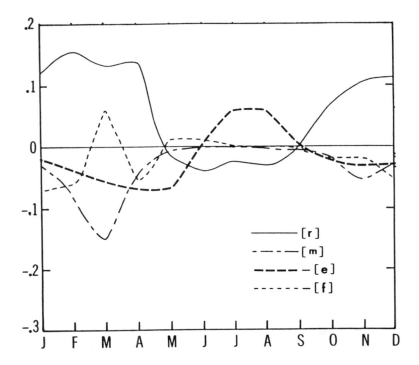

Fig. 1.6. Seasonal variation of zonal mean differences of the soil moisture budget taken at approximately 45° latitude over the idealized continent due to a doubling of carbon dioxide. r = rainfall, e = evaporation, m = snowmelt, and f = runoff. The signs of e and f are reversed to depict soil moisture losses. Units are centimeters per day. From Manabe et al. (1981).

mechanisms responsible for the temperature and soil moisture changes for this GCM are identical to the processes described previously.

The geographic distribution of CO_2-induced surface-temperature change for the December–February period (Fig. 1.8, top portion) shows a relatively large response in middle to high latitudes, which is not present for the June–August period (Fig. 1.8, lower panel). This is due to the recession of continental snow cover and sea ice during the winter and spring seasons, mentioned previously, whereas these processes are relatively inactive during the summer season. As was also previously shown, temperature changes in tropical and subtropical latitudes are smaller and are practically invariant with season.

There is a general increase of soil moisture during December–February for most middle- and high-latitude regions (Fig. 1.9, clear area) and a decrease of soil moisture (Fig. 1.9, shaded area) for the lower portions of the North American continent and Asia. On the other hand, there was a general decrease of soil

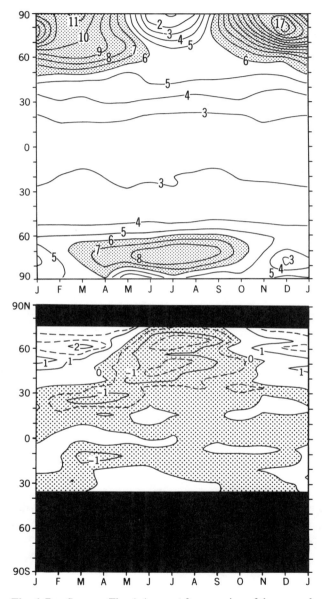

Fig. 1.7. Same as Fig. 1.4 except for a version of the general circulation model with cloud prediction and realistic geography. Soil moisture differences are averaged over all of the continents. From Manabe and Wetherald (1987).

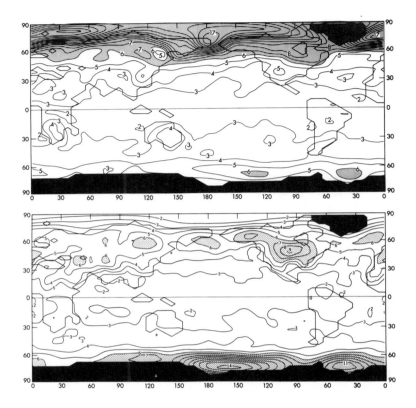

Fig. 1.8. Geographic distributions of surface air temperature difference for December–February (top portion) and for June–August (bottom portion) caused by a doubling of CO_2. Units are in degrees centigrade. From Manabe and Wetherald (1987).

moisture for the June–August period for the entire continents of North America and Asia (Fig. 1.9, bottom). The magnitude of summer dryness is particularly pronounced over the Great Plains and Midwest of the United States. The only exception to this overall summer dryness pattern is an increase of soil moisture over India, which indicates an increase of monsoonal rainfall there. As was previously noted, these features are caused by the earlier disappearance of continental snow cover and changes of precipitation patterns associated with the middle-latitude rainbelt.

Comparisons With Other Modeling Groups

In the early 1980s, GCMs by institutions other than the Geophysical Fluid Dynamics Laboratory (GFDL) were being used for climate-sensitivity studies.

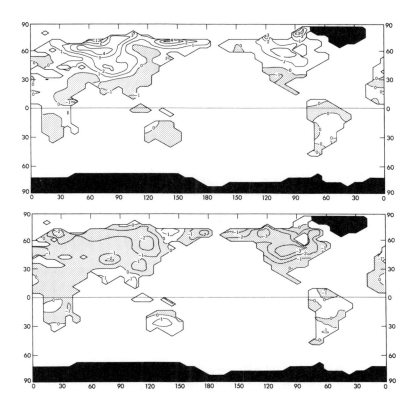

Fig. 1.9. Same as Fig. 1.7 except for differences of soil moisture. Units are in centimeters. From Manabe and Wetherald (1987).

These institutions included the Goddard Institute for Space Studies (GISS), the National Center for Atmospheric Research (NCAR), the United Kingdom Meteorological Office (UKMO), and Oregon State University (OSU).

A detailed comparison was made by Schlesinger and Mitchell (1987) of the results obtained from models by GFDL, GISS, and NCAR. Aside from substantial regional differences of temperature and soil moisture, this study revealed that there was not universal agreement among the three models on middle-latitude continental summer dryness. A comparison is given in Fig. 1.10, which shows the latitude–time differences of soil moisture induced by a doubling of carbon dioxide for the three GCMs. According to this comparison, neither the GISS or the NCAR models produce a significant summer dryness pattern similar to the GFDL model, whereas all three models yield a tendency to produce wetter soil conditions during the winter and early spring seasons. All three models produce more consistent CO_2-induced hydrologic changes during the winter season than they do during the summer season.

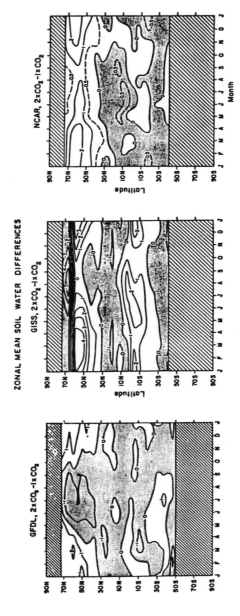

Fig. 1.10. Latitude–time differences of zonal mean soil moisture as obtained from the GFDL model (left panel), the GISS model (middle panel), and the NCAR model (right panel) due to a doubling of atmospheric CO_2. Units are in centimeters. Reproduced from Schlesinger and Mitchell (1987).

However, more recent GCM studies appear to produce results that are more consistent with the GFDL summer hydrologic changes. Kellogg and Zhao (1988) made detailed comparisons of the CO_2-induced hydrologic changes obtained for the United States by all five institutions. A doubling of CO_2 caused three out of the five models (GFDL, UKMO, and OSU) to produce patterns of decreasing soil moisture for the June–August period, although the details of these differences vary considerably from one model to another (Fig. 1.11). The other two models (NCAR and GISS) appear to forecast very small changes of soil moisture, neither significantly positive nor negative, over most of the United States.

To discover the reasons for the discrepancy between the two sets of model results, Meehl and Washington (1988) analyzed and compared the water budgets produced by the NCAR and GFDL models over three different regions of the globe. Figure 1.12 illustrates the monthly variation of area mean soil moisture for both the normal- and high-CO_2 experiments over three selected regions; Northern Canada, the Central United States, and Southern Europe. An inspection of this figure reveals two very interesting features:

1. The 15-cm soil moisture "buckets" in the GFDL model are almost completely saturated for the normal-CO_2 experiment, whereas they are less than half full in the NCAR model in late winter or early spring when the soil moisture attains its maximum value due to snowmelt and spring rainfall.

2. There is still a significant supply of soil moisture in the buckets of the GFDL model during the summer season, whereas it is almost completely depleted in the buckets of the NCAR model for the normal-CO_2 experiment.

The first feature implies that the soil moisture buckets in the NCAR model can accept the additional rainfall that is forecast to occur in the higher CO_2 experiment during the winter season, whereas most of this additional moisture is lost as runoff in the GFDL model. In the NCAR model, this additional moisture must be depleted by increased evaporation before any significant drying out of the soil can occur. In the GFDL model, the buckets of soil moisture in both the normal- and high-CO_2 experiments start out at near their saturation values and, therefore, the drying out process due to increased evaporation can occur soon after the winter season ends. Thus, there is a considerable time lag between the two models in the timing of the summertime dryness.

The second feature is, perhaps, even more important in explaining the difference between the two models. Because the soil moisture is so low in the NCAR model during the summertime for the normal-CO_2 experiment, it cannot be depleted much further in the higher CO_2 experiment. Therefore, there is little change in soil moisture for the NCAR model as compared with the GFDL model. These results suggest that there is too little precipitation in the NCAR model when compared with observation for the control experiment over these regions. However, a detailed analysis of the monthly variation of real soil moisture and

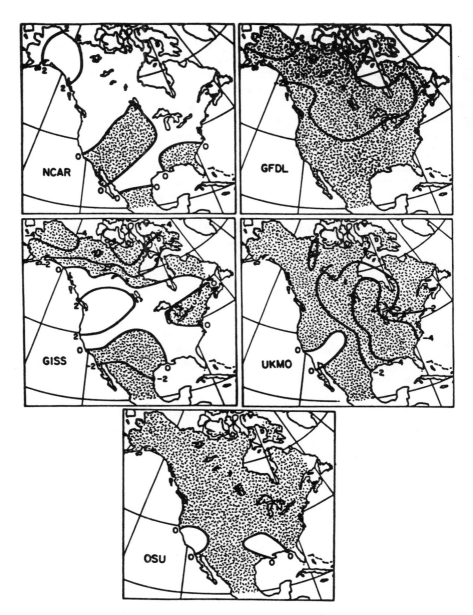

Fig. 1.11. Geographic distribution of soil moisture difference obtained over the North American continent for the NCAR, GFDL, GISS, UKMO, and OSU models for June–August due to a doubling of atmospheric CO_2. Maps are contoured every 2 cm. Reproduced from Kellogg and Zhao (1988).

14

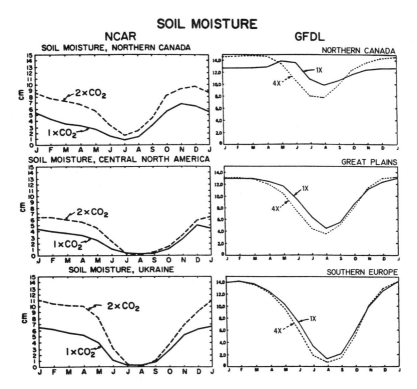

Fig. 1.12. Seasonal variation of mean soil moisture for three selected regions obtained from the GFDL and NCAR models. The normal-CO_2 results are represented by solid lines and the higher CO_2 results by dashed lines. Units are in centimeters. Reproduced from Meehl and Washington (1988).

precipitation must be made for these regions before a determination can be made concerning the accuracy of either of these model scenarios.

Rind et al. (1990) indicated that the GISS model had a deficiency of soil moisture similar to that described above for the NCAR model over the United States. If this is the case, there exists the possibility that all five general circulation models would have produced dryer soil moisture conditions there during the summer season provided enough soil moisture had been present in the control experiments to allow this to occur. A definitive conclusion on this issue must await future modeling studies that incorporate more realistic representations of surface hydrologic processes.

Summary

Although there are many areas of disagreement between the various models, it is worthwhile to highlight the areas of agreement. With regard to temperature, the state-of-the-art GCMs reveal that (1) an increase of global surface temperature due to CO_2 doubling lies in the range 3.5–5.2°C, (2) over the central United States, the average surface temperature increase ranges from 4 to 6°C during the December –February period and from 3 to 6°C for the June–August period, and (3) for all models, the increase of surface temperature is greater in higher latitudes than it is in the tropics. This polar amplification is greatest during the winter and early spring seasons due to the snow/sea ice cover albedo process, which operates mainly at these times.

With regard to hydrology, the latest GCMs reveal that continental snow cover in mid latitudes is less extensive and shallower in depth for the higher CO_2 experiment. This implies that the snow cover there will appear later in fall and disappear earlier in spring and result in less spring runoff from snowmelt (although there will be greater runoff in the form of rainfall). Also, the soil surface is exposed earlier in the winter season and, therefore, higher rates of evaporation will occur from it which will cause greater soil moisture loss from spring to summer.

One of the largest uncertainties in climate-sensitivity studies is the CO_2-induced response of precipitation over the continents during the summer season. Whether or not a given GCM will produce a summer dryness scenario appears to be dependent on a poleward shift of the mid latitude storm track (and accompanying rainbelt) and the state of the soil moisture of the standard experiment for both early spring and summer. In the final analysis, a given GCM will produce a tendency for dryer summertime conditions if the projected rainfall is forecast to either decrease or remain approximately the same. Only if the rainfall is forecast to increase at least as much as the projected increase of evaporation will the desication of soil moisture be prevented.

Other uncertainties include modeling of cloud processes, active ocean currents, and the use of low horizontal resolution. For example, Cess et al. (1989) have shown that there are major differences among GCMs concerning the effects of cloud feedback. In addition, the explicit inclusion of ocean currents can significantly alter the transient or time-dependent phase of a climate sensitivity experiment (Bryan et al. 1988). Until recently, the use of relatively large grid boxes has greatly hampered the successful simulation of climate, particularly on a regional scale. However, the advent of larger and faster supercomputers is making it possible for modelers to rerun their experiments with a considerably higher computational resolution.

In any event, it appears certain that, if the earth's climate becomes warmer, the earth's hydrology will change. If the most pessimistic scenario of CO_2-induced hydrologic change should become reality, then we would do well to consider the possible options available to us concerning agricultural management, water management, water conservation, and energy conservation. Such planning would enable us to either take maximum advantage of the projected climate change or at least mitigate the adverse effects of that climate change. In view of our increasing population, this planning would prove to be extremely beneficial even if there is no significant change in our future climate.

References

Bryan, K., S. Manabe, and M. J. Spelman. 1988. Interhemispheric asymmetry in the transient response of a coupled ocean-atmosphere model to a CO_2 forcing. *Phys. Oceanogr.* 18:851–867.

Cess, R. D., G. L. Potter, J. P. Blanchet, G. J. Boer, S. J. Ghan, J. T. Kiehl, H. Le Treut, Z.-X. Li, X.-Z. Liang, J. F. B. Mitchell, J.-J. Morcrette, D. A. Randall, M. R. Riches, E. Roeckner, U. Schlese, A. Slingo, K. E. Tayler, W. M. Washington, R. T. Wetherald, and I. Yagai. 1989. Interpretation of cloud-climate feedback as produced by 14 atmospheric general circulation models. *Science* 245:513–516.

Keeling, C. D., R. B. Bacastow, A. F. Carter, S. C. Piper, T. P. Whorf, M. Heimann, W. G. Moole, and H. Roeloffzen. 1989. A three-dimensional model of atmospheric CO_2 transport based on observed winds: 1. Analysis of observational data. In *Aspects of Climate Variability in the Pacific and the Western Americas.* D. H. Peterson (ed.) pp. 165–236. Geophysical Monograph 55, American Geophysical Union, Washington, D.C.

Kellogg, W. W. and Z.-C. Zhao. 1988. Sensitivity of soil moisture to doubling of carbon dioxide in climate model experiments. Part I: North America. *J. Climate* 1:348–366.

Manabe, S. and R. T. Wetherald. 1987. Large-scale changes in soil wetness induced by an increase in atmospheric carbon dioxide. *J. Atmos. Sci.* 44:1211–1235.

Manabe, S., R. T. Wetherald, and R. J. Stouffer. 1981. Summer dryness due to an increase of atmospheric carbon dioxide. *Clim. Change* 3:347–386.

Meehl, G. A. and W. M. Washington. 1988. A comparison of soil-moisture sensitivity in two global climate models. *J. Atmos. Sci.* 45:1476–1492.

Rind, D., R. Goldberg, J. Hansen, C. Rosenzweig, and R. Ruedy. 1990. Potential evapotranspiration and the likelihood of future drought. *J. Geophys. Res.* In press.

Schlesinger, M. E. and J. F. B. Mitchell. 1987. Climate model simulations of the equilibrium climate response to increased carbon dioxide. *Rev. Geophys.* 25:760–798.

Wetherald, R. T. and S. Manabe. 1981. Influence of seasonal variation upon the sensitivity of a model climate. *J. Geophys. Res.* 86:1194–1204.

2

Global Climate Change and Water Resources

John T. Hayes

Introduction

The CO_2-rich atmosphere of Venus with temperatures near 460°C and the CO_2-thin atmosphere of Mars with temperatures near −50°C illustrate the importance of the greenhouse effect. Earth's habitable temperatures are principally due to greenhouse gases, which are relatively transparent to incoming solar radiation but are effective absorbers of the infrared radiation emitted by Earth's surface. CO_2 is a greenhouse gas that occurs in trace amounts (0.03% by volume). Other atmospheric trace gases, for example methane (CH_4), nitrous oxide (N_2O), tropospheric ozone (O_3), and the chlorofluorocarbons (CFCs), are equally or more radiatively active per molecule than CO_2, and all are increasing in concentration (Dickinson and Cicerone 1986, NRC 1989, Ramanathan 1988, Ramanathan et al. 1985, 1987, Rasmussen and Khalil 1986). Leading scientists believe attainment of a doubling of "equivalent CO_2" will occur in the second half of the next century (Ramanathan 1988, Schneider 1987, 1989a,b). This doubling will depend upon growth rates in the use of fossil fuels and upon other human activities which release trace gases (Fig. 2.1).

Current atmospheric general circulation models (GCMs) using a doubled atmospheric-CO_2 content (e.g. 600 ppm) predict warming of the Earth's global mean surface air temperature by 2.8–5.2°C (Schlesinger and Zhao 1989, Wetherald, this volume). As Schneider (1989a) states, "What is controversial about the Greenhouse effect is exactly how much Earth's surface temperature will rise given a certain increase in a trace Greenhouse gas such as CO_2", and not whether the planet will experience an increased greenhouse effect. This global warming is predicted to have direct spatial and seasonal effects on climatic patterns of temperature, and therefore indirect climatic effects on precipitation. (Hansen et al. 1984, Manabe and Wetherald 1987, Mitchell et al. 1987, Mitchell and Warrilow 1987, Schlesinger and Zhao 1989, Washington and Meehl 1984). These changes in the spatial patterns of surface air temperature and precipitation will, together, impact on regional and global-scale climate and hydrology.

In this chapter, I review the scientific literature describing the potential climatic

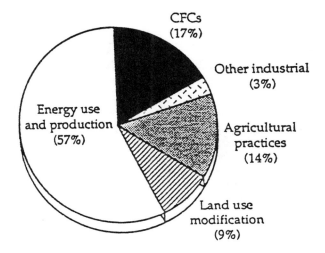

Fig. 2.1. The US Environmental Protection Agency's estimate of greenhouse gas emissions contributing to global warming in the 1980s. From Marshall (1989). Copyright 1989 by the AAAS.

impacts of an enhanced greenhouse effect on terrestrial hydrology and consider the uncertainty about GCMs for regional water-resource and hydrologic-impact studies. If the buildup of greenhouse gases continues at current rates, a significant climatic warming is expected to begin, and to accelerate, within the next few decades. The timing of this expected change is similar to the time required for planning, approval, funding, construction, and useful life of such major water facilities as dams, irrigation canals, treatment plants, and drainage systems. Table 2.1 presents an example of the almost four-decade-long history behind the accession of water from the Delaware River by New York City.

Hydrologic quantities and parameters likely to be affected by the greenhouse effect are atmospheric humidity, evapotranspiration, soil moisture, surface runoff (or overland flow), groundwater recharge and base flow, seasonal snowfall, timing of snowmelt periods, river flows and lake levels, incidence of droughts, hydrologic variability and sensitivity, natural and artificial storage of aboveground and impounded freshwaters, position, depth, and movement of saline (or saltwater) intrusions upstream in rivers that meet the sea, and, of course, sea-level rise and associated coastal flooding (Fig. 2.2). Callaway and Currie (1985) prepared a list of water resource issues that could be influenced by CO_2 buildup for the United States Department of Energy; they organized the issues according to supply, distribution, and use and reuse (Table 2.2). Leatherman (this volume) discusses how greenhouse warming will affect sea-level rise and the resulting implications for coastal resources.

The goals of this chapter are fivefold:

Table 2.1. Example of a past water resource planning timetable and history–New York City municipal system's accession of water from the Delaware River*

Year	Action
1927	NYC Water Board submits plan for development of Delaware River
1928	Project is approved
1931	US Supreme Court upholds the right of New York City to withdraw water from the Delaware River
1937	Construction begins on Delaware River water impoundments and conveyance systems
1944	Delaware aqueduct completed
1950	Neversink reservoir put into operation
1951	Rondout reservoir put into operation
1954	Pepacton reservoir put into operation
1965	Cannonsville reservoir put into operation

*From Waggoner and Schefter (1990).

1. To outline characteristics of five state-of-the-art GCMs that are relevant to predictions of the effect of greenhouse warming on soil moisture, and, in turn, terrestrial hydrology (In most cases I refer only to the GCM results from 2 x CO_2 (doubled CO_2) model experiments.)

2. To attempt to assess the uncertainty of these predictions in examining regional water-resource issues

3. To discuss recent studies that evaluate regional hydrologic impacts and vulnerability of water-supply systems to global climate change

4. To examine the expectations of climate change by water-resource managers and the implications of these expectations on water-resource planning

5. To outline some considerations of the Committee on Earth Sciences 1989 report regarding the strengths and weaknesses of current understanding in modeling of climate and hydrologic systems.

The focus of my discussions of regional hydrologic impacts and water-supply-system vulnerabilities will be confined to the United States and selected water-resource regions within the United States. Additionally, I draw from the report by the American Association for the Advancement of Science (AAAS) Panel on Climatic Variability, Climate Change and the Planning and Management of U.S. Water Resources (Waggoner 1990).

A Review of GCMs and Some of Their Predictions of Soil Moisture Content

Over the last three decades, concentrations of atmospheric-CO_2 levels have increased by approximately 12–13%, and there is evidence that CO_2 concentrations have risen by approximately 25% since 1850–1860 (Houghton, this volume,

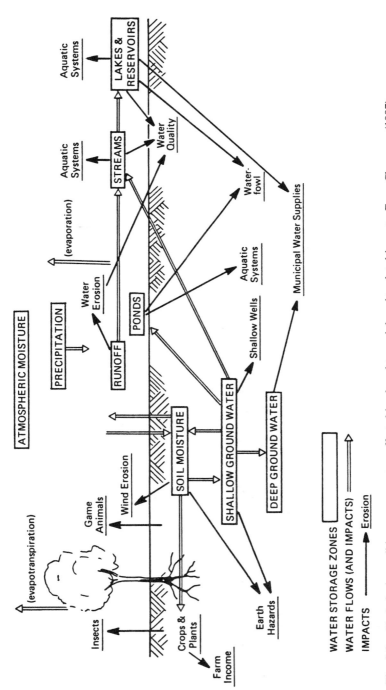

Fig. 2.2. Hydrologic conditions or parameters affected by droughts, and drought-related impacts. From Changnon (1987).

Table 2.2.   Water resource issues that could be influenced by CO_2 buildup in the atmosphere*

Supply Issues	
Surface Water	**Groundwater**
Flooding	Groundwater mining
Drought	(Groundwater overdraft)
Reservoir sedimentation	
Vegetation management	
Water losses from storage systems	
Eutrophication	
Effects of land use change on basin	
Hydrology	
Inadequate surface water supply/storage	

Distribution Issues	
Quantity	**Quality**
River sedimentation	Channel scour/channel erosion
Conveyance losses	
Availability of potable water	

Use and Reuse Issues	
Quantity	**Quality**
Inefficient irrigation practices/management	Saline intrusion of aquifers
Waterlogging (of soils)	Salinity problems
Groundwater infiltration into municipal	Waterborne diseases
sewer systems	Groundwater contamination
Effect of changing water levels	Surface water contamination
Navigation problems	Acidification of lakes
Conflicts in use	Inadequate water treatment facilities
Between instream uses	
Between offstream uses	
Between instream and offstream uses	

*From Callaway and Currie (1985).

Houghton and Woodwell 1989, Schneider 1989a). There is speculation that CO_2 levels could reach 550 ppm (approximately twice the estimated preindustrial level) by the end of the 21st century with the year 2025 being the earliest that this could occur (Trabalka 1985).

Wetherald (this volume) discusses the history of GCM efforts, the basic physics and mathematical structure of these models, their most notable deficiencies and efforts to improve these deficiencies. It is generally considered that there are at least five state-of-the-art three-dimensional GCMs for use in $2 \times CO_2$ experiments. Below are the names and abbreviations of the five models, the affiliation and location of each modeling group, as well as citations of recent publications describing 2 × CO_2-modeling efforts by each of the groups:

GFDL. Geophysical Fluid Dynamics Laboratory/NOAA, Princeton University, Princeton, NJ (Manabe and Stouffer 1980, Manabe and Wetherald 1986, 1987, Manabe et al. 1981, Wetherald and Manabe 1988)

GISS. Goddard Space Flight Center/NASA, Institute for Space Studies, New York, NY (Hansen et al. 1984, 1988, 1989, Rind 1987, 1988a,b)

NCAR. National Center for Atmospheric Research, Boulder, CO (Bates and Meehl 1986, Meehl and Washington 1986, 1988; Washington and Meehl 1984)

OSU. Department of Atmospheric Sciences, Oregon State University, Corvallis, OR (Schlesinger 1984, 1986, 1988, Schlesinger and Mitchell 1987, Schlesinger and Zhao 1989)

UKMO. United Kingdom Meteorological Office, Bracknell, Berkshire, England, UK (Mitchell 1983, Mitchell et al. 1987, 1989, Mitchell and Warrilow 1987, Wilson and Mitchell 1986, 1987)

There are, of course, more than five global climate-modeling groups worldwide, but these five groups have consistently pursued 2 × CO_2-modeling experiments as their models have evolved and improved over time. Over the past decade and a half, GCMs have evolved toward greater sophistication in their depiction of and degree of coupling of the atmosphere to the ocean. Ocean-modeling efforts within GCMs began with observed sea-surface temperatures (SSTs) and sea-ice climatologies, then advanced to what became known as *swamp ocean models* in which the SST and sea ice are calculated but in which the ocean has zero heat capacity and no heat transports. Subsequently, the models evolved to include the mixed-layer ocean model in which the thermal inertia of the ocean is coupled to the GCMs (Nihoul 1985, Schlesinger and Zhao 1989). The five GCMs discussed use mixed-layer ocean models. Because these models do not include oceanic circulation, they are considered to be "intermediate solutions" to the goal of having truly coupled atmosphere/ocean GCMs (Schlesinger and Zhao 1989). All five models are general circulation models of the atmosphere coupled to an ocean consisting of an upper mixed layer (the depth of which varied by model between 50 and 65 m). The models differ in many ways, including spatial resolution, depiction of ocean heat transport, and soil moisture calculations, to name only a few (Table 2.3).

Different grid sizes are used in the GCMs for model calculations (Fig. 2.3). Rind (1988a) studied the GISS GCM's hydrologic cycle for 1 × CO_2 (the control run) and 2 × CO_2 conditions to determine the effect of different grid sizes on sensitivity. He reported that in the winter season of the control run, the differences due to model resolution were not extreme; however, during summer the fine-resolution model was realistically dry in the southwest United States, whereas the coarser grid model was too wet. The fine-grid model was also better at

Table 2.3. General characteristics of five global climate simulation models used in recent $2 \times CO_2$ experiments*

Parameter	Models				
	GFDL[a]	GISS[b]	NCAR[c]	OSU[d]	UKMO[e]
Horizontal spatial resolution [° lat. by ° long.]	4.5 by 7.5	8 by 10 (also 4 by 5 in Rind 1988)	4.5 by 7.5	4 by 5	5 by 7.5 (also 2.5 by 3.75 in Mitchell et al. 1987)
Horizontal spatial resolution [approx. area of grid cell at 45°N/S lat, km², (mi²)]f	295,954 (114,268)	701,520 (270,857)	295,954 (114,268)	175,380 (67,714)	328,838 (126,964)
Vertical resolution (no. of layers)	9	9	9	2	11
Geography of land/ocean distribution	Realistic	Realistic	Realistic	Realistic	Realistic
Topography	Realistic	Realistic	Realistic	Realistic	Realistic
Solar radiation	Seasonally varying, not diurnal	Seasonal and diurnal cycles	Seasonally varying, not diurnal	Seasonally varying, not diurnal	Seasonal and diurnal cycles
Cloud distribution in troposphere: computed or specified	Computed	Computed	Computed	Computed	Computed
Aspects of sea-surface temperature (SST) calculations	Prescribed initial SST; ocean temp change computed from energy budget at ocean surface; includes seasonal variation	Computed SST based on surface energy budget and specified ocean heat transport and mixed-layer heat capacity	Prescribed initial SST; ocean temp change computed from energy budget at ocean surface	Computed oceanic mixed-layed temperature and SST	Computed SST with seasonal variation in SST prescribed from climatology
Aspects of sea ice calculations	Computed sea ice based on energy balance sea ice model; includes seasonal variation	Computed sea ice based on energy balance sea ice model; includes seasonal variation; 2-slab ice model	Computed sea ice based on energy balance sea ice model; includes seasonal variation	Computed sea ice based on energy balance sea ice model	Computed sea ice based on energy balance sea ice model; includes seasonal variation prescribed from climatology
Surface albedo over snow-free land	Prescribed geographically; old data source (Posey and Clapp, 1964)	Depends on local vegetation	Only two values—desert surface and generic vegetated		Prescribed geographically; modern data source (Wilson and Henderson-Sellers, 1985)

Normal atmospheric CO_2 concentration used for $1 \times CO_2$ control run	300 ppmv	315 ppmv	326 ppmv	326 ppmv	323 ppmv
Basis of soil moisture budget calculations	Bucket method; one-layer of soil; only one specified soil field capacity	2-Layer ground; field capacity depends on vegetation type (8 types)	Bucket method		2-Layer ground; field capacity depends on vegetation type
Number of cloud layers permitted	Clouds are allowed to form in each layer	Clouds are allowed to form in each layer	Clouds are allowed to form in all layers except surface atmos. layer	Clouds are allowed to form in each layer	Nonconvective clouds are allowed to form in three layers (low, medium, high); plus convective towers
Type of ocean model; depth of mixed layer	Mixed-layer ocean model; constant 50 m depth of mixed layer	Mixed-layer ocean model; 65 m max depth; depth is prescribed and seasonally varying	Mixed-layer ocean model; constant 50 m depth of mixed layer	Mixed-layer ocean model; constant 60 m depth of mixed layer	Mixed-layer ocean model; constant 50 m depth of mixed layer
Horizontal oceanic heat transport?	No	Prescribed ocean heat transport-specified geographically and seasonally; does not change with $2 \times CO_2$ experiment	No	No	Prescribed oceanic heat flux based on atmospheric simulation with prescribed sea surface temperatures
Oceanic heat exchange between mixed-layer and deeper layer of ocean?	No	No	No	No	No

*Based in part on Kellogg and Zhao (1988), Schlesinger and Mitchell (1987), and Schlesinger and Zhao (1989).

a Manabe and Wetherald (1986); Manabe and Wetherald (1987).

b Hansen et al. (1984); Rind (1988).

c Washington and Meehl (1984).

d Schlesinger and Zhao (1989).

e Wilson and Mitchell (1987); Mitchell et al. (1987).

f Calculated using 1° lat and long at 45° N/S equal to 111 and 79 km, respectively.

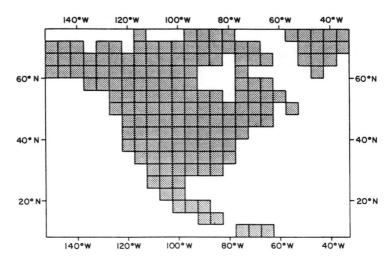

Fig. 2.3. Spatial distribution over North America of grid points and depiction of the 'realism' of the geography of North America and the southern tip of Greenland for one version (4° latitude × 5° longitude horizontal resolution) of the Oregon State University atmospheric GCM. From Katz (1988).

reproducing the standard sea-level atmospheric-pressure patterns. It is generally believed that a doubled CO_2 climate will produce a "vigorous" climate system with a more active hydrologic cycle because the warmer globe will have excess energy available to drive the climate system (e.g. a warmer atmosphere can hold more moisture, Ramanathan 1988). The model-predicted warming is generally not uniform but varies significantly with latitude, longitude, elevation, and season because of the nonlinear interactions among the atmosphere, cryosphere, oceans, and land. Observational data for 1885 to 1984 (Ramanathan 1988) reveal a warming trend of approximately 0.4 to 0.5°C in both the northern and southern hemispheres with "a factor of 2 to 3 poleward amplification of the warming trend." In terms of precipitation, Rind's (1988a) fine-grid model (the GISS GCM) produced warmer sea-surface temperatures, which destabilized the marine atmosphere causing increased storminess and rainfall over the ocean, with consequent decreases in precipitation over land. Since changes in soil moisture result from changes in patterns of rainfall, evaporation, and surface runoff, effects of warming on midlatitude precipitation patterns will have implications for seasonal availability of water in the United States. The fine-resolution version of the GISS GCM predicted decreases in soil moisture occurring from approximately 60–80°N, 20–30°N, and 30–50°S, with increases from approximately 40–60°N and 50–70°S (Rind 1988a).

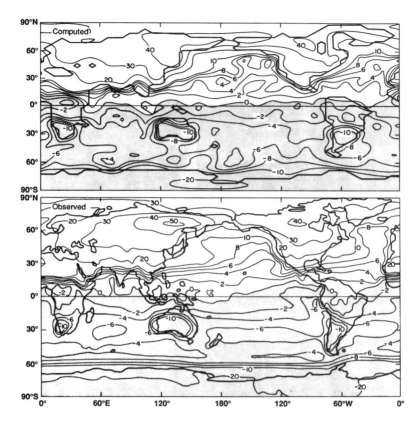

Fig. 2.4. (Top) Use of the GFDL global climate model to compute the winter to summer temperature extremes globally. (Bottom) The model's performance can be compared (verified) against this observed data of the earth's seasonal cycle of air temperature near the surface. From Schneider (1989) based on the work of Manabe and Stouffer (1980). Copyright 1981 by the AAAS.

Verification of GCM Results and Issues of Uncertainty in GCM Predictions

It is appropriate to determine how GCM predictions of climatic change beyond the next several decades might be verified. Examination of the predictions that are obtained from GCMs for normal climate simulations is the preferred way to begin. Computations of winter-to-summer temperature extremes for current conditions (Fig. 2.4, top) reproduces many of the features of the observed seasonal cycle (Fig. 2.4, bottom). There is an underestimation of the continentality effect in the northeast Soviet Union. Reproduction of the seasonal cycle is considered to be a critical test because these natural temperature changes are several times larger, on a hemispheric average, than the change from an ice age to an interglacial period or a projected greenhouse warming (Schneider 1989a).

Other important verification techniques include examination of the computed spatial patterns of variables, such as precipitation, relative humidity, and soil moisture amount (Kellogg and Zhao 1988) and examination of individual physical components of GCMs in isolation, for example, evaporation, sensible heat flux, and average cloud and solar radiation interactions/feedbacks. Finally, the ability of GCMs to reproduce past climates or climates of other planets is considered to be essential (Schneider 1989a). Wetherald (this volume) treats the subject of model verification in more detail.

GCMs have produced a variety of estimates of the magnitude and distribution of the expected response. The calculated global-mean surface warming due to doubling CO_2 concentrations ranges from about 1°C to 5.2°C, with the higher values occurring in recent simulations with model-generated cloud (as opposed to prescribed cloud cover) and mixed-layer ocean models. Although there is some qualitative agreement among existing studies on the more detailed aspects of the response, including enhanced warming and precipitation in higher latitudes in winter and a general reduction in upper tropospheric clouds, there are also marked disagreements. In $2 \times CO_2$ experiments with the UKMO GCM, Mitchell and Warrilow (1987) found that the magnitude of simulated summer drying in northern middle latitudes was dependent on soil texture, soil hydraulic conductivity, and the frozen-soil/surface-runoff relationship. They discovered that by altering these parameters the midcontinent summer drying predicted for $2 \times CO_2$ conditions could be reduced or even reversed. Meehl and Washington (1988) similarly found heightened model sensitivity to the physical representation of the soil surface and subsoil such that "the critical factor determining the magnitude of the summer drying . . . [was] the soil-moisture amount in the control case ($1 \times CO_2$-model run), particularly during spring."

Kellogg and Zhao (1988) found that in winter the areas of agreement among the five GCMs for both drier and wetter conditions were roughly equal. Three of the models agreed with indications of a moister West coast and all five agreed with respect to a drying out of most of the Gulf and Atlantic coasts during the winter. Kellogg and Zhao (1988) compared the summer soil moisture patterns for the five different GCMs by portraying increases and decreases of soil moisture in summer relative to the control when carbon dioxide is doubled (see Fig. 1.11 in Wetherald, this volume). There is reasonable agreement among four of the models (GFDL, UKMO, OSU, and NCAR) for a tendency toward increased aridity for the midcontinent grain-growing areas of North America. Although the NCAR model predicts an increase in soil moisture for all of the upper-middle and high latitudes, the GFDL, OSU, and UKMO models indicate a drying out over most of North America. In the northeastern United States, four of the five models show increased aridity for the summer season. We see a large proportion

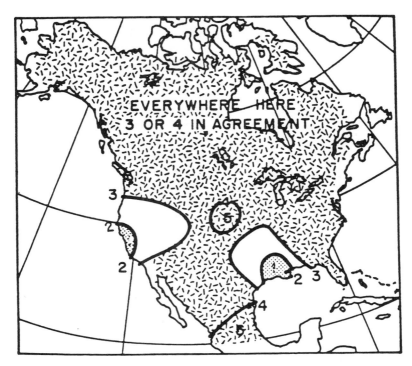

Fig. 2.5. Map showing the degree of agreement among five leading GCMs (the GFDL, GISS, NCAR, OSU, and UKMO) on the direction of the soil moisture change with doubled CO_2 conditions in summer. Areas shaded with hen-scratches show where three or more of the models agreed on a decrease of soil moisture; areas shaded with small dots show where two or fewer of the models agreed on a decrease, i.e., three or more agreed on an increase of soil moisture. From Kellogg and Zhao (1988) in J. Climate, American Meteorological Society.

of the continent with three to four models agreeing on the direction of change of soil moisture; the only place with all five models in agreement for drier soil moisture conditions is western Nebraska and Kansas and eastern Colorado (part of the High Plains region) (Fig. 2.5).

Many scientists are uncomfortable with public discussion of global warming because of the significant uncertainties and the policy implications (Beyea this volume, Topping, 1989, Wyman et al., this volume) associated with such a speculative scientific subject. Schneider et al. (1990) state that the issue of the environmental and societal consequences of climatic changes is "one of the best current examples of a problem in which the public need for reliable scientific knowledge exceeds the state-of-the-art ability to provide it." The complexities of the atmosphere–ocean–ice–land-surface climate system with all of its nonlinear interactive processes still greatly exceed the comprehensiveness of todays GCMs and the capabilities of today's computers. Some scientists believe that many important uncertainties are not likely to be resolved before some noticeable (maybe significant?) climatic changes are felt, and "certainly not before we are committed to some long-term, potentially irreversible (on societal time scales) effects." Society is thus faced with a classic example of the need to make critical decisions with imperfect information (Schneider et al. 1990).

In order to provide impact specialists with ranges of climate changes due to the greenhouse effect, Schneider et al. 1990 provided ranges of climate changes that reflect their interpretation of state-of-the-art modeling results (Table 2.4) The authors hoped to provide plausible estimates about the direction or magnitude of climatic changes over the next 50 years together with high, medium, or low levels of confidence for each variable. As another measure of the nature of the uncertainties, the authors included a rough estimate of the time that may be necessary to achieve a widespread scientific consensus on the direction and magnitude of the change. In the cases of magnitude and changes in sea level and global annual average temperature and precipitation, Schneider et al. (1990) state that such a consensus has almost been reached. In other cases, for example, simulation of the extent of cloud cover or time-evolving patterns of regional precipitation, the large uncertainties associated with current projections will need much more research, on the order of 10–50 years (Cess et al. 1989, Committee on Earth Sciences (CES) 1989, Kerr 1989, Mitchell et al. 1989).

Effects of Global Warming on Terrestrial Hydrology and Water Supply Systems

A profound effect of global warming may be major alterations in regional hydrologic cycles and changes in regional water availability. Callaway and Currie (1985) state that a CO_2 buildup has the potential to influence water availability in two ways:

1. Mean annual runoff may be affected because of changes in patterns of precipitation, air temperature and the transpiration rates of plants, which may be reduced because of increased stomatal resistance of plants in a CO_2-enriched atmosphere

2. The balance between surface water supply and demand may be modified because of climatically induced changes in water consumption and groundwater availability.

Callaway and Currie (1985) also identify water-resource issues with high, medium, and low potential sensitivity to global warming (Table 2.5) The water-resource issues are divided into three categories: supply of surface water and groundwater, distribution issues related to quantity and water quality, and use and reuse issues also related to water quantity and quality. If problems with soil salinization under irrigated agriculture already exists, or if groundwater is

Table 2.4. Estimates of the direction and magnitude of greenhouse gas-induced climate changes, the confidence of global and regional projections, and the time needed for research to lead to consensus for 2 × CO_2 model experiments*

| Phenomena | Projection of Probable Global Annual Average Change[a] | Distribution of Change | | | Significant Transients | Confidence of Projection | | Estimated Time for Research that Leads to Consensus (years) |
		Regional Average	Change in Seasonality	Interannual[b] Variability		Global Average	Regional Average	
Temperature	+2 to +5°C	−3 to +10°C	Yes	Down?	Yes	High	Medium	0–5
Sea Level	+10 to +100 cm	[d]	No	[c]	Unlikely	High	Medium	5–20
Precipitation	+7 to +15%	−20 to +20%	Yes	Up?	Yes	High	Low	10–50
Direct Solar Radiation	−10 to +10%	−30 to +30%	Yes	[c]	Possible	Low	Low	10–50
Evapotranspiration	+5 to +10%	−10 to +10%	Yes	[c]	Possible	High	Low	10–50
Soil Moisture	[c]	−50 to +50%	Yes	[c]	Yes	[c]	Medium	10–50
Runoff	Increase	−50 to +50%	Yes	[c]	Yes	Medium	Low	10–50
Severe Storms	[c]	[c]	[c]	[c]	Yes	[c]	[c]	10–50

*From Schneider et al. (1990).

[a]For an equivalent doubling of atmospheric CO_2 from the preindustrial level. These are equilibrium values, neglecting transient delays and adjustments.

[b]Inferences based upon preliminary results for the U.S. of D. Rind and Colleagues at GISS, 1989. See Rind et al. 1989 *Clim. Change* 14:5-37.

[c]No basis for quantitative or qualitative forecast.

[d]Increases in sea level at approximately the global rate except where local geological activity prevails.

31

Table 2.5. Potential sensitivity of water resource issues to CO_2 buildup

High Potential Sensitivity to CO_2 Buildup

Inadequate surface water supply/storage
Groundwater mining
Conflicts in use
Water losses from storage systems
Vegetation management
Drought
Flooding
River sedimentation
Salinity problems

Moderate Potential Sensitivity to CO_2 Buildup

Waterlogging of soils
Saline intrusion of aquifers
Surface water contamination
Effects of land use change on basin hydrology
Acidification of lakes
Waterborne diseases
Eutrophication
Inefficient irrigation practices/management
Navigation problems

Low Potential Sensitivity to CO_2 Buildup

Reservoir sedimentation
Groundwater contamination
Effect of changing lake levels on aquatic ecosystems
Conveyance losses
Availability of potable water
Inadequate water treatment facilities
Channel scour/Channel erosion
Groundwater infiltration into municipal sewer systems

From Callaway and Currie (1985).

currently being mined (i.e., withdrawn at a rate in excess of natural recharge over the long term), or if drought conditions and inadequate surface water-supply or storage problems already exist, then Callaway and Currie assert that these water-resource issues are potentially highly sensitive to global warming.

Gleick (1986) reviews methods for evaluating regional hydrologic impacts of global climate change and proposes the use of modified water-balance models such as his model of the Sacramento Basin in California (Gleick 1987a,b). Gleick's model is parametric (i.e., it contains both deterministic and statistical empirically based components). It incorporates month-to-month or seasonal variations in climate, snowfall and snowmelt algorithms, groundwater fluctuations, soil moisture characteristics, and watershed lag criteria to account for water-transfer delays in a drainage basin. The model is capable of reproducing both the magnitude and the timing of monthly and seasonal runoff, as well as changes in soil moisture conditions.

Global warming will affect the future design, construction, and operation of water-supply systems. The time horizon for such water accession and development projects is sufficiently long (Table 2.1) that early planning for the hydrologic impacts of climatic changes could prevent the failure of new facilities when conditions change. In light of the current economic outlook for building water-resource projects, Riebsame (1988) suggests that "oversized structural capacity, the traditional adjustment to climate variability in water resources, may prove less feasible in the future as (water resource) projects become smaller and new facilities are delayed by economic and environmental concerns" (see Hanchey et al. 1988 for a description of current problems in water-resource planning faced by the US Army Corps of Engineers). Gleick (1990) discusses the critical vulnerabilities of water supply systems to climatic variability and climatic change and identifies quantitative measures for evaluating these vulnerabilities for water-resource regions within the United States. He separates the vulnerabilities of water-supply systems to climate into three categories: meteorologic and climatologic, hydrologic system and design, and geographic and societal. The most important meteorological events with respect to water resources are the magnitude and time of storms and the magnitude and duration of droughts. Hydrologic system and design vulnerabilities would include physical vulnerabilities related to the design of reservoirs, aqueducts, pumps, and treatment facilities and the physical and economic issues regulating intrabasin and interbasin transfers of water. Examples of geographic vulnerabilities would include regions with a large demand relative to supply, with extensive development in floodplains, with vulnerable groundwater supplies, or with climate-induced changes in aquifer recharge rates.

Reservoirs and dams are the most important components of water supply systems and they are generally constructed to endure climatic variation. However, reservoirs in the United States serve diverse purposes of which water supply is but one. Gleick (1990) reminds us that other functions such as flood control, hydroelectric production, and recreation often conflict with some reservoirs' designated primary purpose of providing water supply.

Five specific quantitative indicators that distinguish different sorts of regional vulnerabilities to climate change can be used to offer insights into such important vulnerabilities as floods and droughts, groundwater overuse, and reliance on hydroelectricity. Gleick evaluated the indicators (which are given in the caption for Fig. 2.6) on an annual basis for the 21 official United States water-resource regions. Figure 2.6 is a map showing the cumulative water-resource vulnerability of hydrologic regions in the United States. The patterns in the map indicate the number of vulnerability factors exceeded by each region. The most vulnerable regions are the Great Basin in Utah and Nevada, the Missouri Basin, and Califor-

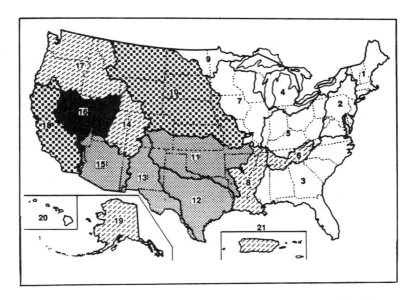

Fig. 2.6. Map showing cumulative water resource vulnerability of hydrologic regions of the United States. Patterns indicate the number of vulnerability factors exceeded by each region: plain, 1 factor; slanted dashes, 2 factors; dots, 3 factors; squares, 4 factors; solid, 5 factors. These five factors are (a) storage capacity as a fraction of supply, (b) ratio of demand to renewable supply, (c) percentage of total electricity produced by hydroelectricity, (d) ratio of groundwater overdraft to total groundwater supply, and (e) variability of streamflow. The regions are 1: New England; 2: Mid-Atlantic; 3: South Atlantic-Gulf; 4: Great Lakes; 5: Ohio; 6: Tennessee; 7: Upper Mississippi; 8: Lower Mississippi; 9: Souris-Red-Rainy; 10: Missouri; 11: Arkansas-White-Red; 12: Texas-Gulf; 13: Rio Grande; 14: Upper Colorado; 15: Lower Colorado; 16: Great Basin; 17: Pacific Northwest; 18: California; 19: Alaska; 20: Hawaii; 21: Caribbean. From *EOS, Transactions of the American Geophysical Union*, 70, 67 (January 31, 1989). Map provided to *Eos* by Dr. Peter Gleick, Pacific Institute, Berkeley, California. Map will appear in Waggoner 1990, reprinted by permission of John Wiley & Sons, Inc.

nia. Although the Great Basin and the Missouri Basin have large storage capacities, they also have high demands, including a high demand for water-produced electricity, and they are experiencing a significant overuse of their groundwater resources. Although the more humid eastern United States is largely characterized by only one of the five vulnerability factors in any one water-resource region, it is well known that the eastern United States experiences drought episodes that affect large numbers of people (Karl and Young 1987, Taylor 1986).

Expectations of Climate Change by Water-Resource Managers

Riebsame (1989) and Schwarz and Dillard (1990) interviewed selected urban water managers and conducted surveys to determine if the water managers incor-

Table 2.6. Response of water managers to convincing evidence for climate change by 2010*

Response	Southwest		Southeast	
	No.	%	No.	%
No response necessary	15	20	1	2
Commit limited resources to monitoring and planning	33	44	23	56
Make changes in operations and/or facilities in anticipation	27	36	17	42
Total	75	100	41	100

*From William E. Riebsame (1989).

porate thoughts and expectations about climate change in their planning and management of water resources. Previous research suggests that natural-resource planners tend to assume long-term stability or "normality" of environmental variables. Riebsame (1989) states that this is especially strong in water-resource planning "where long-term future conditions are assumed to emulate those observed over the past several decades." If detailed and reliable forecasts of future climatic trends are not available, these assumptions may make sense; however, tree-ring research (Cook this volume, Michaelsen et al. 1987) offer proof that more than several decades should be considered in drought management and flood protection. Tree-ring chronologies enable reconstructions of the historical precipitation records to be made over the past several hundred to several thousand years. They can reveal major and minor fluctuations in precipitation variability as well as the kinds of climatic variability inherent in the climate system. Increasingly credible predictions of global warming (Table 2.4) provide a rationale for analyzing and perhaps adjusting expectations of climate in water-resource planning.

Mail surveys (and some interviews) were conducted by Riebsame (1989) of water managers in the southwestern and southeastern United States. These regions were selected because they have experienced marked precipitation anomalies over the past several years. The Southwest has experienced recent dramatic increases in precipitation (e.g., the record heights of the Great Salt Lake in Utah as well as rainfall increases in Arizona, Utah, and Nevada). The Southeast has had to endure a drying trend over several years in the 1980s, especially with respect to summer precipitation. Table 2.6 summarizes the responses of water managers after they were shown convincing evidence during interviews for climate change by the year 2010. Twenty percent of the Southwest managers believed no response was justified and less than 45% of them believed they should commit limited resources to monitoring and planning. In addition to this study, Schwarz and Dillard (1990) used the case study approach to examine the climatic sensitivity of urban water systems by surveying the possible impacts of climate change on the physical structures and management of eight urban water-supply systems in the United States. They analyzed urban water management in terms of supply, waste disposal, storm drainage, flood protection, and amenities. In general, both Schwarz and Dillard (1990) and Riebsame (1989) found that although managers acknowledge that climate change as defined by GCM predictions can significantly affect water systems, they do not see climate change as a cause for immediate major concern or action.

Review of the Report of the Committee on Earth Sciences

The initial research plan for the United States' Global Change Research Program is set forth in the July, 1989 report by the Committee on Earth Sciences of the Office of Science and Technology Policy of the Executive Office of the President (CES, 1989). The report states that the goal of the program "is to provide a sound scientific basis for national and international decision making on global change issues." Seven interdisciplinary research activities were identified by the Committee; one of the seven elements is titled "Climate and Hydrologic Systems." Below is a summary of this Committee's report, which outlines the strengths and weaknesses of current understanding and predictive modeling in climate and hydrologic systems.

Current understanding of climate and hydrologic systems allows the numerical prediction of atmospheric behavior at the shorter time scale of weather events and episodes. We now know the general processes through which water plays a fundamental role in radiation, atmospheric chemistry, and the transport and storage of heat, as well as the major dynamic processes that determine the oceanic circulation, including the El Nino-Southern Oscillation events. Also now understood is glacier mass balance, some aspects of the physics of glacier flow, and the role of the land surface and ice albedo (shortwave reflectivity of ice) in the global radiation balance. In the past decade, significant improvements have been made in the manner in which the process of evapotranspiration of plants or vegetation canopies and their interaction with the climate system are depicted (Abramopoulos et al. 1988, Dickinson 1984, Entekhabi and Eagleson 1989, Sellers et al. 1986, Wilson et al. 1987a,b).

A principal weakness in current understanding of climate and hydrologic systems is our limited knowledge of the way in which small-scale atmospheric processes affect larger scale climate processes and conversely, the influence of large-scale processes on small-scale events. The study of remote-coupling mechanisms between regional processes in the atmosphere and corresponding processes in the ocean needs more work, as does study of the general circulation of the ocean and the processes by which surface water and deep water are exchanged. We also lack proper understanding of the interaction between chemical constituents (such as trace gas species), radiation (both longwave and shortwave), and the dynamics and thermodynamics of the atmosphere. Also important is further study of the role of water throughout the climate system, that is, the functioning of the hydrologic cycle on global and, especially, regional scales (Brutsaert et al. 1988, Eagleson 1986). The dynamics and thermodynamics of the interaction between sea ice and the ocean and atmosphere–land surface–ocean–ice coupling mechanisms, need further attention. Finally, the influence of large-scale atmospheric processes controlling rainfall anomalies (e.g., droughts, monsoon irregularities, hurricane fluctuations, and flood episodes) will be critical to any understanding of water-resource changes.

The Committee further believes that GCMs simulate well the large-scale circulation features of the atmosphere and some of the primary features of past climates and current observed global climate. Models relating the interactions of meteorologic and hydrologic processes over relatively short time scales and small spatial scales have reached a relatively advanced state of development. Substantial improvement in models can be achieved by improvements in computational processing ability alone, and this is continuing to increase rapidly. Because of increased computational capability, major progress in ocean modeling and in ocean model data assimilation has occurred, particularly in ocean basin-scale models. However, despite the available computational capability, the research community is severely limited by the resolution required for climate GCMs.

Finally, the Committee's consensus on the principal weaknesses in current predictive models include the need to improve the ability of these climate models to reproduce the annual cycle of seasonal changes in the oceans and atmosphere and to simulate the changes in the atmosphere or in the hydrologic system observed over the last 100 years. Also important is an improvement in the representation of clouds and their overall effect on the Earth's radiation balance, including how global cloud processes will modulate global warming (Cess et al. 1989, Ramanathan et al. 1989). At the current time, GCMs cannot provide input at ecologically important regional, ecosystem, or watershed scales (Fig. 2.3); climate and hydrology models that can bridge the difference between GCMs and ecosystem scales must be developed. Many key ocean processes are not modeled well, yet are critical to model success; examples include vertical convection, mixing, and parameterization of turbulent eddies and other physical phenomena smaller than grid scale. No global ocean model is yet capable of assimilating ocean observations in the same way that numerical weather prediction models use atmospheric observations, and major progress needs to be made toward the development of truly coupled ocean–atmosphere models. Lastly, despite modest improvements, the adequate parameterization of variables representing the terrestrial phase of the hydrologic cycle remains a major weakness in the capabilities of existing GCMs; principal shortcomings relate to the high degree of spatial variability of land surface characteristics (topography, soils, vegetation), spatial variability of precipitation, representation of lateral as well as vertical movement of water in the subsurface, and orographic (topographic) influences on rainfall and temperature.

Summary

The global rise of atmospheric CO_2 and other trace gases will spatially and seasonally alter temperature and, therefore, precipitation. Together, these will change global as well as regional climates and hydrology. Evapotranspiration, soil moisture content, surface runoff, groundwater recharge, seasonal snowfall, timing of snowmelt periods, river flows, lake levels, hydrologic variability and sensitivity, natural and artificial storage, and, of course, sea-level rise and associated coastal flooding will all be affected.

Although there may be a growing consensus among climate modelers that a greenhouse warming will increase global precipitation (+7 to +15%, Table 2.4), the regional impacts are much less certain (−20 to +20%, Table 2.4); several GCMs show tendencies for midlatitude continental interiors to experience greater aridity under $2 \times CO_2$ equilibrium conditions. Because relatively small changes in precipitation and temperature can have large effects on soil moisture status and the volume and timing of runoff, the impacts of climate change on regional water supplies can be large.

We expect regional predictions of climatic patterns of air temperature and precipitation to improve as the horizontal resolution of the GCMs increases (i.e., the spatial mesh used for calculations becomes finer), as the simulation of heat uptake and transport by the ocean improves, and as the parameterization of modeled clouds improves in all respects. The $2 \times CO_2$ experiments by the climate-modeling groups must also evolve from their equilibrium calculations for doubled CO_2 conditions to the modeling of a transient response to increasing atmospheric CO_2 (Schneider and Thompson 1981). Such models would incorporate a gradual increasing of simulated CO_2 content, a more realistic method, which becomes important when water resource and other policy decisions are being made.

Lastly, because of the interconnectedness of the physical environment and man's use of physical resources, environmental and social scientists must evaluate the impact of long-term, simultaneously occurring environmental problems. For example, Glantz and Ausubel (1984) compare and contrast the implications of existing groundwater mining of the Ogallala aquifer because of agricultural activities in the United States Great Plains with the potential for increased frequency, duration, and severity of droughts in the region with global warming. As the ability of the GCMs to make regional-scale predictions of climate patterns improves, further study of long-term slowly developing, but cumulative, environmental problems that occur simultaneously will be needed.

Acknowledgments

I would like to thank the three anonymous reviewers and R. L. Wyman for their helpful suggestions. The manuscript has benefited from their comments.

References

Abramopoulos, F., C. Rosenzweig, and B. C. Choudhury. 1988. Improved ground hydrology calculations for global climate models (GCMs): Soil water movement and evapotranspiration. *J. Climate* 1:921–941.

Bates, G. T. and G. A. Meehl. 1986. The effect of CO_2 concentration on the frequency of blocking in a general circulation model coupled to a simple mixed layer ocean model. *Monthly Weather Rev.* 114:687–701.

Brutsaert, W., T. J. Schmugge, P. J. Sellers, and F. G. Hall. 1988. Large-scale experimental technology with remote sensing in land surface hydrology and meteorology. *EOS, Trans. Am. Geophys. Union* 69:561, 569–570.

Callaway, J. M. and J. W. Currie. 1985. Water resource systems and changes in climate and vegetation. In *Characterization of Information Requirements for Studies of CO_2 Effects: Water Resources, Agriculture, Fisheries, Forests and Human Health* (DOE/ER–0236), M. R. White (ed), pp. 23–67, US Dept. of Energy, Washington, DC.

Cess, R. D., G. L. Potter, J. P. Blanchet, G. J. Boer, S. J. Ghan, J. T. Kiehl, H. Le Treut, Z. X. Li, X.-Z. Liong, J. F. B. Mitchell, J.-J. Morcrette, D. A. Randall, M. R. Riches, E. Roeckner, U. Schlese, A. Slingo, K. E. Taylor, W. M. Washington, R. T. Wetherald and I. Yagai. 1989. Interpretation of cloud-climate feedback as produced by 14 atmospheric general circulation models. *Science* 245:513–516.

Changnon, S. A., Jr. 1987. *Detecting Drought Conditions in Illinois*. Circular 169, Illinois State Water Survey, Champaign, IL.

Committee on Earth Sciences (CES). 1989. *Our Changing Planet: The FY 1990 Research Plan*. Federal Coordinating Council on Science Engineering, and Technology, Office of Science and Technology Policy, Executive Office of the President, Washington, DC. (Available from the US Geological Survey, Reston, VA.)

Dickinson, R. E. 1984. Modeling evapotranspiration for three-dimensional global climate models. In *Climate Processes and Climate Sensitivity*, J. E. Hansen and T. Takahashi (eds.), p. 58–72. Geophysical Monograph No. 29. American Geophysical Union, Washington, D.C.

Dickinson, R. E. and R. J. Cicerone. 1986. Future global warming from atmospheric trace gases. *Nature* 319:109–115.

Eagleson, P. S. 1986. The emergence of global-scale hydrology. *Water Resources Res.* 22:6s–14s.

Entekhabi, D. and P. S. Eagleson. 1989. Land surface hydrology parameterization for atmospheric general circulation models including subgrid scale spatial variability. *J. Climate* 2:816–831.

Glantz, M. H. and J. H. Ausubel. 1984. The Ogallala aquifer and carbon dioxide: Comparison and convergence. *Environ. Conserv.* 11:123–131.

Gleick, P. H. 1986. Methods for evaluating the regional hydrologic impacts of global climatic changes. *J. Hydrol.* 88:97–116.

Gleick, P. H. 1987a. The development and testing of a water balance model for climate impact assessment: Modeling the Sacramento basin. *Water Resources Res.* 23:1049–1061.

Gleick, P. H. 1987b. Regional hydrologic consequences of increases in atmospheric CO_2 and other trace gases. *Climat. Change* 10:137–160.

Gleick, P. H. 1990. Vulnerabilities of water systems. In *Climate Change and U.S. Water Resources*, P. E. Waggoner (ed.), pp. 223–240. John Wiley, New York. 1990.

Hanchey, J. R., K. E. Schilling, and E. Z. Stakhiv. 1988. Water resources planning under climate uncertainty. In *Preparing for Climate Change, Proceedings of the First North American Confer-*

ence, (Oct. 27–29, 1987, Washington, D.C.), pp. 394–405. Government Institutes, Rockville, MD.

Hansen, J., A. Lacis, D. Rind, G. Russell, P. Stone, I. Fung, R. Ruedy, and J. Lerner. 1984. Climate sensitivity: Analysis of feedback mechanisms. In *Climate Processes and Climate Sensitivity*, J. E. Hansen and T. Takahashi (eds.), Geophysical Monograph No. 29, pp. 130–163. American Geophysical Union, Washington, D.C.

Hansen, J., I. Fung, A. Lacis, D. Rind, S. Lebedeff, R. Ruedy, and G. Russell. 1988. Global climate changes as forecast by Goddard Institute for Space Studies three-dimensional model. *J. Geophys. Res.* 93:9341–9364.

Hansen, J., D. Rind, A. Delgenio, A. Lacis, S. Lebedeff, M. Prather, R. Ruedy, and T. Karl. 1989. Regional greenhouse climate effects. In *Second North American Conference on Preparing for Climate Change* (Dec. 6–8, 1988), pp. 68–81. Climate Institute, Washington, DC.

Houghton, R. A. and G. M. Woodwell. 1989. Global climate change. *Sci. Am.* 260:36–44.

Karl, T. R. and P. J. Young. 1987. The 1986 Southeast drought in historical perspective. *Bull. Am. Meteorol. Soc.* 68:773–778.

Katz, R. W. 1988. Statistics of climate change: Implications for scenario development. In *Societal Responses to Regional Climatic Change: Forecasting by Analogy*, M. H. Glantz (ed.), p. 95–112. Westview Press, Boulder, CO.

Kellogg, W. W. and Z-C. Zhao. 1988. Sensitivity of soil moisture to doubling of carbon dioxide in climate model experiments. Part I: North America. *J. Climate* 1:348–366.

Kerr, R. A. 1989. How to fix the clouds in greenhouse models. *Science* 243:28–29.

Manabe, S. and R. J. Stouffer. 1980. Sensitivity of a global climate model to an increase of CO_2 concentration in the atmosphere. *J. Geophys. Res.* 85:5529–5554.

Manabe, S. and R. T. Wetherald. 1986. Reduction in summer soil wetness induced by an increase in atmospheric carbon dioxide. *Science* 232:626–628.

Manabe, S. and R. T. Wetherald. 1987. Large-scale changes of soil wetness induced by an increase in atmospheric carbon dioxide. *J. Atmos. Sci.* 44:1211–1235.

Manabe, S., R. T. Wetherald, and R. J. Stouffer. 1981. Summer dryness due to an increase of atmospheric CO_2 concentration. *Clim. Change* 3:347–386.

Marshal, E. 1989. EPA's plan for cooling the global greenhouse. *Science* 243:1544–1545.

Meehl, G. A. and W. M. Washington. 1986. Tropical response to increased CO_2 in a GCM with a simple mixed layer ocean: Similarities to an observed Pacific warm event. *Monthly Weather Rev.* 114:667–674.

Meehl, G. A. and W. M. Washington. 1988. A comparison of soil-moisture sensitivity in two global climate models. *J. Atmos. Sci.* 45:1476–1492.

Michaelson, J., L. Haston, and F. W. Davis. 1987. 400 years of central California precipitation variability reconstructed from tree rings. *Water Resources Bull.* 23:809–818.

Mitchell, J. F. B. 1983. The seasonal response of a general circulation model to changes in CO_2 and sea temperature. *Q. J. Roy. Meteorol. Soc.* 109:113–152.

Mitchell, J. F. B. and D. A. Warrilow. 1987. Summer dryness in northern midlatitudes due to increased CO_2. *Nature* 330:238–240.

Mitchell, J. F. B., C. A. Wilson, and W. M. Cunnington. 1987. On CO_2 climate sensitivity and model dependence of results. *Q. J. Roy. Meteorol. Soc.* 113:293–322.

Mitchell, J. F. B., C. A. Senior, and W. J. Ingram. 1989. CO_2 and climate: A missing feedback? *Nature* 341:132–134.

National Research Council (NRC). 1989. *Ozone Depletion, Greenhouse Gases, and Climate Change.* National Academy Press, Washington, DC.

Nihoul, J. C. J. (ed.). 1985. *Coupled Ocean-Atmosphere Models.* Elsevier, New York.

Ramanathan, V. 1988. The greenhouse theory of climate change: A test by an inadvertent global experiment. *Science* 240:293–299.

Ramanathan, V., L. Callis, R. Cess, J. Hansen, I. Isaksen, W. Kuhn, A. Lacis, F. Luther, J. Mahlman, R. Reck, and M. Schlesinger. 1987. Climate-chemical interactions and effects of changing atmospheric trace gases. *Rev. Geophys.* 25:1441–1482.

Ramanathan, V., R. D. Cess, E. F. Harrison, P. Minnis, B. R. Barkstrom, E. Ahmad, and D. Hartmann. 1989. Cloud-radiative forcing and climate: Results from the Earth Radiation Budget Experiment. *Science* 243:57–63.

Ramanathan, V., R. J. Cicerone, H. B. Singh, and J. T. Kiehl. 1985. Trace gas trends and their potential role in climate change. *J. Geophys. Res.* 90:5547–5566.

Rasmussen, R. A. and M. A. K. Khalil. 1986. Atmospheric trace gases: Trends and distributions over the last decade. *Science* 232:1623–1624.

Riebsame, W. E. 1988. Adjusting water resources management to climate change. *Climat. Change* 13:69–97.

Riebsame, W. E. 1989. Expectations of climate and climate change: Results of surveys of water resource managers. Unpublished.

Rind, D. 1987. The doubled CO_2 climate: Impact of the sea surface temperature gradient. *J. Atmos. Sci.* 44:3235–3268.

Rind, D. 1988a. The doubled CO_2 climate and the sensitivity of the modeled hydrologic cycle. *J. Geophys. Res.* 93:5385–5412.

Rind, D. 1988b. Likely effects of global warming on water availability and hydrology in North America. In *Preparing for Climate Change, Proceedings of the First North American Conference* (Oct. 27–29, 1987, Washington, DC), pp. 377–381. Government Institutes, Rockville, MD.

Schlesinger, M. E. 1984. Climate model simulations of CO_2-induced climatic change. *Adv. Geophys.* 26:141–235.

Schlesinger, M. E. 1986. Equilibrium and transient climatic warming induced by increased atmospheric CO_2. *Climate Dynamics* 1:35–51.

Schlesinger, M. E. (ed.). 1988. *Physically-Based Modelling and Simulation of Climate and Climatic Change,* NATO Advanced Science Institute Series. Kluwer Academic Publishers, Boston, MA.

Schlesinger, M. E. and J. F. B. Mitchell. 1987. Climate model simulations of the equilibrium climatic response to increased carbon dioxide. *Rev. Geophys.* 25:760–798.

Schlesinger, M. E. and Z-C. Zhao. 1989. Seasonal climatic changes induced by doubled CO_2 as simulated by the OSU atmospheric GCM/Mixed-layer ocean model. *J. Climate* 2:459–495.

Schneider, S. H. 1987. Climate modeling. *Sci. Am.* 256:72–80.

Schneider, S. H. 1989a. The Greenhouse effect: Science and policy. *Science* 243:771–781.

Schneider, S. H. 1989b. The changing climate. *Sci. Am.* 261:70–79.

Schneider, S. H. and S. L. Thompson. 1981. Atmospheric CO_2 and climate: importance of the transient response. *J. Geophys. Res.* 86:3135–3147.

Schneider, S. H., P. H. Gleick, and L. O. Mearns. (1990). Prospects for climate change. In *Climate Change and U.S. Water Resources,* P. E. Waggoner (ed.). pp. 41–73. John Wiley, New York.

Schwarz, H. E. and L. A. Dillard. 1990. Urban water. In *Climate Change and U.S. Water Resources,* P. E. Waggoner (ed.). pp. 341–366. John Wiley, New York.

Sellers, P. J., Y. Mintz, Y. C. Sud, and A. Dalcher. 1986. A simple biosphere model (SiB) for use within general circulation models. *J. Atmos. Sci.* 43:505–531.

Taylor, R. S. 1986. New York City's water supply drought of 1985. In *Conference on Climate and Water Management—A Critical Era.* (Aug. 4–7, 1986, Asheville, NC), pp. 1–6. American Meteorological Society, Boston, MA.

Topping, J. C., Jr. (ed.). 1989. *Coping With Climate Change: Proceedings of the Second North American Conference on Preparing for Climate Change—A Cooperative Approach.* The Climate Institute, Washington, D.C.

Trabalka, J. R. (ed.). 1985. *Atmospheric Carbon Dioxide and the Global Carbon Cycle* (DOE/ER–0239). US Dept. of Energy, Washington, DC.

Waggoner, P. E. (ed.). 1990. *Climate Change and U.S. Water Resources.* John Wiley, New York.

Waggoner, P. E. and J. Schefter. 1990. Future water use in the present climate. In *Climate Change and U.S. Water Resources,* P. E. Waggoner (ed.). pp. 19–39. John Wiley, New York.

Washington, W. M. and G. A. Meehl. 1984. Seasonal cycle experiment on the climate sensitivity due to a doubling of CO_2 with an atmospheric general circulation model coupled to a simple mixed-layer ocean model. *J. Geophys. Res.* 89:9475–9503.

Wetherald, R. T. and S. Manabe. 1988. Cloud feedback processes in a general circulation model. *J. Atmos. Sci.* 45:1397–1415.

Wilson, C. A. and J. F. B. Mitchell. 1986. Diurnal variation and clouds in a general circulation model. *Q. J. Roy. Meteorol. Soc.* 112:347–369.

Wilson, C. A. and J. F. B. Mitchell. 1987. A doubled CO_2 climate sensitivity experiment with a global climate model including a simple ocean. *J. Geophys. Res.* 92:13,315–13,343.

Wilson, M. F., A. Henderson-Sellers, R. E. Dickinson, and P. J. Kennedy. 1987a. Sensitivity of the biosphere-atmosphere transfer scheme (BATS) to the inclusion of variable soil characteristics. *J. Climate App. Meteorol.* 26:341–362.

Wilson, M. F., A. Henderson-Sellers, R. E. Dickinson, and P. J. Kennedy. 1987b. Investigation of the sensitivity of the land-surface parameterization of the NCAR Community Climate Model in regions of tundra vegetation. *J. Climatol.* 7:319–343.

3

The Role of Forests in Affecting the Greenhouse Gas Composition of the Atmosphere

Richard A. Houghton

Introduction

The high summer temperatures and unusual drought in the United States in 1988, along with the burning of forests in Yellowstone National Park and extremes of weather in other parts of the world, raised public awareness of the greenhouse effect. Whether or not 1988 marked the arrival of climatic change, there is a scientific consensus that such summers will occur more frequently if the concentrations of greenhouse gases in the atmosphere continue to increase. The major greenhouse gases are carbon dioxide (CO_2), methane (CH_4), nitrous oxide (N_2O), the chlorofluorocarbons (CFCs), and tropospheric ozone (O_3). They are called greenhouse gases because they are more transparent to the short-wave radiation of the sun's energy than they are to the long-wave radiation of the energy re-radiated from the Earth. Thus, the equilibrium temperature of the Earth is greater as a result of these gases and will increase as the concentrations of the gases increase.

The greenhouse effect is "one of the most well-established theories in atmospheric science" (Schneider 1989). It was hypothesized by scientists almost 100 years ago (Arrhenius 1896, Chamberlin 1899), and today the radiative properties of trace gases are well known. The greenhouse effect is essential for life on earth. Without it the Earth's average temperature would be about $-18°C$, 33° cooler than it is presently (Schneider and Mesirow 1976). The recent notoriety of the greenhouse effect is due to the increasing concentrations of greenhouse gases and to the increased temperatures and other changes in climate that seem to be underway as a result.

The increase in the concentration of greenhouse gases in the atmosphere over the last decades and centuries is a fact. Continuous measurements of CO_2 were begun in 1957 by C. D. Keeling at Mauna Loa, Hawaii, and at the South Pole. The concentration of CO_2 at Mauna Loa increased from 315 ppm (parts per million by volume) in 1958 to about 351 ppm in 1988 (Keeling et al. 1989) (Fig. 1). In addition to these measurements over the last 30 years, there is now information on the concentrations of trace gases in preindustrial air. Analysis of

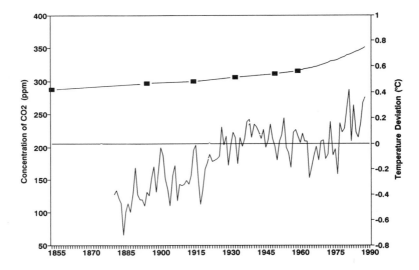

Fig. 3.1. (Upper) Atmospheric concentrations of CO_2 measured in air trapped in bubbles of glacial ice (Neftel et al. 1985) and, after 1958, measured continuously in air at Mauna Loa, Hawaii (Keeling et al. 1989). (Lower) Annual deviations of mean global surface air temperatures from the 30-year mean for the period 1951–1980. From Hansen and Lebedeff (1987).

air trapped in the bubbles of glacial ice shows that the preindustrial concentration of CO_2 was about 280 ppm (Neftel et al. 1985). Thus the amount of CO_2 in the atmosphere has increased by approximately 25% since 1750 or so. The concentration of methane has increased by 100% over the same time period (Stauffer et al. 1985).

Most scientists agree that the average temperature of the Earth's surface has increased by approximately 0.5°C since 1880 (Jones et al. 1986, Hansen and Lebedeff 1987) (Fig. 3.1). The decade of the 1980s was the warmest decade in the 100-year record, and 1988 was the warmest year (Anonymous 1990). There are other indications of a global warming. The temperature profile in the permafrost of the Alaskan and Canadian Arctic shows it (Lachenbruch and Marshall 1986). Observed changes in the distribution of precipitation (Bradley et al. 1987) are consistent with the patterns predicted for a warmer earth (Hansen et al. 1988), and the sea level is rising (Peltier and Tushingham 1989). None of these changes by itself establishes unequivocally that the earth is warming as a result of the changes in the composition of the atmosphere, but together they provide strong evidence that the warming is underway.

The warming might be part of a natural fluctuation, not related to the increasing concentrations of greenhouse gases. However, if the radiative properties of these gases are known, how is this uncertainty possible? The reason is that the climate of

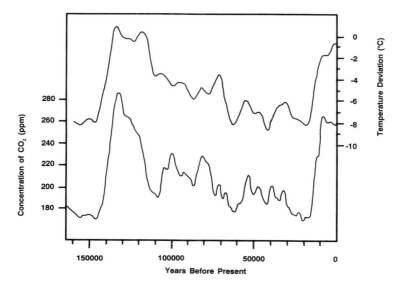

Fig. 3.2. Variations in atmospheric CO_2 concentration and temperature over the past 160,000 years as recorded in glacial ice at Vostoc, Antarctica. From Lorius et al. (1988).

the earth is more complicated than the greenhouse effect. The latter, technically, concerns only the radiative properties of a gas. The earth's climate, on the other hand, includes many linkages and feedbacks between atmospheric temperature, oceanic heat storage, clouds, humidity, ice cover, energy budgets, heat transport, and so on.

The evidence that the warming today is the result of the greenhouse effect comes from two sources. First, global climate models, based on the physics of the atmosphere and the linkages and feedbacks listed above, predict an average global warming of 1.5 to 4.5°C when the concentration of CO_2 in the simulated atmosphere is doubled above preindustrial concentrations (Wetherald, this volume) (current concentrations are approximately 25% above preindustrial levels). These models cannot provide geographically detailed predictions of such factors as soil moisture, but they are generally consistent in their predictions of temperature change. Their credibility is based on their demonstrated ability to capture the geographical patterns of seasonal temperatures in the present climate and to reproduce climates of the past.

The second type of evidence that atmospheric CO_2 and the Earth's temperature are linked comes from the strong correlation between the two over-time scales ranging from decades (Keeling et al. 1989, Kuo et al. 1990) to tens of thousands of years (Barnola et al. 1987, Lorius et al. 1988) (Fig. 3.2). During cold years or glacial periods, the concentrations of CO_2 are lower than during warm years or interglacial periods. The same correlation with temperature exists for the other greenhouse gases CH_4 and N_2O (Raynaud et al. 1988, Khalil and Rasmussen 1989). It is not clear whether increasing concentrations of the greenhouse gases caused the warming or whether the warming caused increased concentrations of the gases. It is clear that the warming is much too great to have been caused either by variations in the Earth's orbit or by the radiative properties of the gases alone (Lorius et al. 1988). For example, the statistical correspondence between CO_2 and temperature in the 160,000-year record is more than five times the radiative forcing expected for the gas. Despite the uncertainty as to cause and effect, the tight coupling of the gas concentrations with temperature is consistent with a positive feedback. That is, increased concentrations of CO_2 cause increases in temperature, increased temperatures cause further releases of CO_2, and so on. Once begun, the process amplifies itself.

Releases of CO_2 to the Atmosphere During the Last Century

At least two activities have been responsible for the increased concentrations of atmospheric CO_2: (1) emissions of CO_2 from combustion of fossil fuels and (2) releases of CO_2 from deforestation. A third contributor may have been the warming itself through its effect on terrestrial metabolism, including decomposition (Houghton and Woodwell 1989, Woodwell 1989). This third contribution has probably been small during the last 100 years, but it could become substantial if the Earth continues to warm. The temperature-enhanced release of CO_2 is an example of the positive feedback described above.

Emissions from Combustion of Fossil Fuels

The annual, global release of CO_2 from combustion of fossil fuels since 1860 shows that the rate of combustion has increased exponentially (Fig. 3.3). One can recognize interruptions in the trend by the two World Wars and a reduction in the rate of increase following the jump in oil prices in 1973. Despite the jump in price, the use of fossil fuels and the CO_2 released annually to the atmosphere increased each year until 1980. From 1980 through 1983 the annual emissions decreased each year. But the downward trend was temporary. Starting in 1984, the annual emissions increased again, such that by 1985 they were similar to 1979, and by 1986 they were the highest on record, 5.55 billion metric tons (bmt) (Marland 1989). Between 1860 and 1986, the total emission of carbon to the atmosphere from fossil fuels was about 190 bmt (Keeling et al. 1989).

Net Releases of Carbon from Deforestation

The release of carbon to the atmosphere from deforestation is calculated from rates of deforestation, documented from land-use statistics and satellite imagery

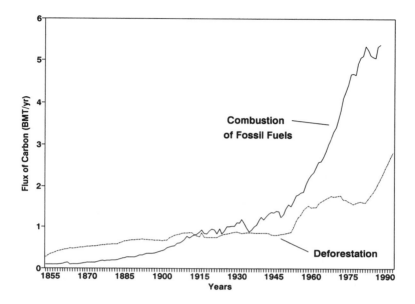

Fig. 3.3.   Annual global emissions of carbon from combustion of fossil fuels (Rotty and Marland 1986, Keeling et al. 1989, Marland 1989) and from deforestation (Houghton and Skole 1990).

(Woodwell et al. 1987) (Fig. 3.4), and from ecological data pertaining to the changes in vegetation and soil that accompany the transformation of forests to agricultural land. Deforestation releases CO_2 to the atmosphere because carbon stored in the organic matter of trees and soils is oxidized during the processes of clearing. This oxidation may occur rapidly through burning or may occur slowly through decay. If agricultural lands are abandoned and return to forests, the flux of carbon is reversed. Growing forests withdraw CO_2 from the atmosphere and store it again in trees and soil. In 1980 the ratio of deforestation to reforestation was 10:1 in the tropics (FAO/UNEP 1981).

The net release of carbon to the atmosphere from deforestation is estimated to have been between 1 and 2 bmt in 1980 and between 1.5 and 3 bmt in 1990 (Houghton 1990b). Almost the entire release was from the tropics; outside the tropics the releases and accumulations of carbon were small and approximately balanced (Houghton et al. 1987). The highest biotic release of carbon was not always from tropical countries, however. The large current releases from tropical America, Africa, and Asia did not begin until about 1950. In the nineteenth century the major regions of deforestation were the regions now industrialized, North America, Europe, and the Soviet Union. The total release from global deforestation between 1850 and 1985 is calculated to have been about 120 bmt (Houghton and Skole 1990) (Fig. 3.3).

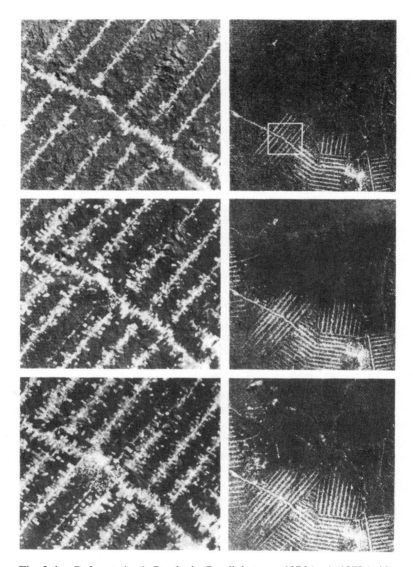

Fig. 3.4. Deforestation in Rondonia, Brazil, between 1976 (top), 1978 (middle), and 1981 (bottom). Images on the right are full Landsat scenes, 185 km on a side. Images on the left are enlargements of segments of the full scenes. The enlargements cover an area on the ground 30 km × 30 km. From Woodwell et al. (1987).

Deforestation and Reforestation in the Next Century

To estimate how much carbon might be released to the atmosphere in the future, projections of tropical deforestation and its associated release of carbon were computed to the year 2100. The purpose of the projections was to evaluate a range of possible exchanges of carbon between tropical ecosystems and the atmosphere. The projections are not predictions, but possibilities.

In the first two projections, the rates of deforestation between 1980 and 1985 were assumed to increase, linearly and exponentially, to the year 2100. The rate of deforestation in the tropics in 1980 was about 11.3 million ha per year (1 ha = 1 hectare = 2.47 acres). Thus an area slightly less than the area of New York State was deforested every year in the late 1970s. Under the first two projections, the total rate of deforestation increased from 11.3 million ha per year in 1980 to between 16 and 20 million ha per year in 2079, when the available area of closed forests in Latin America was eliminated. A small area of legally inaccessible forest was assumed to remain after 2079, but as the only area of forest left, it is unlikely to escape deforestation.

The annual net release of carbon increased from about 2.5 to 2.8 bmt in the linear projection and to about 3.3 in the exponential projection (Fig. 3.5) before forests could no longer be cleared in Latin America. The total net flux over the period 1980 to 2100 was 288 bmt carbon, more than twice the release that occurred in the 130-year period preceding 1980.

In the third projection, based on expected population growth, the rate of deforestation increased from 11.3 million ha per year in 1980 to about 29.7 million ha per year in 2045, when the available area of forest in Asia was exhausted. Forests in the rest of the tropics were eliminated within the next 30 years.

The projection gave a maximum annual release of carbon of about 5.0 bmt (Fig. 3.5), approximately equal to the annual emission of carbon from fossil fuels in the early 1980s. The total release of carbon from deforestation between 1980 and 2100 according to this projection was about 340 bmt.

All of the projections were based on rates of deforestation determined for the late 1970s (FAO/UNEP 1981). It is noteworthy that even the highest of the projections gave rates of deforestation in 1990 lower than the actual rates reported recently by Myers (1989). According to his estimates, the rate of tropical deforestation almost doubled in the 10 years between 1980 and 1989.

Deforestation need not continue until the tropical forests are gone. In the fourth projection deforestation was assumed to stop completely in 1991, and to be replaced by massive reforestation. The area available for reforestation in each region was estimated from the area of previously forested land that is currently neither forest, agricultural land, nor settled land. More than 500 million ha of such land is estimated to be available in the tropics. In addition, 365 million ha of fallow lands might be reforested by replacing shifting cultivation with low

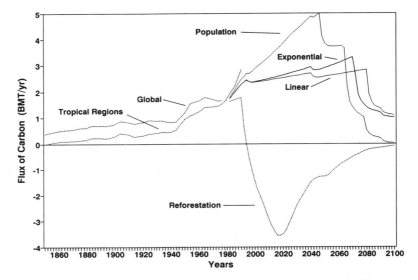

Fig. 3.5. Recent and projected annual fluxes of carbon between tropical forests and the atmosphere. The four projections are based on different assumptions of future rates of deforestation and reforestation. Positive values indicate a net release of carbon to the atmosphere; negative values indicate a withdrawal of carbon from the atmosphere. Abrupt decreases in the emissions of carbon occur after the loss of forests from a major region in the tropics. From Houghton (1990a).

input, permanent agriculture. These estimates are optimistic and crude, but if such an area were reforested in the tropics, about 100 bmt carbon could be withdrawn from the atmosphere and sequestered in new tropical forests (Houghton 1990a). The timing of the reforestation was arbitrarily chosen in the fourth projection, but rates of withdrawal reached values as high as 3 bmt carbon per year (Fig. 3.5), a rate equal to the current annual increase of carbon in the atmosphere.

A Third Strategy for Management of Atmospheric CO_2 Concentrations

The global warming of 1.5–4.5°C expected as a result of continued emissions of all greenhouse gases may occur by the middle of the next century, perhaps by 2030 (WMO/UNEP 1988). Such a warming is 10–100 times more rapid than the warming that has occurred since the last glacial maximum about 10,000 years ago (Fig. 3.2). The consequences of a warming this rapid include a 0.3- to 0.5-m rise in sea level, shifts in agricultural zones across national boundaries, mass mortality of trees, and an increased frequency of weather extremes. Such changes are likely to be difficult for most of the people of the world, for the changes will be rapid and continuous. Efforts to adapt to climatic changes are likely to produce adaptations to climates that no longer exist. The changes in climate will also be irreversible within human lifetimes. There is no way to cool the Earth or lower sea level if the changes are unacceptable. In fact, the Earth is already committed to a warming of 1–2°C from greenhouse gases already emitted to the atmosphere. This commitment to an irreversible warming increases with further emissions.

The only way to avoid these changes is to stabilize the concentrations of greenhouse gases in the atmosphere, and the only way to stabilize the concentrations is to *reduce emissions*. Stabilization of emissions keeps the concentrations increasing as they are currently. Without a stabilization of atmospheric concentrations the changes in climate are open-ended. Most discussion of the effects of climatic change are based on global climatic models that simulate a doubling of CO_2 concentrations (Wetherald, this volume) . The emphasis on a doubling seems to suggest that the Earth will reach a new equilibrium with warmer climates. The fact is that unless stopped by overt and deliberate human action the warming will continue for the indefinite future. Estimated reserves of recoverable fossil fuels are enough to increase the atmospheric concentration of CO_2 by a factor of five to ten, and the amount of organic carbon thought to be readily oxidizable in the world's plants and soils is at least as large as the amount of carbon in the atmosphere currently.

Stabilization of greenhouse gases in the atmosphere is not out of the question. Three measures are required. The most important is a large reduction in the use of fossil fuels. Increased energy efficiency in the industrialized world might reduce emissions by 50%, or by 2.5 bmt carbon, without changing living standards (Goldemberg et al. 1988). The second and third measures concern forests. Halting deforestation would reduce current emissions by 1.5–3.0 bmt, and a massive program in reforestation might withdraw as much as 2–3 bmt from the atmosphere annually for a few years.

But reforestation withdraws carbon from the atmosphere only for as long as the forests are gaining mass. Once they have matured, forests are approximately in balance with respect to carbon. They continue to hold the carbon they have accumulated, but they do not accumulate additional carbon. Thus reforestation helps stabilize the concentration of CO_2 only temporarily. On the other hand, forests could stabilize the concentration nearly indefinitely if wood fuels replaced fossil fuels as the major energy source. To replace fossil fuels indefinitely, forests have to be managed sustainably. That is, the wood harvested annually would have to be replaced by the regrowth of wood in large areas of managed forests. If forests required 20 years to grow to a harvestable size, for example, the total area of managed forests would have to be at least 20 times greater than the area annually harvested. Over a period of 20 years, the whole area would be harvested, but each year a different area would be cut; and after 20 years, the same area could be cut again.

The combustion of wood releases carbon to the atmosphere just as fossil fuels

Table 3.1. The current net flux of carbon to the atmosphere (bmt carbon per year) under different strategies of tropical forest management

Source of Carbon to the Atmosphere	Strategy		
	1 Current Land Use Practices	**2** Reforestation to Accumulate Carbon on Land	**3** Fossil Fuels Replaced with Wood Fuels
Fossil fuel	5.6	5.6	0
Deforestation	1.5 to 3.0	0	0
Reforestation	0	−1.5 (avg.)	0
Plantations	0	0	0*
Total release of carbon to the atmosphere (bmt per year)	7 to 9	4	0

*6.9 bmt carbon released annually from the combustion of 15×10^9 tons of wood harvested from 50 million ha, and 6.9 bmt carbon accumulated annually in 500 to 1000 million ha plantations regrowing from earlier harvests (see text).

do. In fact, it would release slightly more carbon than fossil fuels because the energy-to-carbon ratio for wood is lower than for oil and gas. However, as long as forests were managed sustainably, the carbon released each year by combustion would be accumulated again in forests regrowing from earlier harvests. The net flux of carbon to the atmosphere would be zero instead of the 7–9 bmt currently (Table 3.1).

Thus, one can consider three strategies for the use of forests in the tropics (Table 3.1). The first strategy is "business as usual," in which tropical forests will be eliminated from the earth in the next 75–100 years, releasing 120–335 bmt carbon to the atmosphere in the process. A second strategy, the withdrawal of carbon from the atmosphere, includes a cessation of deforestation and massive reforestation, estimated to be possible on 500 to 850 million ha of tropical lands. On the order of 1.5 bmt carbon per year might be withdrawn from the atmosphere over the next century (Table 3.1). The larger the forests, the more carbon that could be stored under this strategy, but the removal of carbon from the atmosphere would be temporary.

Only the third strategy provides a potentially permanent solution to stabilizing the concentration of CO_2 in the atmosphere. This strategy is the substitution of wood fuels for fossil fuels. The total use of energy from fossil fuels in 1980 was approximately 2.7×10^{14} MJ (1 MJ = 1 megajoule = 10^6 joules) (Goldemberg et al. 1988). This energy is equivalent to the energy in approximately 15×10^9 tons of wood, assuming an energy content of 17.5 MJ/kg dry wood (or 39 MJ/kg C) (Lieth 1975). Sustainable production of this amount of wood would require on the order of 500 to 1000 million ha, approximately 50 million ha harvested each year and the rest regrowing for future harvests. The area is approximately the area estimated to be available for reforestation in the tropics currently. At the high end of the range, it is roughly the size of the United States. The prospect of managing that area sustainably is sobering. On the other hand, the area currently managed for crop production, globally, is larger, almost 1500 million ha.

In the final analysis, stabilization of the concentration of CO_2 in the atmosphere, if the stabilization is to last into the indefinite future, must include a reduction of fossil fuel use, a cessation of deforestation, and an initiation of reforestation. Despite the emphasis here on the tropics, the measures are at least as appropriate and important in the temperate and boreal regions of the world, where approximately 75% of the world's fossil fuel is used currently (Rotty and Marland 1986). Furthermore, each of the measures for reducing emissions of greenhouse gases is good for reasons quite apart from climatic change. An improvement in the efficiency of energy use, for example, whether fossil or wood energy, would not only reduce the emissions of CO_2. It would also reduce the emissions of sulfur and nitrogen oxides, reduce acid deposition, help restore the balance of payments for many nations, and help reduce the international tension associated with purchase of oil from a limited market. Halting deforestation would help maintain the genetic diversity of the planet, reduce erosion, stabilize local and regional climates, and cleanse water and air. Steps taken to reduce one problem help to reduce others. Finally, substitution of renewable energy for fossil fuel satisfies the long-term need to consume no more than can be produced.

Summary

The atmospheric concentrations of CO_2, CH_4, and other greenhouse gases have increased during the last century from fossil fuel combustion, industrial activity, deforestation, and probably from the global warming during this same period. Atmospheric CO_2 has increased by approximately 25% since the 18th century; atmospheric CH_4 has doubled. The rates of increase are accelerating. Approximately 70% of the total annual emissions of CO_2 to the atmosphere is currently from combustion of coal, oil, and gas; 30% is from deforestation. Most of this deforestation is in the tropics. Outside the tropics, smaller releases of carbon to the atmosphere are approximately in balance with accumulations of carbon in regrowing forests.

The reason for the release of carbon following deforestation is that forests hold 20 to 100 times more carbon per unit area than agricultural lands. With deforestation the carbon held in trees and in the organic matter of soil is oxidized by burning and decay and is released to the atmosphere as CO_2.

Future policies can lead either to the complete elimination of tropical forests in the next century, with a release of enough CO_2 to increase atmospheric concentrations by another 50%, or to an expansion of forest area and a withdrawal of CO_2 from the atmosphere. The latter alternative would contribute significantly to a stabilization of atmospheric greenhouse gases and would limit the extent of global warming, but the contribution would be temporary. The substitution of sustainably managed wood fuels for nonrenewable fossil fuels could reduce the net emissions of CO_2 to the atmosphere indefinitely and reverse the century-long accumulation of that greenhouse gas in the atmosphere.

References

Anonymous. 1990. Last decade warmest on record. *Sci. News* 137:92.

Arrhenius, S. 1896. On the influence of carbonic acid in the air upon the temperature of the ground. *Phil. Mag.* 41:237.

Barnola, J. M., D. Raynaud, Y. S. Korotkevich, and C. Lorius. 1987. Vostoc ice core provides 160,000-year record of atmospheric CO_2. *Nature* 329:408–414.

Bradley, R. S., H. F. Diaz, J. K. Eischeid, P. D. Jones, P. M. Kelly, and C. M. Goodess. 1987. Precipitation fluctuations over northern hemisphere land areas since the mid-19th century. *Science* 237:171–175.

Chamberlin, T. C. 1899. An attempt to frame a working hypothesis of the cause of glacial periods on an atmospheric basis. *J. Geol.* 7:575, 667, 751.

Food and Agricultural Organization/United Nations Environment Programme (FAO/UNEP). 1981. *Tropical Forest Resources Assessment Project.* FAO, Rome.

Goldemberg, J., T. B. Johansson, A. K. N. Reddy, and R. H. Williams. 1988. *Energy for a Sustainable World.* Wiley Eastern Limited, New Delhi. (Summarized in two publications by the same authors, *Energy for Development* and *Energy for a Sustainable World,* World Resources Institute, Washington, DC.)

Hansen, J., I. Fung, A. Lacis, D. Rind, S. Lebedeff, R. Ruedy, and G. Russell. 1988. Global climate changes as forecast by Goddard Institute for Space Studies three-dimensional model. *J. Geophys. Res.* 93:9341–9364.

Hansen, J. and S. Lebedeff. 1987. Global trends of measured surface air temperature. *J. Geophys. Res.* 92:13345–13372.

Houghton, R. A. 1990a. The future role of tropical forests in affecting the carbon dioxide concentration of the atmosphere. *Ambio.* in press.

Houghton, R. A. 1990b. Tropical deforestation and atmospheric carbon dioxide. *Clim. Change.* In press.

Houghton, R. A., R. D. Boone, J. R. Fruci, J. E. Hobbie, J. M. Melillo, C. A. Palm, B. J. Peterson, G. R. Shaver, G. M. Woodwell, B. Moore, D. L. Skole, and N. Myers. 1987. The flux of carbon from terrestrial ecosystems to the atmosphere in 1980 due to changes in land use: geographic distribution of the global flux. *Tellus* 39:122–139.

Houghton, R. A. and D. L. Skole. 1990. Changes in the global carbon cycle between 1700 and 1985. In *The Earth Transformed by Human Action,* B. L. Turner (ed.). Cambridge University Press, Cambridge. In press.

Houghton, R. A. and G. M. Woodwell. 1989. Global climatic change. *Sci. Am.* 260:36–44.

Jones, P. D., S. C. B. Raper, R. S. Bradley, H. F. Diaz, P. M. Kelly, and T. M. L. Wigley. 1986. Northern hemisphere surface air temperature variations: 1851–1984. *J. Climatol. Appl. Meteorol.* 25:161–179.

Keeling, C. D., R. B. Bacastow, A. F. Carter, S. C. Piper, T. P. Whorf, M. Heimann, W. G. Mook, and H. Roeloffzen. 1989. A three-dimensional model of atmospheric CO_2 transport based on observed winds: 1. Analysis of observational data. In *Aspects of Climate Variability in the Pacific and the Western Americas*, D. H. Peterson (ed.) pp. 165–236, Geophysical Monograph 55. American Geophysical Union, Washington, DC.

Khalil, M. A. K. and R. A. Rasmussen. 1989. Climate-induced feedbacks for the global cycles of methane and nitrous oxide. *Tellus* 41:554–559.

Kuo, C., C. Lindberg, and D. J. Thomson. 1990. Coherence established between atmospheric carbon dioxide and global temperature. *Nature* 343:709–714.

Lachenbruch, A. H. and B. V. Marshall. 1986. Changing climate: Geothermal evidence from permafrost in the Alaskan Arctic. *Science* 234:689–696.

Lieth, H. 1975. Measurement of calorific values. In *Primary Productivity of the Biosphere*, H. Lieth and R. H. Whittaker (eds.), pp. 119–129. Springer-Verlag, New York.

Lorius, C., N. I. Barkov, J. Jouzel, Y. S. Korotkevich, V. M. Kotlyakov, and D. Raynaud. 1988. Antarctic ice core: CO_2 and climatic change over the last climatic cycle. *Eos* 69:681, 683, 684.

Marland, G. 1989. Fossil fuels CO_2 emissions: Three countries account for 50% in 1986. *CDIAC Commun. Winter*. Carbon Dioxide Information Analysis Center, Oak Ridge National Laboratory, Oak Ridge, Tennessee.

Myers, N. 1989. *Deforestation Rates in Tropical Forests and their Climatic Implications*. Friends of the Earth, London.

Neftel, A., E. Moor, H. Oeschger, and B. Stauffer. 1985. Evidence from polar ice cores for the increase in atmospheric CO_2 in the past two centuries. *Nature* 315:45–47.

Peltier, W. R. and A. M. Tushingham. 1989. Global sea level rise and the greenhouse effect: Might they be connected? *Science* 244:806–810.

Raynaud, D., J. Chappellaz, J. M. Barnola, U. S. Korotkevich, and C. Lorius, 1988. Climatic and CH_4 cycle implications of glacial-interglacial CH_4 change in the Vostok ice core. *Nature* 333:655–657.

Rotty, R. M. and G. Marland. 1986. Fossil fuel combustion: recent amounts, patterns, and trends of CO_2. In *The Changing Carbon Cycle. A Global Analysis*, J. R. Trabalka and D. E. Reichle (eds.), pp. 474–490. Springer-Verlag, New York.

Schneider, S. H. 1989. The greenhouse effect: Science and policy. *Science* 243:771–781.

Schneider, S. H. and L. E. Mesirow. 1976. *The Genesis Strategy*. Plenum Press, New York.

Stauffer, B., G. Fischer, A. Neftel, and H. Oeschger. 1985. Increase of atmospheric methane recorded in Antarctic ice cores. *Science* 229:1386–1389.

WMO/UNEP. 1988. *Developing Policies for Responding to Climatic Change*, A summary of the discussions and recommendations of the workshops held in Villach (September 28–October 2, 1987) and Bellagio (November 9–13, 1987) under the auspices of the Beijer Institute, Stockholm. WMO/TD-No. 225, World Meteorological Organization, Geneva.

Woodwell, G. M. 1989. The warming of the industrialized middle latitudes 1985–2050: Causes and consequences. *Clim. Change* 15:31–50.

Woodwell, G. M., R. A. Houghton, T. A. Stone, R. F. Nelson, and W. Kovalick. 1987. Deforestation in the tropics: New measurements in the Amazon Basin using Landsat and NOAA advanced very high resolution radiometer imagery. *J. Geophys. Res.* 92:2157–2163.

4

Tree Rings as Indicators of Climatic Change and the Potential Response of Forests to the Greenhouse Effect

Edward R. Cook

Introduction

The response of forests to future climatic change is an important research topic given the anticipated changes in regional and global climate due to the greenhouse effect (Manabe and Wetherald 1980, Wetherald, this volume). Based on stand simulation model results, Solomon (1986) has estimated that the forests in eastern North America will undergo enormous changes in response to regional climatic change. These changes include the migration of tree species into new areas, the disappearance of some species in areas they now occupy, changes in forest community structure, and a large reduction in live-tree biomass for some regions. Similar effects are also indicated in an analysis by Emanuel et al. (1985). All of these changes will have profound ecological and potentially large economic effects in eastern North America.

The greenhouse effect is likely to produce climatic changes not yet seen in the Holocene if the simulations of general circulation models (e.g., Manabe and Wetherald 1980, Wetherald, this volume) are basically correct. Given that the climatic conditions of a high-CO_2 world are likely to have no historical analogs, it is equally likely that forests will respond in ways that also have no historical analogs. This suggests that changes in past vegetation and tree growth cannot be used to estimate future changes of the forests. However, much can still be learned from studying tree growth in the past that is relevant to predicting future changes in forests. For example, the variations in annual tree rings for the past few centuries can provide information about the natural background variability in tree growth and climate prior to the rapid increase of CO_2 and other greenhouse gases in the atmosphere caused by human activities. This information would be valuable in detecting the true response of forests to anthropogenic perturbations of climate. In addition, the relationships between tree rings and climate can be modeled and mapped to identify tree species and forest types having high sensitivity to climate in the past and, by logical extension, in the future (Cook and Cole 1990). This information could lead to the development of better process-based models of tree and forest growth for producing more accurate predictions of forest response to climatic change (Cook and Cole 1990).

In this chapter, I emphasize how tree-ring records from old trees can provide centuries of baseline information on how forests respond to climate. Examples of large-scale variations in tree growth will be described for two regions of North America: (1) the high-latitude boreal forest treeline of North America extending from western Alaska to eastern Canada, where seasonal and annual temperature changes are believed to limit tree growth most strongly; and (2) the mid-latitude eastern deciduous forest, where variations in growing season rainfall and drought strongly influence tree growth. These two examples are contrasts in how climate can influence tree growth. In addition to these contrasts are additional differences in regional climatology, with the boreal forest region being more sensitive to changes in global air temperature than the temperate deciduous forest region (Lamb and Morth 1978). Thus, trees growing along the boreal forest treeline should reflect large-scale climatic trends more clearly then trees growing in the more temperate eastern deciduous forest.

The Boreal Forest Treeline

The position of the boreal forest treeline is generally thought to be determined in part by growing season temperatures and heat-sums (Jacoby and Ulan 1981, Larson 1974, Mikola 1961). These variables affect rates of photosynthesis and respiration, which determine net photosynthesis and the ability of trees to survive through the long, dark winter. Bryson (1966) also showed that the latitudinal position of the treeline boundary could be well approximated by the mean summer position of the Arctic front. Other variables, such as available soil moisture (Goldstein 1981) and permafrost (Larson 1980) may also be important in some regions and for some species. However, variations in ring width of trees growing along the boreal treeline often reflect variations in the thermal regime of the trees' micro- and macro-environments (Jacoby and Cook 1981, Jacoby et al. 1985). Thus, temperature-related variables are likely to cause much of the annual ring-width variations of trees growing along the boreal forest-tundra ecotone.

In this region of study, 11 tree-ring chronologies of white spruce (*Picea glauca* [Moench] Voss), larch (*Larix laricina* [Du Roi] K. Koch), and northern white cedar (*Thuja occidentalis* L.) were examined using principal components analysis (PCA) (Cooley and Lohnes 1971). The chronologies cover the time period 1670–1974, although only the period from 1700 on will be described here. Principal components analysis allows one to distill a large body of information down to a smaller number of important modes of common variation that may be easier to analyze and interpret. In particular, the first principal component accounts for the most common mode of variation in each of the series and, therefore, will represent

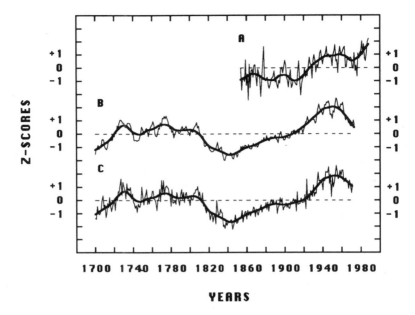

Fig. 4.1. Plots of actual temperature data averaged over the Northern Hemisphere (A), a reconstruction of those temperatures from tree rings (B), and the 1st-eigenvector scores of 11 boreal forest tree-ring chronologies (C). Each series has been normalized to unit-variance and has also been smoothed to emphasize long-term fluctuations of climate and tree growth.

the largest scale pattern of tree growth common to all series over the region. Only this first component is described here.

The chronologies selected for PCA all exhibited high ring-width sensitivity to variations in seasonal and annual temperature (Jacoby and D'Arrigo 1989) and covered an east-west transect from eastern Canada to Alaska that spans approximately 90° of longitude across North America. The first principal component estimated from these 11 series affectively selected all of the series as being similar, meaning that there was a geographically coherent pattern of tree growth across the North American boreal forest treeline. This common signal, expressed as a time series of dimensionless indices or scores, is shown in Fig. 4.1C. The scores have also been smoothed to emphasize the long-term growth fluctuations. The tree-ring scores reveal strong long-period fluctuations in tree growth. These fluctuations are dominated by a sustained growth decline from about 1810 to 1840 followed by a long-term trend of increasing ring width that peaks in about 1950 and then declines to the end of the series. The upward trend in growth since 1850 is consistent with known increases in Northern Hemisphere temperature (Jones et al. 1986, Fig. 4.1A), which indicates that boreal treeline forests have been responding to this recent large-scale warming trend.

Using sophisticated statistical procedures, Jacoby and D'Arrigo (1989) subsequently developed an actual reconstruction of Northern Hemisphere temperatures extending back to 1671 from these boreal forest tree-ring chronologies. This reconstruction is shown in Fig. 4.1B for comparison with the original uncalibrated tree-ring scores. There is an enormous similarity between the two time series, which emphasizes the degree to which the information in the original tree-ring chronologies is dominated by temperature trends.

The pattern of abrupt decline after 1810 and the subsequent long-term recovery in boreal tree rings has been previously described by Jacoby (1986). The decline coincides with a period of intense volcanic activity (Lamb 1971), which may have had a strong effect on climate in the high northern latitudes. The latter upward trend parallels changes in recorded surface air temperature since 1854 (Fig. 4.1A). However, most of this trend predates the large increase in atmospheric CO_2 and, therefore, is unlikely to be related to CO_2-induced warming. Thus, the growth fluctuations seen in Fig. 4.1C (especially before 1900) are probably reflecting the natural background variability of the climate system (perturbed or not by volcanic activity) from which the effects of greenhouse warming must depart. Also, note in Fig. 4.1A that the most recent annual temperatures have exceeded those seen in the previous 1940–1960 warm period. The boreal forest trees used in this study were sampled before this newest temperature increase occurred. Given the strong temperature response in these tree-ring chronologies, it is likely that these forests are growing at an even more accelerated pace now compared to the past few centuries.

Because of the way in which boreal treeline forests appear to track long-term trends in temperature, these forests should be sensitive indicators of changing climate due to greenhouse warming. It is generally believed that the greatest changes in global temperature will happen in the high northern latitudes (Manabe and Wetherald 1980). This being the case, the boreal forests will be heavily affected by CO_2-induced climatic change, and they may well be one of the best natural indicators of global environmental change presently available.

The Eastern Deciduous Forest Region

The eastern deciduous forest region or biome (Braun 1950) of North America is a complex mosaic of broadleaf and evergreen tree species and forest types. It is situated in the temperate region of North America where there is a mean annual surplus of precipitation. This surplus increases from the Atlantic coast to the Appalachian Mountains and then systematically decreases to zero roughly along the 96°W meridian (Barry and Chorley 1976). This meridian approximates well the westerly limit of this forest region in the Great Plains (Cook 1982). Even though the overall distribution of precipitation is sufficient to sustain the characteristic forest types in this region, droughts of varying severity and spatial extent are common. These droughts significantly reduce ring widths of trees (Cook and

Jacoby 1977) by reducing the availability of soil moisture and increasing the frequency of internal water deficits in the affected trees. Thus, variations in growing season moisture availability cause variations in ring width of trees growing in these forests, in contrast to temperature-caused variations at the boreal forest treeline.

In this forest region, 97 tree-ring chronologies covering the period 1700–1973 were also examined for large-scale common signals using PCA. The chronology set is dominated by eastern hemlock (*Tsuga canadensis* [L.] Carr.) and white oak (*Quercus alba* L.), with some other oak (*Quercus*), pine (*Pinus*), spruce (*Picea*), hemlock (*Tsuga*), and juniper (*Juniperus*) species also present in the set. Oak species are dominant in the western and southern quadrants of the network, whereas eastern hemlock is dominant in the northern and eastern quadrants. No attempt was made to select or stratify any of the 97 chronologies by species, climatic response, or site characteristics. However, the majority of sites can be classified as upland and moderately well-drained. The exceptions are the cool-moist spruce sites in the Appalachian Mountains and a few poorly drained hemlock and pine sites.

The result of this PCA showed more variation among chronologies compared to the boreal example. As before, the first principal component indicated the presence of a common, broadscale pattern of tree growth among all 97 chronologies, which was best expressed in the Great Lakes, Pennsylvania-New York, and Iowa-Illinois regions dominated by either hemlock or white oak chronologies. However, compared to the boreal treeline chronologies, the common signal in the eastern forest trees was considerably weaker. This probably reflected the fact that more tree species were used in this PCA, resulting in greater genetic differences among chronologies compared to the more homogeneous boreal set. In addition, the use of different species implies some differences in climatic sensitivity, that is, each species tends to react to climate somewhat differently from the other species.

Figure 4.2C shows the tree-ring scores of the first principal component. As before, the series has also been smoothed to emphasize the longer period fluctuations. In comparing this series with that from the boreal forest (Fig. 4.1C), it is obvious that tree growth in the two regions differs enormously in terms of year-to-year persistence and trend. In contrast to the boreal forest tree rings, tree growth in the eastern deciduous forest rarely departs from the mean for more than 3–4 years. However, there are some rhythmical, growth fluctuations in the series with a tendency for above- or below-average growth across the region every 15–25 years.

To more easily interpret the climatic meaning of these fluctuations, the tree-ring scores were compared to tree-ring reconstructions of summertime (June–August) drought across the same region (Cook et al. 1990). These reconstructions were derived from a subset of the same 97 tree-ring chronologies after screening the chronologies for drought sensitivity. The drought reconstructions were inde-

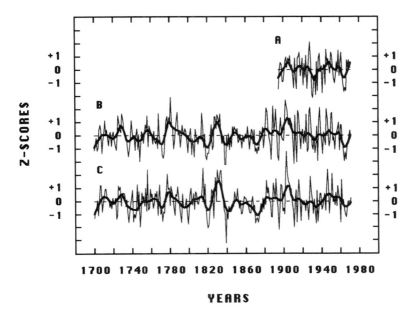

Fig. 4.2. Plots of actual summertime (June–August) drought index scores (A), the principal component scores of 17 drought reconstructions from tree rings (B), and the principal component scores of 97 deciduous forest tree-ring chronologies (C). Each series has been normalized to unit-variance and smoothed to emphasize multiyear fluctuations of climate and tree growth.

pendently developed for 18 separate states or subregions within the eastern deciduous forest biome. In 17 of the 18 cases, the tree-ring reconstructions were successfully verified as accurate when compared to drought data not used to develop the reconstructions. The 17 verified reconstructions, which also extend back to 1700, were then subjected to PCA for comparison with the raw tree-ring scores.

The drought reconstruction scores (Fig. 4.2B) and the raw tree-ring scores (Fig. 4.2C) are very similar, especially in the behavior of their multiyear fluctuations. The correlation between the series is 0.73, which is statistically significant at the 99% confidence level. In addition, the raw tree-ring and drought reconstruction scores were compared with actual drought index data (1895–1971) computed from meteorological records in the 18 states or subregions. The actual drought index data were previously used to both calibrate and verify the tree-ring reconstructions used in PCA to produce the scores in Fig. 4.2B. The correlation between the raw tree-ring and actual drought data is 0.58, whereas the correlation between the reconstructed and actual drought data is 0.82. Each correlation exceeds the 99% confidence level. Given these results, it is highly probable that the large-scale variations in tree growth seen in the raw tree-ring scores are largely driven by changes in growing season moisture supply. Although it is not possible to say that these scores are representative of tree growth for all important tree species in the eastern deciduous forest, it is a biologically reasonable first approximation.

From this finding, it appears that any future impact of CO_2-induced climatic change on eastern deciduous forests will come from the interaction of changing patterns of growing season temperature and precipitation that lead to changes in soil moisture availability and drought frequency. Because of this interaction and the considerable uncertainty in modeling CO_2-induced changes in regional precipitation climatology (Schlesinger and Mitchell 1985, Wetherald, this volume), the identification of a clear greenhouse effect on eastern deciduous forests may be difficult. However, some estimates of climate change for this region (Wigley et al. 1980, Rind et al. 1990) suggest that an increase in droughts will occur. If so, then a clear decline in tree growth will result with the potential loss of certain more drought sensitive species in some areas.

Summary

The boreal and eastern deciduous forest examples have provided insights into the large-scale background fluctuations of climate and tree growth that must be considered when searching for the occurrence of CO_2-induced climatic change and its effect on forests. The boreal example shows that substantial, long-term changes in tree growth have occurred. These changes are believed to reflect long-term changes in surface air temperature. This complicates the statistical assessment of future changes in both instrumental temperature data and ring widths, making the identification of an anomalous greenhouse effect difficult. Given the high year-to-year persistence in boreal forest tree-rings seen in Fig. 4.1B, an anomalous climatic effect on tree growth might have to last several years or decades before it emerges unequivocally from the background variance in the tree rings. The same basic problems of high background variance and trend also exist in the hemispheric temperature data. However, it appears to be amplified in the boreal tree-ring series used here by the physiological processes of the trees.

Yet given these problems, the temperature-sensitive nature of latitudinal and elevational timberline tree species still makes such sites highly appealing in the search for temperature-related effects on tree growth. General circulation model estimates of regional climatic change are considered much more reliable for temperature than for precipitation (Schlesinger and Mitchell 1985, Wetherald, this volume). This means that there may be a reliable expectation of CO_2-induced temperature change that can be used to predict the way in which boreal timberline trees will grow in the future. Thus, it may be possible to reduce the uncertainty in interpreting future ring-width trends in the boreal forest.

The eastern deciduous forest example indicates that past large-scale changes in climate and tree growth have been less extreme and persistent compared to the boreal example. Potentially, this makes the identification of CO_2-induced climatic change and its effect on ring width easier to identify in this forest region because an unusual series of climatic events caused by greenhouse warming might emerge more quickly from the natural background variance. However, the presence of a summertime drought signal in the tree rings means that both changes in temperature and precipitation will impact tree growth in the future.

The large uncertainty in the GCM estimates of CO_2-induced precipitation patterns (Schlesinger and Mitchell 1985, Wetherald, this volume) means that there is presently no reliable expectation of climatic change that can be used to predict the way in which deciduous forest trees will grow in the future. At the very best, the expectations of climatic change and the simulations of forest response to those changes (e.g., Solomon 1986) can only be regarded as scenarios of possible future change in the region. However, it is clear from this analysis that any CO_2 effect on the summertime climatology of the eastern deciduous forest that leads to increased droughtiness will ultimately be translated into a significant reduction of tree growth in this forest biome.

References

Barry, R. G. and R. J. Chorley. 1976. *Atmosphere, Weather and Climate*. Methuen, London.

Braun, E. L. 1950. *Deciduous Forests of Eastern North America*. Hafner Press, New York.

Bryson, R. A. 1966. Air masses, streamlines, and the boreal forest. *Geog. Bull.* 8:228–269.

Cook, E. R. 1982. Eastern North America. In *Climate from Tree Rings*. M. K. Hughles, P. M. Kelley, J. R. Pilcher, and V. C. LaMarche (eds.), pp. 126–133. Cambridge University Press, Cambridge.

Cook, E. R. and J. Cole. 1990. On predicting the response of forests in eastern North America to future climatic change. *Climatic Change*, in press.

Cook, E. R. and G. C. Jacoby, Jr. 1977. Tree-ring drought relationships in the Hudson Valley, New York. *Science* 198:390–392.

Cook, E. R., D. W. Stahle, and M. K. Cleaveland. 1990. Evidence in tree rings from eastern North America. In *Climate Since 1500 A.D.*, R. S. Bradley and P. D. Jones (ed.). Unwin Hyman, London, in press.

Cooley, W. W. and P. P. Lohnes. 1971. *Multivariate Data Analysis*. John Wiley, New York.

Emanuel, W. R., H. H. Shugart, and M. P. Stevenson. 1985. Climatic change and the broad-scale distribution of terrestrial ecosystem complexes. *Clim. Change* 7:29–43.

Goldstein, G. H. 1981. Ecophysiological and demographic studies of white spruce (*Picea glauca* [Moench] Voss) at treeline in the central Brooks Range of Alaska. Ph.D. thesis. University of Washington, Seattle.

Jacoby, G. C. 1986. An abrupt temperature decline in the early 1800's as evidenced by high-latitude tree growth. In *The Book of Abstracts and Reports from the Abrupt Climatic Change Conference*, W. H. Berger and L. D. Labeyrie (conveners), pp. 131–137. SIO Reference 86–8. Scripps Institute of Oceanography, La Jolla, CA.

Jacoby, G. C., Jr. and E. R. Cook. 1981. Past temperature variations inferred from a 400-year tree-ring chronology from Yukon Territory, Canada. *Arctic Alpine Res.* 13:409–418.

Jacoby, G. C., Jr. and R. D'Arrigo. 1989. Reconstructed northern hemisphere annual temperature since 1671 based on high-latitude tree-ring data from North America. *Clim. Change* 14:39–59.

Jacoby, G. C., Jr. and L. D. Ulan. 1981. Review of dendroclimatology in the forest-tundra ecotone of Alaska and Canada. In *Climatic Change in Canada,* Vol. 2, C. R. Harington (ed.), pp. 97–128. Syllogeus 33-Publication of the National Museums of Canada, Ottawa.

Jacoby, G. C., Jr., E. R. Cook, and L. D. Ulan. 1985. Reconstructed summer degree days in central Alaska and northwestern Canada since 1524. *Quat. Res.* 23:18–26.

Jones, P. D., T. M. L. Wigley, and P. B. Wright. 1986. Global temperature variations between 1861 and 1984. *Nature* 322:430–434.

Lamb, H. H. 1971. Volcanic dust in the atmosphere; with a chronology and assessment of its meteorological significance. *Phil. Trans. R. Soc. Lond.* 226:425–533.

Lamb, H. H. and H. T. Morth. 1978. Arctic ice, atmospheric circulation and world climate. *Geog. J.* 144:1–22.

Larson, J. A. 1974. Ecology of the northern continental forest border. In *Arctic and Alpine Environments,* J. D. Ives and R. G. Barry (eds.), pp. 341–369. Methuen and Co. Ltd., London.

Larson, J. A. 1980. *The Boreal Ecosystem.* Academic Press. New York.

Manabe, S. and R. T. Wetherald. 1980. On the distribution of climate change resulting from an increase in CO_2-content of the atmosphere. *J. Atmos. Sci.* 37:99–118.

Mikola, P. 1961. Temperature and tree growth near the northern timberline. In *Tree Growth,* T. T. Kozlowski (ed.), pp. 265–274, Ronald Press, New York.

Rind, D., R. Glodberg, J. Hansen, C. Rosenzweig, and R. Ruedy. 1990. Potential evapotranspiration and the likelihood of future drought. *J. Geophys. Res.,* in press.

Schlesinger, M. E. and J. F. B. Mitchell. 1985. Model projections of the equilibrium climatic response to increased carbon dioxide. In *The Potential Climatic Effects of Increasing Carbon Dioxide,* M. C. MacCracken and F. M. Luther (eds.), pp. 81–148. US Department of Energy Document DOE/ER–0237.

Solomon, A. 1986. Transient response of forests to CO_2-induced climatic change: Simulation modeling experiments in eastern North America. *Oecologia* 68:567–579.

Wigley, T. M. L., P. D. Jones, and P. M. Kelley. 1980. Scenario for a warm, high-CO_2 world. *Nature* 283:17–21.

5

Ecosystem Sensitivity to Climate Change and Complex Responses

James S. Clark

Introduction

By the time atmospheric CO_2 concentrations double, south and central portions of North America may be warmer and drier, and higher latitudes and the western United States may become moister (Kellogg and Zhao 1988, Zhao and Kellogg 1988). These predictions are tenuous to be sure, and the global circulation models (GCMs) that generate them disagree concerning many aspects of the future climate (Hayes, this volume, Kellogg and Zhao 1988, Rind 1988, Wetherald, this volume). The projections are sensitive to model resolution, gradients in sea-surface temperatures that influence atmospheric circulation, and assumptions regarding withdrawal of soil moisture. Moreover, the transient climate we see on the way to doubled CO_2 may be quite different from these "equilibrium" predictions and much harder to anticipate (Solomon 1986).

As concentrations of greenhouse gases increase in the atmosphere, the radiation balance changes the distribution of temperatures change, and thus the large-scale circulation patterns that determine storm tracks, convective activity, and rainfall distribution also change. Predicting what these changes may be is complicated by the uncertainty regarding how the climate system responds to enhanced CO_2, where the precipitation will fall, and what the atmosphere demand will be for that soil moisture after we allow for cloudiness and temperature redistribution by the air masses. It is generally true that warmer temperatures increase evapotranspiration, leading to more clouds and more precipitation (Rind 1988). We therefore have the potential for more evaporation *and* more precipitation, in short, a stepped-up hydrologic cycle. The forecasts for any given region, however, are exceedingly difficult to evaluate.

Because of these problems with prediction, it is useful to focus on the more general topic of climate sensitivity, which is potentially knowable from existing data and studies that can be done on existing ecosystems. Although we may not possess the knowledge required to predict regional climates of the year 2050, we can say and/or learn something about the sensitivity to water balance of the important processes in natural ecosystems. Knowledge of sensitivity does not substitute for predictive ability. It is perhaps the next best thing. Knowledge of sensitivity tells us whether a given change in temperature or precipitation matters, and it helps us to gauge the responses that might occur under a range of scenarios.

I begin by establishing a historical context for climate change in natural ecosystems and by providing examples of the complexity of climate changes in North America since the last ice age, together with evidence that forests are indeed responsive to these changes. These considerations are presented at a rudimentary level, for knowledge of past climates is limited to what can be learned from geology, fossils, knowledge of the earth's orbital fluctuations, and atmospheric physics. Broad redistribution of plant species since the last ice age indicate sensitivity to those climate changes that have occurred during the last 18,000 years. I then focus on the concept of climate sensitivity and the ecosystem-level processes that are likely to respond to changing climate. It is possible to estimate relative sensitivities of some of these processes to climate variables, thus allowing statements regarding the direction and perhaps even the magnitude of change that might result from change in a given climate variable. Other processes display complex responses to a range of variables that are likely to change, making broad statements concerning magnitude, and even direction, of change almost impossible.

Climate Change and Forest Response

Climate Change

Fossil evidence for forest composition during times of past climate change provides one of the most important demonstrations of sensitivity of forest ecosystems to climate variables. Changes in some variables that affect climate, such as atmospheric CO_2 and aerosols, ice sheets, orbitally induced changes in solar radiation, and sea-surface temperatures have been used as boundary conditions (i.e., they influence the climate system, but are, for simplicity, themselves held constant) in GCM runs to approximate conditions for the last 18,000 years (COHMAP 1988, Kutzbach and Wright 1985). This greatly simplified picture of the climate system produces complex responses and some dramatic shifts in air masses and circulation patterns. These climate changes help to explain changes in forest composition that is indicated by analysis of fossil pollen in lake sediments.

One of the more important boundary conditions in these models is represented by variation in the earth's orbit, which influences the seasonal distribution of solar radiation at the earth's surface. The details of the geometry that result in this variation and the cycles themselves are beyond the scope of this paper. The following discussion of climate changes of the recent past is clarified somewhat, however, given the knowledge that the maximum 'seasonality' of the last 18,000 years occurred approximately 9,000 years ago—less radiation was received during winters than today and more was received during summers. Eighteen thousand years ago, the amount and seasonal distribution of solar radiation was similar to that of today, but the climate was much different, because of the presence of continental ice sheets, sea ice, and lower sea-surface temperatures (COHMAP 1988).

At 18,000 years before present (yr BP), the jet stream was strong and split over the North American ice sheet, with the northern branch following the arctic coast, emerging over the North Atlantic, and producing cold northerly winds that drove sea ice to the latitude of Spain (Fig. 5.1A). The southern branch followed a more southerly route than does the existing jet stream, bringing moist westerlies to the Southwest. Meanwhile, anticyclonic circulation prevailed over the North American ice sheet and was responsible for dry easterly winds in the Pacific Northwest (COHMAP 1988) and eastern North America was colder and drier than today (Kutzbach and Wright 1985). The effects of a large ice sheet over the center of the continent included moister conditions in the Southwest and drier conditions in the Northwest and East.

From 12,000 to 9,000 yr BP, summer insolation and temperatures in the Pacific Northwest increased, although conditions were still generally cooler than at present south of the ice (Fig. 5.1B). The ice sheet had diminished, and the jet stream was no longer split, although it was still stronger than it is today. Only a small anticyclone remained over the ice sheet, and a strengthening Pacific subtropical high resulted in northwesterly winds being replaced by westerlies in the Pacific Northwest.

By roughly 6,000 yr BP, summer insolation and continentality reached maximum levels for the Holocene (Fig. 5.1C). Summers were perhaps warmer than now in the interior [mean July temperatures predicted from pollen data by Bartlein et al. (1984) for the upper Midwest and from pollen and tree-ring data of Diaz et al. (1989) for Canada are 0.5–1°C higher than today; COHMAP's (1988) GCM predictions for the Midwest generally are 2–4°C higher than today], and they have declined since, as solar insolation has decreased. Southerly flow dominated in the East, and the westerlies of the present day developed in the Midwest (COHMAP 1988). Among the most important climate changes in North America since 6,000 yr BP are a general cooling trend, changes in latitudinal temperature gradients, with attendant changes in magnitude of westerlies, and temperature and precipitation oscillations having greatest amplitude along the southern boundary of the Arctic air mass (Diaz et al. 1989).

These rather intricate model responses to changes of a few boundary conditions demonstrate the complexity of the climate system and the difficulties with prediction, particularly when more of the feedbacks and variables present in the real world are included. Changes in vegetation and land use, for example, can have important effects on albedo, soil moisture, and temperature, all of which influence regional heat balance and thus circulation (Graham et al. 1990, Schlesinger et al. 1990). Models also suggest the potential for important effects on ecosystems. Although climate changes of the future will likely differ in magnitude and kind

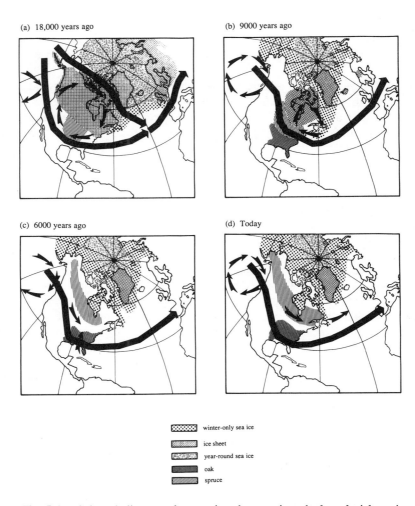

(a) 18,000 years ago

(b) 9000 years ago

(c) 6000 years ago

(d) Today

winter-only sea ice
ice sheet
year-round sea ice
oak
spruce

Fig. 5.1. Selected climate and vegetation changes since the last glacial maximum in North America summarized by COHMAP members. Redrawn from COHMAP (1988).

from those of the last 18,000 years, the fact that climate changes have occurred and that forests have responded is one reason to be concerned over increased atmospheric concentrations of greenhouse gases. It is instructive to consider some of the more dramatic changes in forest composition that have attended this reshuffling of air masses in the past for the information it provides on sensitivity.

Forest Ecosystems

Existing vegetation types correspond to recognizable patterns in the dominant air masses (Bryson 1966), suggesting a close link between the two (Bernabo and

Webb 1977). Not surprisingly, the dramatic climate shifts from full-Glacial times to the present have resulted in widespread rearrangement of plant assemblages (Davis 1983, Jacobson et al. 1987, Webb et al. 1983, Webb 1988). The ranges of tree species changed during this period, with most extending their range limits to higher latitudes. But the spatial and temporal patterns of change varied widely among taxa. Black ash (*Fraxinus nigra*), for example, appeared within the spruce woodland near the ice margin of the Upper Midwest between 18,000 and 14,000 yr BP (Fig. 5.1A). Ash and elm (*Ulmus* spp.) species both appear to have played a more important role over a large geographic area early in the Holocene than they do today (Webb et al. 1983, Webb 1988). Some species extended their range limits rapidly (e.g., many of the oaks), whereas others moved into new areas more slowly (e.g., chestnut, *Castanea dentata*, Davis 1983). White pine (*Pinus strobus*) expanded from the Atlantic Coastal Plain north into New England by 11,000 yr BP and then moved slowly west toward the prairie-forest border in the Upper Midwest. With cooler/moister conditions of the last two millennia (Gajewski 1988), white pine (Jacobson 1979), and red pine (*Pinus resinosa*) (McAndrews 1966) extended their range limits west to the prairie-forest border, whereas beech (*Fagus grandifolia*) populations became established in more westerly sites at the present range margin (Woods and Davis 1989), and spruce (*Picea* spp.) became more important in forests of the Northeast (Gajewski 1987, Webb 1981). The more positive water balance of the 16th century in the upper Midwest saw the westward expansion of Bigwoods vegetation of southeastern Minnesota (Grimm 1983).

The fact that each taxon responded differently to climate change during the Holocene (Davis 1981), suggests differential sensitivities to climate change. These rearrangements of taxa further imply more fundamental shifts in ecosystem processes, because species differ in how they cycle nitrogen (Chapin 1980, Pastor et al. 1984, Pastor and Post 1988, Vitousek 1982), how they use soil moisture (Abrams 1988, Bunce et al. 1977, Hinckley et al. 1978), and the degree to which they intercept light (Jarvis and Leverenz 1983). It is certain that many ecosystem-level processes have experienced profound transition as direct (e.g., temperature, wind speed, precipitation) and indirect (e.g., changing species composition) consequences of these recent climate changes (Clark 1990b, c).

Sensitivity to Climate Change

It is difficult to think of an ecosystem process that does not depend directly or indirectly on climate. Rather than attempt to catalog them all here (most would be obvious and many trivial), I focus instead on responsiveness, or "sensitivity," to climate variables. Although all respiring organisms metabolize at rates that depend on temperature, the exponential form of that temperature dependency implies that respiration response depends not only on how much temperature changes, but also on the temperature at which we begin observing the processes. If a particular enzymatic reaction possesses a Q_{10} of 2, the rate of that reaction

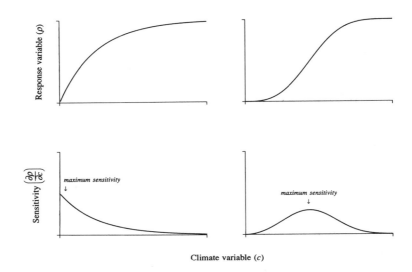

Climate variable (c)

Fig. 5.2. The relationship between climate dependencies (above) and climate sensitivity (below) for simple saturating (left) and sigmoid (right) responses, where c represents some climate variable, and $\rho(c)$ represents some ecological process that depends on c. The nonlinearities in these response functions $\rho(c)$ results in sensitivities that depend on the initial value c.

doubles with every 10°C increase in temperature. Suppose respiration is proceeding at a rate of 1 mg $CO_2 m^{-2} h^{-1}$ per gram of dry matter. A temperature increase from 10 to 15°C results in a respiration-rate increase of 0.4 mg $m^{-2} h^{-1}$. The same change in temperature from 25 to 30°C, where the respiration rate is already proceeding at 5.6 mg $m^{-2} h^{-1}$, however, results in an increased respiration rate of 2.4 mg $m^{-2} h^{-1}$. The sixfold difference in magnitude of the responses results from higher sensitivity to temperature at the higher temperature.

This sensitivity consideration arises anytime a response variable depends in a nonlinear way on a climate variable (Fig. 5.2). Because nonlinear responses are the norm in the biological world (linear relationships are useful primarily over restricted ranges), sensitivity to climate change will vary greatly at all levels of biological organization, from enzymatic reactions to ecosystem processes. Thus, although it is easy to say that all processes will respond to climate change, it is much more difficult to say which will change in an appreciable way and which will appear unchanged.

Figure 5.2 demonstrates some common functional forms used to describe climate dependencies at the level of an ecosystem. These responses differ from process to process, and they also depend on initial conditions, that is, the current location along the climate gradient. Thus, even though both response variables shown in Fig. 5.2 show positive tendencies along the climate gradient, the first is most sensitive to climate change at one extreme, whereas the second

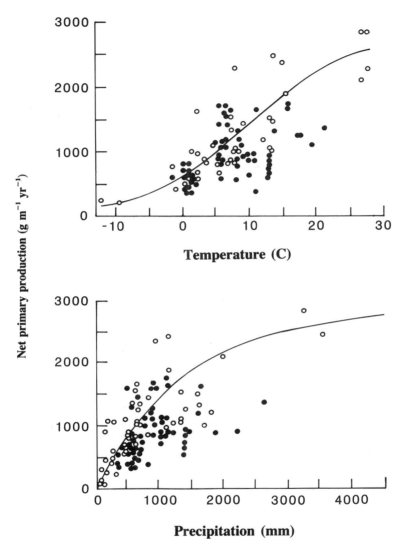

Fig. 5.3. The effect of temperature and precipitation on net primary production from data sets described in O'Neill and DeAngelis (1981). Redrawn from O'Neill and DeAngelis (1981).

demonstrates greatest sensitivity at intermediate values. It is not possible to say that one process is more sensitive than the other without specifying the initial condition.

The way in which existing relationships can be used to gauge sensitivity is illustrated with a simple example. This example uses the relationships in Fig. 5.3

as a rough estimate of sensitivity of grasslands to temperature and precipitation. This exercise is intended only as an example, because the relationships in Fig. 5.3 are coarse and because a single response surface to both temperature T and precipitation P would be preferable to the two individual relationships in Fig. 3A and 3B. The Appendix to this chapter illustrates how these relationships between a response variable, such as net primary production (NPP), and climate variables, such as T and P, can be used to derive sensitivity coefficients. These coefficients are used to answer questions such as: At which site is temperature most important? Is NPP more sensitive to temperature or precipitation? What would be the proportionate change in NPP with a percentage change in temperature or precipitation?

Before attempting to answer these questions, let us consider the results from a simulation of NPP response in grasslands to climate change (Schimel et al. 1990). The predicted changes in temperature and precipitation used by Schimel et al. (1990) for a northern grid cell characterized by lower temperatures and precipitation versus a southern grid cell having higher values of both produced increased NPP in both cases. The increases occurred at both sites despite the fact that predicted precipitation increased in the north and decreased in the south, although the increases in NPP were greater in the north than they were in the south.

A sensitivity analysis supports the overwhelming effect of temperature on NPP response found by Schimel et al. (1990), despite the fact that NPP is more sensitive to precipitation than it is to temperature at both sites. The precipitation sensitivity is highest in the north, whereas the temperature sensitivity is highest in the south. Despite the fact that NPP is more sensitive to precipitation, the temperature response dominates at both sites, because the predicted increases are so massive (44% in the north; 27% in the south). In contrast, the changes in precipitation are modest (7.7% increase in the north; 3.5% decrease in the south). The parallel changes in temperature and precipitation in the north serve to exaggerate the response there. The offsetting effects of these two climate variables in the south may tend to diminish the response.

It is difficult to draw close parallels between sensitivity and simulation results in this case, because the sensitivity analysis is based on a crude model. The model serves to demonstrate the approach, however. It also demonstrates the ways in which simulation models and sensitivity analysis may produce complementary results, where sensitivity to a particular variable summarizes the direct and indirect effects of a climate variable on a response variable, and simulation models can aid identification of the complexity of interactions for particular climate scenarios.

Because the steepness of a gradient provides a rough guide to climate sensitivity, manipulation of climate variables or observation of the response variable across a gradient in a climate variable can suggest sensitivity to climate change. Manipulation represents a more difficult but more direct approach, because the confounding effects of correlated variables along spatial gradients that have acted with a long and unknown history can be constrained. Unfortunately, the response time may be so great (e.g., Clark 1990b, Davis and Botkin 1985, Schimel et al. 1990, Solomon 1986) as to make manipulation impractical.

For processes that respond more rapidly, manipulations of variables can, in some cases, be conducted in either direction. For example, it is easier to add water to an ecosystem than it is to remove it (although water addition may also involve undesirable side effects). Thus, the response of an ecosystem process to the predicted decreases in soil-moisture availability in the coming decades might be explored by "increasing" moisture availability. The degree of change in the response variable represents sensitivity, and it provides a guide to the extent to which that process might respond to future climate change. If there is no significant change in the process when water is added, then it is likely that modest decreases in moisture availability will have little effect. If the response is large, variables contributing to that process may be moisture-limited, and decreased moisture is expected to have important consequences.

This concept of amendment to assess sensitivity is the basis for the long tradition of fertilization trials in agriculture and forestry. Rather than remove nitrogen, for example, nitrogen limitation is assessed by adding nitrogen. If no growth response to increased nitrogen ensues, then nitrogen probably does not limit growth. The alternative approach of removing nitrogen, would be difficult and would likely involve undesirable side effects. Moreover, the degree of sensitivity is given by the magnitude of the growth response. Thus, the effect of nitrogen decline on plant growth is inferred from the way in which growth responds to nitrogen addition.

Several experiments of this nature that involve sensitivity to water balance are available from forest ecosystems. For example, irrigation of Douglas fir stands in New Mexico (White et al. 1988) in combination with carbon and nitrogen additions showed that several aspects of the nitrogen cycle responded to water addition, depending on the nitrogen-cycling characteristics of different stands. Irrigation of Scots pine plantations in Sweden resulted in changes in root-to-shoot ratios (Ågren et al. 1980), as would be expected from results of solution-culture experiments on seedlings (Ingestad and Kahr 1985). Greater use of irrigation experiments might be used to address water-balance sensitivity of ecosystem-level processes.

Conclusions regarding responses to decreased moisture availability derived from such manipulations must be more conservative for processes that are irreversible, that is, for a process that depends on the direction of change (Poulovassilis 1962). This hysteresis would be represented in Fig. 5.2 by pairs of curves, one for the situation where the climate variable is increasing, and a second where the climate variable is decreasing. Where hysteresis occurs, manipulation of a climate variable results in a different trajectory of the response variable, depending on the direction of the manipulation. There are aspects of water availability in ecosystems that display hysteretic effects, for example, soil-moisture potential

(Hillel 1980) and photosynthetic capacity during drying versus rehydration phases (e.g., Ghashghaie and Sangier 1989). Because this trajectory *is* the sensitivity, different sensitivities would result, depending on whether water is being added or removed. Both results are valid, but they are dependent on direction.

Manipulation of climate variables must also recognize the indirect effects of climate variables on ecosystem processes. Wright (1921) introduced *path analysis* to identify the composite effects of correlated explanatory variables on a response variable (Provine 1971). For example, temperature influences growth rates of trees directly and indirectly, through its effects on evaporation and on mineralization rates (Fig. 5.4). If temperature has a positive direct effect on growth rate and a negative effect on mineralization rate (e.g. in dry soils where soil-moisture availability limits mineralization), then the observed low correlation between temperature and growth rates will suggest that temperature is less important than it is actually. The positive direct and negative indirect correlations tend to cancel one another (Fig. 5.4A). Where mineralization is not limited by soil moisture, increased mineralization rate would serve to amplify the positive, direct response of growth rate to increased temperature (Fig. 5.4B). Wright (1921) observed that the problem of identifying the composite effects of correlated environmental variables on nongenetic variance could be accommodated by allowing for the correlations that can exist among explanatory variables. This approach has now been applied to many biological questions (Sokal and Rohlf 1981), including the problem of understanding how local microclimate, which depends on topography, and litter quality and disturbance history influence nitrogen mineralization rates (Clark 1990d) (see below). Path analysis represents an approach that could be widely applied to questions of climate effects on ecosystems, where explanatory variables are almost always correlated and have many indirect effects (Jenny 1980, Van Cleve et al. 1983).

Because manipulations of climate variables across broad scales are limited, however, I focus here on some of the existing relationships of ecosystem variables across climate gradients as examples of how they can be used to suggest sensitivity to climate changes that could occur in the future.

Climate Gradients and Sensitivity to Climate Change

Despite the disagreements among GCM predictions, all climate models forecast changes in water balance. The simplest approach to understanding water-balance sensitivity is to consider how ecosystem processes vary across existing water-balance gradients. Unfortunately, all of these water-balance dependencies may be altered by the direct and the many indirect responses of water-use efficiency to atmospheric CO_2 concentrations. Although water-use efficiencies tend to be positively related to CO_2 concentrations, differing sensitivities and many indirect pathways, such as those discussed in the previous section, make it extremely difficult to assess what will be the composite influence of altered CO_2 concentra-

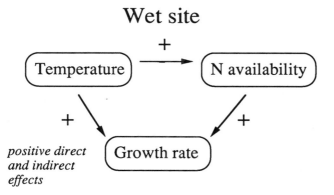

Fig. 5.4. Example of the ways in which indirect effects may complement or offset direct effects. In this example, temperature may increase growth of trees directly, whereas indirect effects depend on local water balance. On dry sites, temperature increase may reduce water availability and nitrogen mineralization, so that the net effect on growth may actually be negative. On moist sites, increased temperature might have the indirect effect of increasing the nitrogen mineralization rate, thereby exaggerating the positive direct effect on growth.

tions on ecosystem processes. Many of the potential effects are reviewed by Graham et al. (1990).

Production, Decomposition, and Nutrients

Net primary production is a variable for which existing climate dependencies suggest a range of sensitivities. In much of the United States, growing season temperatures are predicted to increase, whereas soil moisture may decline (Kellogg and Zhao 1988). Consideration of temperature and precipitation dependencies in existing forests (Fig. 5.3) suggests opposing effects of rising temperatures and falling precipitation on NPP. The dependencies shown in Fig. 5.3 imply maximum sensitivity to precipitation at low precipitation values and maximum sensitivity to temperature at intermediate temperatures. At precipitation values where sensitivity is high, deserts, grasslands and temperate forests are located. The high end of this gradient includes tropical forests, which are predicted to be little affected by modest changes in precipitation of a magnitude that could have important effects where annual precipitation is lower. The maximum temperature sensitivity is predicted to occur in boreal and temperate forests. A rough guide to the relative importances of these two climatic variables for NPP in any given region is provided by a comparison of temperature-versus-precipitation gradients at the average values of those variables for the region.

It is important to recall, however, that the sensitivities relate to factors being discussed. Although the relationship in Fig. 5.3 implies that boreal or temperate forests may be more sensitive to temperature change than will arctic ecosystems, that prediction applies only to the temperature response, only to NPP, and it assumes that the temperature change is small. The observed response to a temperature change will also depend on the magnitude of that response. For example, a larger change in temperature might have more profound effects on arctic ecosystems if it involves an important change in the heat balance of permanently frozen soils. Moreover, most GCMs agree that water-balance changes will be of greatest magnitude at high latitudes. The sensitivity analysis of the last section demonstrated how temperature responses could dominate in grasslands, despite the fact that sensitivity to precipitation is higher than is that to temperature. Unfortunately, these considerations of magnitude get into the problems of prediction, rather than sensitivity, and prediction is difficult for reasons given earlier. The quality of NPP can also be more sensitive to climate change than is the quantity (Schlesinger et al. 1990), so it is important to consider climate effects on a range of ecosystem processes.

Actual evapotranspiration (AET) is another climate variable that has been widely used to predict ecosystem processes like production and decomposition of litter (Clark 1990b, Meentenmeyer 1978, Meentenmeyer et al. 1982, Pastor and Post 1986). It is argued that AET incorporates the effects of temperature (used as a surrogate for evaporative demand) and precipitation, and it provides a good fit. Linear responses provide a reasonable description of the production and decomposition dependencies on AET. An aspect of linear responses important for this discussion is that linearity implies constant sensitivity. Thus, although litter production generally increases with AET (Fig. 5.5A), the sensitivity is everywhere roughly the same. To point out that the overall pattern is described by a linear model is not to imply that the component processes each proceed at rates proportional to AET. It is simply an empirical description that implies constant sensitivity to AET at the level of the response variables discussed here.

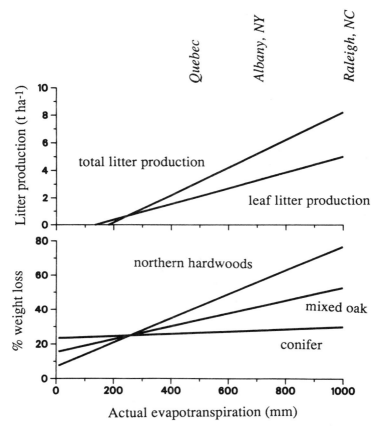

Fig. 5.5. (a) Litter production (Meentenmeyer et al. 1982) and (b) decomposition rate (Pastor and Post 1986) responses to regional variability in actual evapotranspiration. Responses are regression lines fit to collections of data sets from many different studies.

A given change in AET in Raleigh, NC produces a change in magnitude of production similar to what would be observed in Quebec. Sensitivity of decomposition rates to AET is likewise described by a linear relationship (Fig. 5.5B). Here again, the sensitivity is rather constant, but that sensitivity now depends on litter quality, with the highest quality litters of northern hardwood stands displaying the greatest sensitivity. The sensitivities of mixed oak stands in Raleigh, NC might be similar to those of Quebec, but the sensitivities of mixed oak versus conifer forests in Raleigh, NC might be quite different.

There are limitations to AET as a predictor of decomposition processes, however, in desert habitats (Whitford et al. 1981), along steep gradients in elevation (Reiners and Lang 1987), and in regions where the water balance can shift from

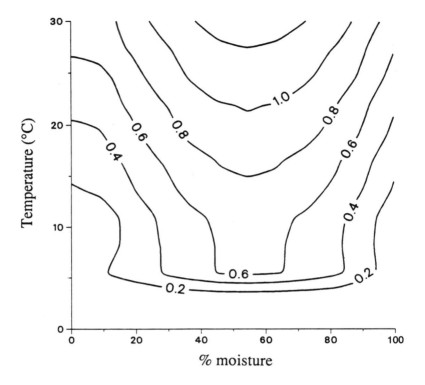

Fig. 5.6. CO_2 evolution from soil as a response surface of temperature and moisture content fit to data of Ino and Monsi (1969).

positive to negative (Clark 1990b). Although AET depends on both temperature and precipitation, a given change in AET might signal a shift to a more positive or a more negative water balance, depending on whether atmospheric demand for soil moisture (insolation) or precipitation were the cause of the change in AET (Clark 1990b).

These relationships between ecosystem processes and climate relate to the average responses to regional climate, summarized by total annual AET. The more local implications of altered water balance for decomposition processes depend on local drainage and therefore topography. Decomposition rates decline when soils are too wet, because they become anaerobic and respiration of carbon depends on electron acceptors that are used less efficiently than is oxygen. Microbial mineralization can also be limited by insufficient moisture when soils become too dry (Clarholm et al. 1981, Vitousek and Matson 1985) (Fig. 5.6), perhaps because microbial biomass may be roughly proportional to moisture content in dry soils (West et al. 1988). During a drying phase, for example, decomposition rates may increase in areas previously saturated and decrease in drier upland areas. Thus, the local response can be much different from the regional response, and each portion of a landscape may exhibit responses that depend on its own initial condition.

The nonlinear response surface for temperature and precipitation (Fig. 5.6) also demonstrates the difficulty with predicting the response to a scenario like "warmer and drier." Whether rates increase or decrease for a soil at 20% moisture content and 10–20°C depends on how much drier versus how much warmer. If the change in moisture status predominates, rates decrease, whereas, if the temperature change dominates, rates increase (Fig. 5.6).

The cycling of nutrients is closely tied to production and decomposition (Aber and Melillo 1980), because plant uptake, nutrient return in litter and with mortality, and decomposition rates all control the turnover of nutrients derived from the atmosphere (e.g., nitrogen) or weathered from parent material (e.g., phosphorus) (Gorham et al. 1979). Temperature decreases that slow growth rates have the indirect consequences of decreasing uptake (Knapp and Seastedt 1986) and thus might have a positive effect on availability. The same temperature decrease may reduce the rate at which nitrogen is mineralized from organic matter (Van Cleve et al. 1983). The simulated responses of grasslands to projected climate change discussed earlier (Schimel et al. 1990) suggest that decomposition sensitivity to temperature may dominate the decade-scale dynamics. Increased respiration of the soil-organic pool at the 4°C increased annual temperature, predicted by GCMs for the region, elevated nitrogen availability and, hence, NPP both in areas where precipitation is predicted to increase and decrease. Over long periods of time, however, this organic pool may be depleted and NPP may decline.

Rates of mineralization and uptake affect soil-nutrient pools, which determine removal of labile nutrients, such as NO_3^-, by water percolating through the soil profile. NO_3^- is an example of a nutrient that may adversely affect water quality if losses are sufficiently high (Vitousek 1983), although such high losses generally might not occur (Vitousek et al. 1982), except following large disturbances (Tiedemann et al. 1978, Likens et al. 1977).

These variable responses of decomposition rate to climate change are responsible for local variability in mineralization across landscapes. Landscape variability in nitrogen mineralization rates is tied to the quality of litter produced by the stand (Clark 1990d, Pastor et al. 1984, Van Cleve et al. 1983, Zak et al. 1986) and local microclimate and drainage (Schlesinger et al. 1990) (Fig. 5.7). The response of a local stand to climate change will therefore depend on whether mineralization rates are limited by water or temperature and the lignin-to-nitrogen ratio of litter (Melillo et al 1982). The response further depends on the feedback effect of mineralization rate on nitrogen returned in litterfall (Vitousek 1982). The more nitrogen-limited plant growth becomes, the more nitrogen is translocated from leaves to woody tissues before leaf abscission in autumn. Plants become more conservative with nitrogen, and better nitrogen competitors may replace poorer nitrogen competitors (Pas-

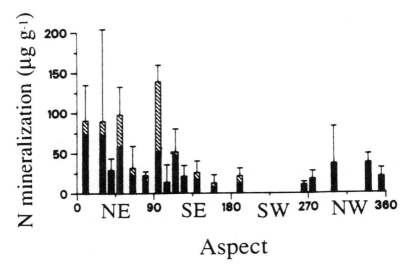

Fig. 5.7. Net nitrogen mineralization rates in old-growth forests of northwestern Minnesota varies with topography. Xeric southwest aspects support conifer species having lower litter quality, and low soil moisture may limit mineralization rates during part of the growing season. Mesic northeast aspects support northern hardwoods species having high litter quality, and local water balance may be more conducive to microbial respiration. From Clark (1990d).

tor et al. 1984, Tilman 1982). Over long periods of time, even the disturbance regime may play a role in this complex interaction between nutrient cycling and species composition. Using path analysis to assess the direct and indirect correlations among topography, species composition, and fire history, Clark (1990d) showed that the modest direct correlation between soil moisture and fertility is substantially improved when one incorporates the indirect interactions among soil moisture and other variables that control fertility (Fig. 5.8). Much of the strong control of soil moisture over fertility results from its indirect influences on litter quality and quantity and fire regime. These results also suggested that topographic control over water balance represents a stronger influence over vegetation pattern and nitrogen availability than does fire history. Despite the fact that fires were frequent in mixed pine/hardwood forests of northwestern Minnesota, and fires favor the establishment of pines in the region, the composite topographic effects of water balance on nutrient cycling and species composition appeared more as a cause than a consequence of fire regime. More frequent fires on drier sites may enhance composition differences, but fire is only one of several influences on species composition. The response of nutrient cycles to climate change might therefore be complex and protracted, as plant and microbial assemblages and disturbance regimes respond to changing conditions.

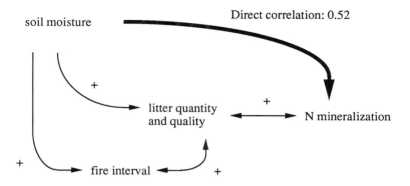

Composite correlation: 1.0

Fig. 5.8. An example of indirect effects that complement the direct effects of soil moisture on fertility (Clark 1990d). The direct correlation between soil moisture and nitrogen mineralization rate is significant but rather low. Using path analysis to include the indirect effects of soil moisture that result from influence on litter types and fire regime revealed a correlation of 1.0. This complete determination is embarrassingly high, and it cannot be interpreted to say that soil moisture is the only influence on fertility (Clark 1990d). It does illustrate how these indirect interactions serve to enhance the control a variable like soil moisture can exert on forest ecosystems.

Simulation results of Pastor and Post (1988) provide a nice illustration of how these complex interactions may influence forest composition and nutrient cycling under warmer and drier conditions. Climate change could result in an increase in forest heterogeneity as a consequence of the differing sensitivities of water and nutrient cycles at different locations along the moisture gradient (Fig. 5.9). On portions of the landscape that maintain a more positive water balance (moist site, Fig. 5.9), the increase in temperature results in increased nitrogen mineralization, which in turn promotes establishment of species that return proportionately more nitrogen to the forest floor in annual leaf fall. This positive feedback exaggerates the initial changes brought about by rising temperatures. On the other hand, a moisture response may prevail on a somewhat drier site (dry site, Fig. 5.9). The positive effect of higher temperature on the mineralization rate is not realized, because mineralization is limited by low moisture availability. Establishment of species more conservative in their use of nitrogen lead to a tighter nitrogen cycle, which is advantageous to such species. These species tend to drop only modest amounts of nitrogen in their litter (Vitousek 1982). Therefore, the changes in species composition that can result from the initial responses of the nitrogen cycle to climate serve to exaggerate these changes as the trend in litter quality mirrors that of nitrogen availability.

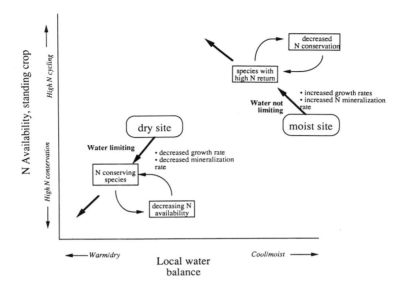

Fig. 5.9. Potential feedback effects of warmer and drier climates on forests suggested by simulation models of Pastor and Post (1988). Sites that initially are rather similar could become increasingly different when subjected to warm/dry conditions as a result of modest initial differences in local water balance. On the moist site, higher temperatures lead to increased mineralization rate, whereas, on the dry site, moisture is limiting and mineralization rate decreases. Subsequent changes in species composition, and thus litter chemistry, provide feedback effects that exaggerate these differences.

Leaching losses of a large number of dissolved ions are sensitive to precipitation, because their concentrations may be relatively constant in the soil solution (Likens et al. 1977). Sensitivity of leaching losses to change in precipitation and evapotranspiration that determine streamflow appear to vary substantially among study areas. Some are rather constant for any given substance (Fig. 5.10), others show decreasing sensitivity with streamflow (Iwatubo and Tsutsumi 1968, Nakane et al. 1983) and still others suggest a weak dependency (Johnson and Swank 1973). But the substances differ among themselves in sensitivity depending on relative abundances and mobilities in the soil profile (Fig. 5.8). Sensitivities are therefore difficult to predict and are sure to vary among watersheds and among substances.

Fire

The occurrence of fire is also likely to increase in areas where conditions become warmer and drier. Fire occurrence depends on accumulation of fuels, the

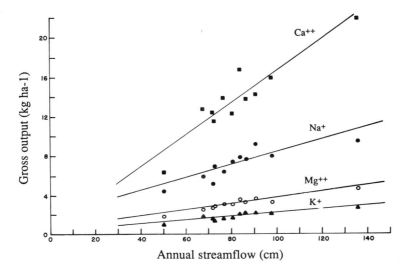

Fig. 5.10. The relatively constant concentrations of cations in streamwater result in linear relationships between streamwater losses of these substances and streamflow at Hubbard Brook Experimental Forest during 1963–1974. Redrawn from Likens et al. (1977).

moisture content of those fuels, and ignition incidence. Fuel accumulation depends in turn on production and decomposition, which varies within and among vegetation types. The effects of climate change on these processes mentioned above can influence fuel regimes. Fuel-moisture content depends on weather variables, among the most important of which are precipitation duration, time between precipitation events, and relative humidity. These variables will all be affected by changes in circulation patterns and convective storms (Overpeck et al. 1990). But will these changes be sufficiently dramatic to have a noticeable effect on fire regimes?

Fires burn more frequently in drier areas (Fig. 5.11), and fire incidence and area burned increases during years with high moisture deficit (Clark 1989a, Haines et al. 1973, 1978, Heinselman 1973, Payette et al. 1989). Long-term data from northwestern Minnesota, Missouri, Pennsylvania, and northern Quebec suggest that climate fluctuations have noticeable effects on fire regimes (Clark 1990a). In Minnesota, fire frequency responded to water-balance fluctuations of years to decades as far back as the climate records go (1830, Fig. 5.12), and to climate fluctuations lasting centuries (Fig. 5.13). The warm/dry 15th and 16th centuries saw an increase in fire frequency, followed by decreased fire frequency with the onset of the cooler/moister conditions near 1600 (Clark 1988). These cool/moist conditions, representing the regional expression of a global climate event known as the Little Ice Age (Gajewski 1988), persisted until the mid-19th

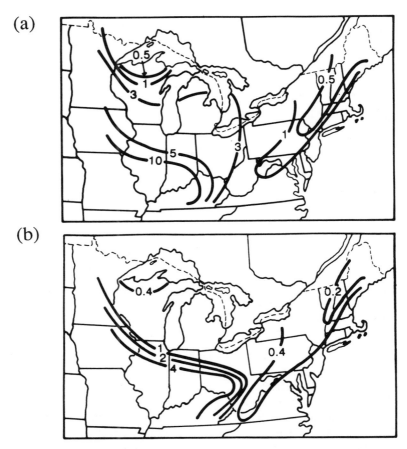

Fig. 5.11. Geographic variability in the importance of fire in the Northeast and Upper Midwest forests expressed as numbers of fires per unit area (a) and area burned (b) annually. Constructed from data in Haines et al. (1975).

century. These climate changes of decades to centuries (Fig. 5.13) interacted with the buildup of fuels to produce changing distributions of fire probability as a function of time since the last fire (Fig. 5.13). During warm/dry times (1400–1640, 1770–1820, 1865–1920), fires occurred at 8–13 yr intervals. This period represents the approximate time required for accumulation of a continuous litter layer that could support another fire. During cooler/moister periods (1640–1770, 1820–1860) the intervals were longer. Together these results suggest that fire probability was sufficiently high during the warm/dry times that fires tended to occur as soon as a suitable fuel layer developed (Clark 1989b, 1990b). When conditions were moister, fire tended to depend more on the occurrence of unusually dry years (Clark 1989a).

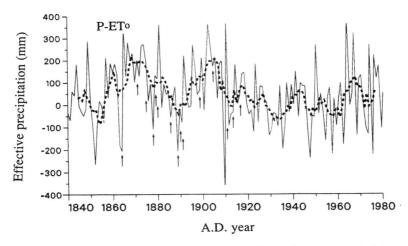

Fig. 5.12. The probability of fire increased with increasing moisture deficit at Lake Itasca Forestry and Biological Station before fire suppression was instituted in 1910. Fire years are indicated by arrows on this plot of effective precipitation, i.e. precipitation (P)—potential evapotranspiration $(ET°)(P=0.003)$ From Clark (1989a).

Simulation models of these stands (Clark 1990b) suggest that fire frequency would have increased by 10–25% with the warmer dry conditions of the mid-20th century, had fire suppression not been instituted in 1910.

Comparisons of fire records with water balances from Missouri (Haines et al. 1973) and Pennsylvania (Haines et al. 1978) show similar increases in fire occurrence during dry times in the 1950s and 1960s, respectively. Payette et al. (1989) found fires to be more frequent during the warm/dry 1950s in northern Quebec, and the probability of fire increased during individual years of high deficit. These data indicate that the importance of fire is likely to increase with increased moisture deficits, even in rather mesic forests like the mountainous areas of the eastern United States, where droughts of the 1950s and 1960s saw increased fire incidence (Haines et al. 1975, 1978). The responsiveness of fire regimes to climate change may be higher now than was the case before European settlement, because ignition incidence is so high as a result of human activity (Haines et al. 1975). Presettlement forests in areas where lighting is rare and Indian burning was low might not have experienced an ignition during the critical times when fire weather conditions were right, for example, the mesic forests of the Northeast, where lightning is generally associated with rainfall (Fahey and Reiners 1981).

Although these studies indicate fire sensitivity to climate change even in mesic regions, there may still exist a gradient in sensitivity to climate change across eastern North America, with highest sensitivity in dryer mixed conifer forests.

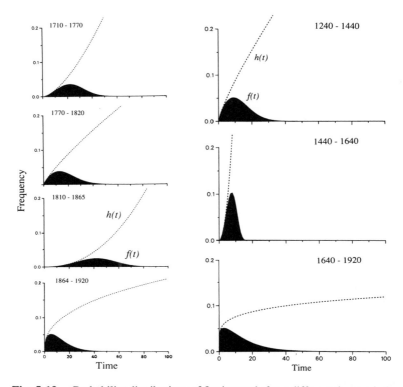

Fig. 5.13. Probability distributions of fire intervals from different time periods (given by dates) in northwestern Minnesota. Fire intervals on the left are taken from stratigraphic charcoal data. Those on the right are from fire scars. The distributions represent the probability that the interval between the occurrence of two fires will of a given length. From Clark (1989b).

One expression of this higher sensitivity may be the better correlation between area burned and weather variables in dryer western Canada than in the moister East (Flanningan and Harrington 1988). It is possible that the low flammability of eastern forests also results in low sensitivity of fire regime to climate and that relatively large changes in water balance (compared with drier regions) are required to increase fire risk. Whereas a 10-cm increase in annual effective precipitation in northwestern Minnesota (where the annual mean effective precipitation can be near zero) results in a 10% decrease in fire probability (Clark 1989a), the same change in effective precipitation in a northern hardwoods forest (where effective precipitation is much higher) may be much less. Decreases of this magnitude are also likely to have occurred in the eastern United States over the last several centuries, but there is not evidence for frequent fires in the mesic forests of the region, except where soils are excessively drained or where Native American burning was important (primarily coastal areas) (Patterson and Sassaman 1988). Taken together, it is likely that fire regimes may show important responses to climate changes throughout North America, but drier mixed conifer forests in the Midwest may respond to a greater extent than more mesic forests of the Northeast.

Species Composition

Existing patterns of species composition across climatic gradients also suggest a range of sensitivities. These sensitivities can be roughly approximated by turnover of vegetation types on the coordinate system defined by mean annual precipitation and mean annual temperature (Fig. 5.14). At mean annual temperatures of 15°C, the dominant vegetation type changes from desert to grassland to deciduous or conifer forest over a 50-cm range of precipitation values, that is, from 30 to 80 cm. The same precipitation change where precipitation is already 150 cm does not result in such dramatic transitions in the dominant vegetation type. Likewise, a change of 50 cm, where the annual mean is already 350 cm, does not result in a change in the dominant tropical forest vegetation type. Vegetation type is most sensitive to precipitation in drier climates.

At the coarser spatial and temporal scales provided by pollen analysis, it appears that more xeric forests (McAndrews 1966) and ecotones (Davis 1978, Gajewski 1987) are most sensitive to climate fluctuations that result from nonlinearities such as those in Fig. 5.2. Although climate changes have varied regionally through the past, it is also possible that the degree of sensitivity to climate change has played a role in the more dramatic changes in species composition.

Although these results apply to the level of the "vegetation type," climate effects on distributions of individual species is also certain. Among the life stages most sensitive to climate change is seedling establishment (Barr 1930, Toumey and Neethling 1924). Kullman (1983) demonstrated correlations in establishment of birch (*Betula pubescens*) along an altitudinal gradient in Sweden with summer temperatures in the 20th century. Declining temperatures since the 1930s have resulted in decreased establishment at high elevations, whereas establishment at lower elevations has continued at a low rate. Establishment of sugar maple (*Acer saccharum*) seedlings in understory of old-growth forests of northwestern Minnesota has also varied with water balances in the 20th century (Fig. 5.15). Trees did not regenerate during the dust-bowl years of the 1930s. Clearly species composition is sensitive to climate changes of the magnitudes experienced during the Holocene and even as recently as this century.

Stand simulation models further suggest responses of species composition to future climate changes. Overpeck and Bartlein (1989) used GCM output for future climate variables together with a stand simulation model to predict decline of conifer forests in the Upper Midwest and Northeast and increased oaks and other hardwoods (Fig. 5.16). Solomon's (1986) results using a similar model made similar predictions, with southern boreal forest being replaced by deciduous

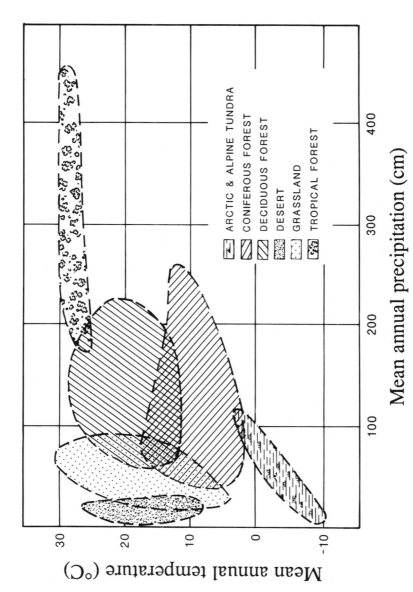

Fig. 5.14. Vegetation formations on the coordinate system defined by mean annual temperature and total annual precipitation. Redrawn from MacMahon (1981).

Mean annual temperature (°C)

Mean annual precipitation (cm)

ARCTIC & ALPINE TUNDRA

CONIFEROUS FOREST

DECIDUOUS FOREST

DESERT

GRASSLAND

TROPICAL FOREST

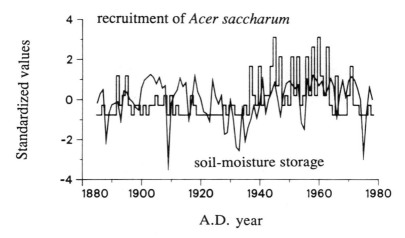

Fig. 5.15 Age distribution of *Acer saccharum* trees and soil-moisture content calculated from temperate and precipitation data (Clark 1989a) in northwestern Minnesota. Series are standardized to unit variance. The dust-bowl years of the 1930s are characterized by low regeneration rates, suggesting sensitivity of tree reproduction to climate changes in this century.

stands. Pastor and Post's (1988) results point out the potential for changes in species composition at smaller spatial scales as a result of the ways in which changes in regional climate are modified by local landscape variability (Fig. 5.9). The uncertainty associated with effects of future disturbance regimes is further suggested by model results of Overpeck et al. (1990).

Seasonality

The foregoing discussion focused on very generalized climate changes, because GCM predictions are still rather coarse. Not surprisingly, the GCMs predict changes in seasonality, and trends in seasonality throughout the Holocene appears to have been one of the more important influences on vegetation (Kutzbach and Wright 1985). These changes in the timing of water-balance transitions throughout the year can be among the most important effects of climate change on ecosystems. Whether precipitation falls during the growing season determines runoff, evapotranspiration, nutrient losses, and fire regimes. The losses of NO_3^- and cations that occur during snowmelt in the Northeast (Likens et al. 1977) are, in part, a result of the rather even distribution of precipitation throughout the year. The accumulated snowpack is released over a relatively short period of time, flushing labile anions with it. In midwestern regions, winter precipitation is lower, and the accumulation of snow that results in higher runoff at snowmelt is less dramatic.

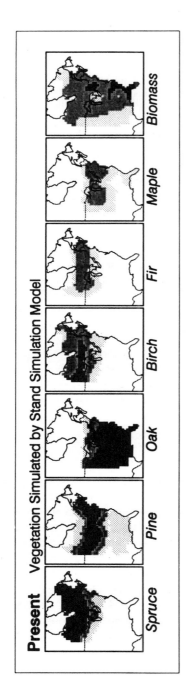

Fig. 5.16. Vegetation under (top) modern and (bottom) $2 \times CO_2$ climate scenarios as simulated by Overpeck and Bartlein (1989) using a stand simulation model. Shading is relative biomass for individual species and tons ha^{-1} for the total biomass plot. Shading intensities are <50 (lightest), 50–100, and >50 (darkest). From Overpeck and Bartlein (1989).

Fire occurrence is also sensitive to seasonality, because fires tend to occur early in spring before greenup or after leaf fall in autumn. Because the phenology of plant growth and snowfall depend on seasonality, fire regimes depend not only on average climate and daily weather, but also on the seasonal progression of vegetation growth and water balance. The duration of snow cover into the spring and the heat sink provided by developing leaves provide a rather narrow window during which fires can burn before summer. Except in dry summers, fires will not burn in many forests, because understory vegetation contains much moisture. The time between leaf fall in autumn and the first snows provide a second window for fire occurrence (Haines et al. 1975). Seasonality represents one of the most important aspects of climate, it is likely to change, and ecosystem processes will depend on that change.

Summary

The lessons of history and existing climate dependencies in ecosystems indicate ranges of sensitivities and complex responses. Broad-scale ecosystem processes, such as NPP, may be most sensitive to *small* changes in water balance in deserts, grasslands, and temperate and conifer forests. Decomposition rates and accumulation rates of detritus may be more sensitive in temperate hardwood forests, because decomposition rates slow with increasing latitude to a greater degree than do production rates. Because of their higher litter quality, decomposition rates in hardwood forests are likely to be more sensitive to small climatic shifts than are those in conifer stands. This statement refers only to sensitivity, however, as protracted climate change and changes of large magnitude could have potentially greater effects in boreal conifer forests due to the greater accumulation of organic matter in those areas. Nutrient cycling is sensitive to all aspects of macroclimate, microclimate, seasonality, local vegetation cover, and disturbance. Different aspects of nutrient cycles respond in different ways to climate change; therefore it is difficult to speculate on the composite effects in given ecosystems. Fire regime appears sensitive to climate change throughout most of the temperate forests, but it is likely that drier conifer forests will display greater sensitivity to climate change than will mesic forests.

As long as we have only the vaguest notion of how climate will change in any given area (Bryson 1988), however, it is going to be impossible to predict accurately how ecosystems will change. Even if the boundary conditions used in GCMs could be forecast with high confidence, it would still be exceedingly difficult to predict ecosystem transition at local scales because of the complexities of the climate system and of the ecosystem responses. Prediction of ecosystem change must build from this shaky foundation; ecosystem simulations using GCM output are logically only as good as the climate assumptions they contain. In fact, they are much worse, because they contain their own uncertainties. Perhaps half of the papers regularly published on forest ecosystems in leading journals investigate processes that stand-simulation models must assume we already understand. They contain dozens of functional forms and tens to hundreds of parameters. These problems that result from lack of empirical data and ecosystem understanding are no reason to abandon simulation models. They are cause to question model output and to explore the more fundamental question of climate sensitivity, either through field manipulation or synthesis of climate/ecosystem relationships. We have better potential for assessing ecosystem sensitivity than we do for prediction. There is much existing evidence to suggest which processes are sensitive and where, and much could be done to increase this knowledge.

Appendix

This appendix contains sensitivity estimates from the relationships presented in Fig. 5.3 and compares them with predictions of Schimel et al. (1990). Ideally, one would prefer to replace Fig. 5.3A and 5.3B with a single response surface of NPP to the combined effects of temperature and precipitation. It is nonetheless possible to analyze the two different relationships in a general way. For purposes of demonstration, we will construct a composite function as

$$\text{NPP} = N_m \, [\text{lim by } P] \, [\text{lim by } T],$$

Where N_m is that which is realized when neither P (millimeters) not T (in degrees Centigrade) are limiting to NPP (in grams per meter^2). From the two individual responses to P,

$$\text{NPP}_P = N_m \, (1 - e^{-k_1 P}),$$

and T,

$$\text{NPP}_T = \frac{N_m}{1 + k_2 e^{-k_3 T}},$$

(Kimmins 1988), we can write a composite response

$$\text{NPP} = N_m \left[\frac{1 - e^{-k_1 P}}{1 + k_2 e^{-k_3 T}} \right].$$

This relation assumes a product form of limitation (e.g., Powell and Richerson 1985), it does not contain the full interactive effects of T and P, and parameter values fitted to individual relationships contain a bias that results from the fact that they are fit independently. Our analysis is thus but a rough guide to relative

Table 5.1. Changes in climate variables in two prairie grid cells used in the analysis of Schimel et al. (1990) and sensitivity analysis given in the Appendix

	North cell		South cell	
	$1 \times CO_2$	$2 \times CO_2$	$1 \times CO_2$	$2 \times CO_2$
Annual precipitation (mm)	460	495	600	579
% change	+ 7.7		− 3.5	
Mean annual temperature (°C)	9	13	15	19
% change	+44		+27	
% change in NPP	+35		+14	
S_P*	0.86		0.82	
S_T†	0.60		0.68	

*NPP sensitivity to total annual precipitation or the proportionate change in NPP with a percentage change in total annual precipitation (see Appendix).

†NPP sensitivity to mean annual temperature or the proportionate change in NPP with a percentage change in mean annual temperature (see Appendix).

sensitivities. The parameter values are $N_m = 3000$ gm^{-2}, $k_1 = 0.00063$ mm^{-1}, $k_2 = 3.72$ (dimensionless), and $k_3 = 0.119°C^{-1}$.

Sensitivities to P and T are described by dimensionless sensitivity coefficients

$$S_P = \left(\frac{\partial NPP/NPP}{\partial P/P} \right) = \frac{Pk_1 e^{-k_1 P}}{1 - e^{-k_1 P}},$$

and

$$S_T = \left(\frac{\partial NPP/NPP}{\partial T/T} \right) = \frac{Tk_2 k_3 e^{-k_3 T}}{1 + k_2 e^{-k_3 P}},$$

that express the proportionate change in NPP with a percentage change in P and T, respectively. The coefficients are taken in dimensionless form to permit comparison among sensitivities to variables having different units. Values for the example discussed in the text are given in Table 5.1.

Acknowledgments

I thank Schimel et al. (1990) and John Pastor for providing their unpublished results and Jon Overpeck for Fig. 5.15. This chapter benefited from comments of J. Pastor and R. Wyman, and two anonymous reviewers.

References

Aber, J. D. and J. M. Melillo. 1980. Litter decomposition: Measuring relative contributions of organic matter and nitrogen to forest soils. *Can. J. Bot.* 58:416–421.

Abrams, M. D. 1988. Comparative water relations of three successional hardwood species in central Wisconsin. *Tree Physiol.* 4:263–273.

Agren, G. I., B. Axelsson, G. G. K. Flower-Ellis, S. Linder, H. Persson, H. Staff, and E. Troeng. 1980. Annual carbon budget for a young scots pine. *Ecol. Bull.* 32:307–313.

Barr, P. M. 1930. The effect of soil moisture on the establishment of spruce reproduction in British Columbia. *Yale Univ. Sch. Forestry Bull.* 26:1–77.

Bartlein, P. J., T. Webb III, and E. Fleri. 1984. Holocene climatic changes estimated from pollen data from the northern midwest. *Quat. Res.* 22:361–374.

Bernabo, J. C. and T. Webb, III. 1977. Changing patterns in the Holocene pollen record or northeastern North America: A mapped summary. *Quat. Res.* 8:64–96.

Bryson, R. 1966. Air masses, streamlines and the boreal forest. *Geogr. Bull.* 8:228–269.

Bryson, R. A. 1988. Civilization and rapid climate change. *Environ. Conserv.* 15:7–15.

Bunce, J. A., L. E. Miller, and B. F. Chabot. 1977. Competitive exploitation of soil water by five eastern North American tree species. *Bot. Gaz.* 138:168–173.

Chapin, F. S. III. 1980. The mineral nutrition of wild plants. *Ann. Rev. Ecol. Syst.* 11:233–260.

Clarholm, M., P. Budimir, T. Rosswall, B. Soderstrom, B. Sohlenius, H. Staff, and A. Wiren. 1981. Biological aspects of nitrogen mineralization in humus from a pine forest podsol incubated under different moisture and temperature conditions. *Oikos* 37:137–145.

Clark, J. S. 1988. Effects of climate change on fire regime in northwestern Minnesota. *Nature* 334:233–235.

Clark, J. S. 1989a. Effects of long-term water balances on fire regime, northwestern Minnesota. *J. Ecol.* 77:989–1004.

Clark, J. S. 1989b. Ecological disturbance as a renewal process: theory and application to fire history. *Oikos* 56:17–30.

Clark, J. S. 1990a. Fire occurrence during the last 750 years in northwestern Minnesota. *Ecol. Monogr.*, in press.

Clark, J. S. 1990b. Twentieth century climate change, fire suppression and forest production and decomposition in northwestern Minnesota. *Can. J. Forest Res.*, in press.

Clark, J. S. 1990c. Disturbance, climate change, and forest rehabilitation. In *Environmental Rehabilitation: Preamble to Sustained Development*, M. K. Wali (ed.). Wiley, New York, in press.

Clark, J. S. 1990d. Landscape interactions among nitrogen mineralization, species composition, and long-term fire frequency. *Biogeochemistry*, in press.

COHMAP. 1988. Climatic changes of the last 18,000 years: Observations and model simulations. *Science* 241:1043–1052.

Davis, M. B. 1978. Climatic interpretation of pollen in Quaternary sediments. In *Biology and Quaternary Environments*, D. Walker and J. C. Guppy (eds.), pp. 35–51. Australian Academy of Sciences, Canberra City, Australia.

Davis, M. B. 1981. Quaternary history and the stability of forest communities. In *Forest Succession: Concepts and Application*, D. C. West, H. H. Shugart, and D. B. Botkin (eds.), pp. 132–153. Springer-Verlag, New York, New York.

Davis, M. B. 1983. Quaternary history of the deciduous forests of eastern North America and Europe. *Ann. Missouri Bot. Garden* 70:550–563.

Davis, M. B. and D. B. Botkin. 1985. Sensitivity of cool temperate forests and their fossil pollen record to rapid temperature change. *Quat. Res.* 23:327–340.

Diaz, J. F., J. T. Andrews, and S. K. Short. 1989. Climate variations in northern North America (6000 BP to present) reconstructed from pollen and tree-ring data. *Arctic Alpine Res.* 21:45–59.

Fahey, T. J. and W. A. Reiners. 1981. Fire in the forests of Maine and New Hampshire. *Bull. Torrey Bot. Club* 108:362–373.

Flannigan, M. D. and J. B. Harrington. 1988. A study of the relation of meteorological variables to monthly provincial area burned by wildfire in Canada (1953–80). *J. Appl. Meteorol.* 27:441–452.

Gajewski, K. 1987. Climatic changes on the vegetation of eastern North America during the past 2000 years. *Vegetatio* 68:179–190.

Gajewski, K. 1988. Late Holocene climate changes in eastern North America estimated from pollen data. *Quat. Res.* 29:255–262.

Ghashghaie, J. and B. Sangier. 1989. Effects of nitrogen deficiency on leaf photosynthetic response of tall fescue to water deficit. *Plant, Cell Environ.* 12:261–271.

Gorham, E., P. M. Vitousek, and W. A. Reiners. 1979. The regulation of chemical budgets over the course of terrestrial ecosystem succession. *Ann. Rev. Ecol. Syst.* 10:53–84.

Graham, R. L., M. G. Turner, and V. H. Dale. 1990. Increasing atmospheric CO_2 and climate change: Effects on forests. *BioScience,* in press.

Grimm, E. C. 1983. Chronology and dynamics of vegetation change in the prairie-woodland region of southern Minnesota, U.S.A. *New Pathologist* 93:311–350.

Haines, D. A., V. J. Johnson, and W. A. Main. 1975. *Wildfire Atlas of the Northeastern and North Central States,* US Dept. of Agriculture Forest Service General Technical Report NC–16, Washington, DC.

Haines, D. A., W. A. Main, and J. S. Crosby. 1973. *Forest Fires in Missouri,* US Dept. of Agriculture Forest Service Research Paper NC–87, Washington, DC.

Haines, D. A., W. A. Main, and E. F. McNamara. 1978. *Forest Fires in Pennsylvania,* US Dept. of Agriculture Forest Service Research Paper NC–158, Washington, DC.

Heinselman, M. L. 1973. Fire in the virgin forest of the Boundary Waters Canoe Area, Minnesota. *Quat. Res.* 3:329–382.

Hillel, D. 1980. *Applications of Soil Physics.* Academic Press, New York.

Hinckley, T. M., J. P. Lassoie, and S. W. Running. 1978. Temporal and spatial variations in the water status of forest trees. *Forest Science Monogr.* 20:1–72.

Ingestad, T. and M. Kahr. 1985. Nutrition and growth of coniferous seedlings at varied relative nitrogen addition rate. *Physiol. Plants* 65:109–116.

Ino, T. and M. Monsi. 1969. An experimental approach to the calculation of CO_2 amount evolved from several soils. *Jap. J. Botany* 20:153–188.

Iwatubo, G. and T. Tsutsumi. 1968. On the amount of plant nutrients supplied to the ground by rain water in adjacent open plot and forest. III. On the amount of nutrient contained in run-off water. *Bull. Kyoto Univ.* 40:140–156.

Jacobson, G. L. 1979. The palaeoecology of white pine (*Pinus strobus*) in Minnesota. *J. Ecol.* 67:697–726.

Jacobson, G. L., T. Webb, and E. C. Grimm. 1987. Patterns and rates of vegetation change during the deglaciation of eastern North America. In *North America and Adjacent Oceans During the Last*

Deglaciation, W. F. Ruddiman and H. E. Wright (eds.), pp. 277–288. Geological Society of America, Boulder, CO.

Jarvis, P. G. and J. W. Leverenz. 1983. Productivity of temperate, deciduous and evergreen forests. In *Ecosystem Processes: Mineral Cycling, Productivity and Man's Influence,* Physiological Plant Ecology: New Series, Vol 12D, O. L. Land, P. S. Nobel, C. B. Osmond, and H. Zeigler (eds.), pp. 233–280. Springer-Verlag, New York.

Jenny, H. 1980. *Soil Genesis with Ecological Perspectives.* Springer-Verlag, New York.

Johnson, P. J. and E. T. Swank. 1973. Studies of cation budgets in the southern Appalachians on four experimental watersheds with contrasting vegetation. *Ecology* 54:70–80.

Kellogg, W. W. and Z. -C. Zhao. 1988. Sensitivity of soil moisture to doubling of carbon dioxide in climate model experiments. Part I: North America. *J. Climate* 1:348–366.

Kimmins, J. P. 1988. Community organization: Methods of study and prediction of the productivity and yield of forest ecosystems. *Can. J. Botany* 66:2654–2672.

Knapp, A. K. and T. R. Seastedt. 1986. Detritus accumulation limits productivity of tallgrass prairie. *BioScience* 36:662–668.

Kullman, L. 1983. Past and present tree lines of different species in the Handolan Valley, Central Sweden. In *Tree Line Ecology,* P. Morisset and S. Payette (eds.), pp. 25–26. Centre d'etudes nordique de l'Universite Laval, Quebec.

Kutzbach, J. E. and H. E. Wright. 1985. Simulation of the climate of 18,000 years BP; results for the North American/North Atlantic/European sector and comparison with the geologic record of North America. *Quat. Sci. Rev.* 4:147–187.

Likens, G. E., F. H. Bormann, R. S. Pierce, J. S. Eaton, and N. M. Johnson. 1977. *Biogeochemistry of a Forested Ecosystem.* Springer-Verlag, New York.

MacMahon, J. A. 1981. Successional processes: comparisons among biomes with special reference to probable roles of and influences on animals. In *Forest Succession: Concepts and Application,* D. C. West, H. H. Shugart, D. B. Botkin (eds.), pp. 277–304. Springer-Verlag, New York.

McAndrews, J. H. 1966. Postglacial history of prairie, savanna, and forest in northwestern Minnesota. *Mem. Torrey Bot. Club* 22:1–72.

Meentenmeyer, V. 1978. Macroclimate and lignin control of litter decomposition rates. *Ecology* 59:465–472.

Meentenmeyer, V., E. O. Box, and R. Thompson. 1982. World patterns and amounts of terrestrial plant litter production. *BioScience* 32:125–128.

Melillo, J. M., J. D. Ager, and J. F. Muratore. 1982. Nitrogen and lignin control of hardwood leaf litter decomposition dynamics. *Ecology* 63:621–626.

Nakane, K., S. Kusaka, M. Mitsudera, and H. Tsubota. 1983. Effect of fire on water and major nutrient budgets in forest ecosystems II. Nutrient balances, input (precipitation) and output (discharge). *Jap. J. Ecol.* 33:333–345.

O'Neill, R. V. and D. L. DeAngelis. 1981. Comparative productivity and biomass relations of forest ecosystems. In *Dynamic Properties of Forest Ecosystems,* D. E. Reichle (ed.), pp. 411–449. Cambridge University Press, London.

Overpeck, J. T. and P. J. Bartlein. 1989. Appendix D. Assessing the response of vegetation to future climate change: ecological response surfaces and paleoecological model validation. In *The Potential Effects of Global Climate Change on the United States,* EPA–230–05–89–054, US Environmental Protection Agency, Washington, DC.

Overpeck, J. T., D. Rind, and R. Goldberg. 1990. Climate-induced changes in forest disturbance and vegetation. *Nature* 343:51–53.

Pastor, J. J., J. D. Aber, C. A. McClaugherty, and J. M. Melillo. 1984. Aboveground production and N and P cycling along a nitrogen mineralization gradient on Blackhawk Island, Wisconsin. *Ecology* 65:256–268.

Pastor, J. and W. M. Post. 1986. Influence of climate, soil moisture, and succession on forest carbon and nitrogen cycles. *Biogeochemistry* 2:3–27.

Pastor, J. and W. M. Post. 1988. Response of northern forests to CO_2-induced climate change. *Nature* 334:55–58.

Patterson, W. A. III, and K. E. Sassaman. 1988. Indian fires in the prehistory of New England. In *Holocene Human Ecology in Northeastern North America*, G.P. Nicholas 9 (ed.), pp. 107–135. Plenum, New York.

Payette, S., C. Morneau, L. Sirois, and M. Desponts. 1989. Recent fire history of the northern Quebec biomes. *Ecology* 70:656–673.

Poulovassilis, A. 1962. Hysteresis of pore water, an application of the concept of independent domains. *Soil Sci.* 93:405–412.

Powell, T. and P. J. Richerson. 1985. Temporal variation, spatial heterogeneity, and competition for resources in plankton systems: a theoretical model. *Am. Nat.* 125:431–464.

Provine, W. B. 1971. *The Origins of Theoretical Population Genetics*. University of Chicago Press, Chicago.

Reiners, W. A. and G. E. Lang. 1987. Changes in litterfall along a gradient in altitude. *J. Ecol.* 75:629–638.

Rind, D. 1988. The doubled CO_2 climate and the sensitivity of the modeled hydrologic cycle. *J. Geophys. Res.* 93:5385–5412.

Schimel, D. S., W. J. Parton, T. G. F. Kittel, D. S. Ojima, and C. V. Cole. 1990. Grassland biogeochemistry: links to atmospheric processes. *Clim. Change,* in press.

Schlesinger, W. H., J. F. Reynolds, G. L. Cunningham, L. F. Huenneke, W. M. Jarrell, R. A. Virginia, and W. G. Whitford. 1990. Biological feedbacks in global desertification. *Science* 247:1043–1048.

Sokal, R. R. and F. J. Rohlf. 1981. *Biometry*. Freeman, New York.

Solomon, A. M. 1986. Transient response of forests to CO_2-induced climate change: Simulation modeling experiments in eastern North America. *Oecologia* 68:567–579.

Tiedemann, A. R., J. D. Helvey, and T. D. Anderson. 1978. Stream chemistry and watershed nutrient economy following wildfire and fertilization in eastern Washington. *J. Environm. Qual.* 7:580–588.

Tilman, D. 1982. *Resource Competition and Community Structure*. Princeton University Press, Princeton.

Toumey, J. W. and E. J. Neethling. 1924. Insolation a factor in the natural regeneration of certain conifers. *Yale Univ. Sch. Forestry Bull.* 11:1–63.

Van Cleve, K., L. Oliver, R. Schlentner, L. A. Viereck, and C. T. Dyrness. 1983. Productivity and nutrient cycling in taiga forest ecosystems. *Can. J. Forest Res.* 13:553–572.

Vitousek, P. M. 1982. Nutrient cycling and nutrient use efficiency. *Am. Nat.* 119:553–572.

Vitousek, P. M. 1983. The effects of deforestation on air, soil, and water. In *The Major Biogeochemical Cycles and Their Interactions*, B. Bolin and R. B. Cook (eds.), pp. 222–225. Scientific Committee on Problems of the Environment/UNEP. Wiley, Chichester, UK.

Vitousek, P. M., J. R. Gosz, C. C. Grier, J. M. Nelillo, and W. A. Reiners, 1982. A comparative analysis of potential nitrification and nitrate mobility in forest ecosystems. *Ecol. Monogr.* 52:155–157.

Vitousek, P. M. and P. A. Matson. 1985. Disturbance, nitrogen availability, and nitrogen losses in an intensively managed loblolly pine plantation. *Ecology* 66:1360–1376.

Webb, T. III. 1981. The past 11,000 years of vegetations change in eastern North America. *BioScience* 31:501–506.

Webb, T. III. 1988. Eastern North America. In *Vegetation History*, B. Huntley and T. Webb III (eds.), pp. 385–414. Kluwer Academic, The Hague.

Webb, T. III, E. J. Cushing, and H. E. Wright. 1983. Holocene changes in the vegetation of the Midwest. In *Late Quaternary Environments of the Eastern United States, Vol. 2, the Holocene,* H. E. Wright, Jr. (ed), pp. 142–165. University of Minnesota Press, Minneapolis.

West, A. W., G. P. Sparling, T. W. Speir, and J. M. Wood. 1988. Dynamics of microbial C, N-flush and ATP, and enzyme activities of gradually dried soils from a climosequence. *Australian J. Soil Res.* 26:519–530.

White, C. S., J. R. Gosz, J. D. Horner and D. I. Moore. 1988. Seasonal, annual, and treatment induced variation in available nitrogen pools and nitrogen cycling processes in soils of two Douglas fir stands. *Biol. Fertility Soils* 6:93–99.

Whitford, W. G., V. Meentenmeyer, T. R. Seastedt, K. Cromack, D. A. Crossley, P. Santos, R. L. Todd, and J. B. Waide. 1981. Exceptions to the AET model: Deserts and clearcut forest. *Ecology* 62:275–277.

Woods, K. D. and M. B. Davis. 1989. Paleoecology of range limits: beech in the upper peninsula of Michigan. *Ecology* 70:681–696.

Wright, S. 1921. Correlation and causation. *J. Agric. Res.* 20:557–585.

Zak, D. R., K. S. Pregitzer, and G. E. Host. 1986. Landscape variation in nitrogen mineralization and nitrification. *Can. J. Forest Res.* 16:1258–1263.

Zhao, Z. -C. and W. W. Kellogg. 1988. Sensitivity of soil moisture to doubling of carbon dioxide in climate model experiments. Part II: The Asian Monsoon region. *J. Climate* 1:367–378.

6

Consequences of Global Warming for Biological Diversity

Robert L. Peters

Introduction

Our understanding of how atmospheric composition affects global climate is still in its infancy, but an increasing body of knowledge suggests that rising concentrations of CO_2 and other anthropogenic polyatomic gases will raise global average temperatures substantially (National Research Council 1983, Schneider and Londer 1984, World Meteorological Organization 1982). Associated with global warming will be regional and local changes in average temperature, changes in the distribution of hot and cold periods, and changes in a number of other chemical and physical variables, including precipitation, evaporation rates, sea level, and soil and water chemistry.

We can infer how the biota might respond to climate change by observing present and past distributions of plants and animals, which are heavily determined by temperature and moisture patterns. For example, one race of the dwarf birch (*Betula nana*) can only grow where the temperature never exceeds 22°C (Ford 1982), suggesting that it would disappear from those areas where global warming causes temperatures to exceed 22°C. Recent historical observations of changes in range or species dominance, as observed in the gradual replacement of spruce (*Picea rubens*) by deciduous species during the past 180 years in the eastern United States (Hamburg and Cogbill 1988), can also suggest future responses. Insight into long-term responses to large climatic changes can be gleaned from studies of fossil distributions of pollen (Davis 1983) and small mammals (Graham 1986).

Such observations tell us that plants and animals are very sensitive to climate. Their ranges move when the climate patterns change—species die out in areas where they were once found and colonize new areas where the climate becomes newly suitable.

We can expect similar responses to projected global warming during the next 50 to 100 years, including disruption of natural communities and extinction of populations and species. Even many species that are today widespread will experience large range reductions. Efficient dispersers may be able to shift their ranges to take advantage of newly suitable habitat, but most species will at best experience a time lag before extensive colonization is possible and hence in the short-term will show range diminishment. At worst, many species will never be able to recover without human intervention, because migration routes are cut off by development or other human-caused habitat loss.

Although this chapter focuses on the terrestrial biota, ocean systems may show similar shifts in species ranges and community compositions if warming of ocean water or alteration in the patterns of water circulation occur. For example, recent El Nino events demonstrate the vulnerability of primary productivity and species abundances to changes in ocean currents and local temperatures (e.g., Duffy 1983, Glynn 1984).

The Nature of Ecologically Significant Changes

Although the exact rate and magnitude of future climate change is uncertain given imperfect knowledge about the behavior of clouds, oceans, and biotic feedbacks, there is widespread consensus among climatologists that ecologically significant warming will occur during the next century. For example, the National Academy of Sciences (NAS 1987) concluded that both global mean surface warming and an associated increase in global mean precipitation are "very probable." Hansen et al. (1988a) have stated "we can confidently state that major greenhouse climate changes are a certainty."

It is expected that, within the next 40 years, greenhouse trace gases in the atmosphere, including carbon dioxide, chlorofluorocarbons, and methane, will reach a concentration equivalent to double the preindustrial concentration of carbon dioxide. The National Academy of Sciences and others have estimated that this concentration of greenhouse gases will be sufficient to raise the Earth's temperature by $3 +/- 1.5°C$ (Hansen et al. 1988b, NAS 1987, NRC 1983, Schneider and Londer 1984, WMO 1982). More recent estimates suggest the possibility that warmings as high as $4.2 +/- 1.2°C$ (Schlesinger 1989), or even 8–10°C (Lashof 1989), are possible. Because of a time lag caused by thermal inertia of the oceans, some of this warming will be delayed by 30–40 years beyond the time that a doubling equivalent of carbon dioxide is reached (EPA 1988), but substantial warming could occur soon; the Goddard Institute for Space Studies (GISS) model projects a 2°C rise by 2020 AD (Rind 1989). Such general circulation models have many uncertainties, but they provide the best estimates possible. As discussed below, this transitional warming would cause profound ecologic change well before 3 or 4°C is reached; warming of less than 1°C would have substantial ecological effects.

It should be stressed that although projections can be made about global averages, regional projections are much less certain (Schneider 1988). It is known that warming will not be even over the earth, with the high latitudes, for example, predicted to be warmer than the low latitudes (Hansen et al. 1988a). Regional and local peculiarities of typography and circulation will play a strong role in determining local climates.

For the purpose of discussion in this chapter, I use 3°C as the average global warming, because this is a commonly used benchmark, but it must be recognized that additional warming well beyond 3°C may be reached during the next century if the production of anthropogenic greenhouse gases continues. I also make the conservative assumption that 3°C warming is not reached until 2070 AD. Additional warming or faster warming would cause additional biological disruption beyond what is described here.

The threats to natural systems are serious for the following reasons. First, 3°C of warming would present natural systems with a warmer world than has been experienced in the past 100,000 years (Schneider and Londer 1984). A 4°C rise would make the earth its warmest since the Eocene, 40 million years ago (Barron 1985, see Webb 1990). This warming would not only be large compared to recent natural fluctuations, but it would be very fast, perhaps 15 to 40 times faster than past natural changes (Gleick et al. 1990). For reasons discussed below, such a rate of change may exceed the ability of many species to adapt. Even widespread species are likely to have drastically curtailed ranges, at least in the short-term. Moreover, human encroachment and habitat destruction will make wild populations of many species small and vulnerable to local climate changes.

Second, ecological stress would not be caused by temperature rise alone. Changes in global temperature patterns would trigger widespread alterations in rainfall patterns (Hansen et al. 1988b, Kellogg and Schware 1981, Manabe et al. 1981), and we know that for many species precipitation is a more important determinant of survival than temperature *per se*. Indeed, except at treeline, rainfall is the primary determinant of vegetation structure, trees occurring only where annual precipitation is in excess of 300 mm (Woodward 1990, also see Cook, this volume). Because of global warming, some regions would see dramatic increases in rainfall and others would lose their present vegetation because of drought. For example, the United States Environmental Protection Agency (1988) concluded, based on several studies, that a long-term drying trend is likely in the midlatitude, interior continental regions during the summer. Specifically, Kellogg and Schware (1981), based upon rainfall patterns during past warming periods, projected that substantial decreases in rainfall in North America's Great Plains are possible, perhaps decreasing as much as 40% by the early decades of the next century.

Other environmental factors important in determining vegetation type and health would change because of global warming. Soil chemistry would change (Kellison and Weir 1987), as, for example, changes in storm patterns alter leaching and erosion rates (Harte et al. 1990). Increased carbon dioxide concentrations may accelerate the growth of some plants at the expense of others (NRC 1983, Strain and Bazzaz 1983), possibly destabilizing natural ecosystems. Rises in sea level may inundate coastal biological communities (Hansen et al. 1988a, Hoffman et al. 1983, NRC 1983, Titus et al. 1984).

As previously mentioned, a variety of computer projections have concluded that warming will be relatively greater at higher latitudes (Hansen et al. 1987). This suggests that, although tropical systems may be more diverse and are currently under great threat because of habitat destruction, temperate zone and arctic species may ultimately be in greater jeopardy from climate change. Arctic vegetation would experience widespread changes (Edlund 1987). A recent attempt to map climate-induced changes in world biotic communities projects that high-latitude communities would be particularly stressed (Emanuel et al. 1985), and the boreal forest, for example, was projected to decrease by 37% in response to global warming of 3°C.

A final point, important in understanding species response to climate change, is that weather is variable, and extreme events, like droughts, floods, blizzards, and hot or cold spells may have more effect on species distributions than average climate *per se* (e.g., Knopf and Sedgwick 1987). For example, in northwestern forests, global warming is expected to increase fire frequency, leading to rapid alteration of forest character (Clark, this volume, Franklin 1990).

Species' Range Shifts in Response to Climate Change

We know that when temperature and rainfall patterns change, species' ranges change. Not surprisingly, species tend to track their climatic optima, retracting their ranges where conditions become unsuitable and expanding them where conditions improve (Peters and Darling 1985, Ford 1982). Even very small temperature changes of less than one degree within this century have been observed to cause substantial range changes. For example, the white admiral butterfly (*Ladoga camilla*) and the comma butterfly (*Polygonia c-album*) greatly expanded their ranges in the British Isles during the past century as the climate warmed approximately 0.5°C (Ford 1982). The birch (*Betula pubescens*) responded rapidly to warming during the first half of this century by expanding its range north into the Swedish tundra (Kullman 1983).

On a larger ecological and temporal scale, entire vegetation types have shifted in response to past temperature changes no larger than those that may occur during the next 100 years or less (Baker 1983, Bernabo and Webb 1977, Butzer 1980, Flohn 1979, Muller 1979, Van Devender and Spaulding 1979). As the Earth warms, species tend to shift to higher latitudes and altitudes. From a simplified point of view, rising temperatures have caused species to colonize new habitats toward the poles, often while their ranges contracted away from the equator as conditions there became unsuitable.

During several Pleistocene interglacials, the temperature in North America was apparently 2–3°C higher than presently. Sweet gum trees (*Liquidambar*) grew in southern Ontario (Wright 1971); Osage oranges (*Maclura*) and papaws (*Asimina*) grew near Toronto, several hundred kilometers north of their present distributions; manatees swam in New Jersey; and tapirs and peccaries foraged in North Carolina (Dorf 1976). During the last of these interglacials, which ended more than 100,000 years ago, vegetation in northwestern Europe, which is now boreal, was predominantly temperate (Critchfield 1980). Other significant changes in species' ranges have been caused by altered precipitation accompanying past global warming, including expansion of prairie in the American Midwest during a global warming episode approximately 7,000 years ago (Bernabo and Webb 1977).

It should not be imagined, because species tend to shift in the same general direction, that existing biological communities move in synchrony. Conversely, because species shift at different rates in response to climate change, communities often disassociate into their component species (Fig. 6.1). Recent studies of fossil packrat (*Neotoma* spp.) middens in the southwestern United States show that during the wetter, moderate climate of 22,000–12,000 years ago, there was not a concerted shift of plant communities. Instead, species responded individually to climatic change, forming stable, but, by present-day standards, unusual assemblages of plants and animals (Van Devender and Spaulding 1979). In eastern North America, too, postglacial communities were often ephemeral associations of species, changing as individual ranges changed (Davis 1983, Graham 1986).

A final aspect of species response is that species may shift altitudinally as well as latitudinally. When climate warms, species shift upward. Generally, a short climb in altitude corresponds to a major shift in latitude: for 3°C cooling, 500 m in elevation equals roughly 250 km in latitude (MacArthur 1972). Thus, during the middle Holocene, when temperatures in eastern North America were 2°C warmer than at present, hemlock (*Tsuga canadensis*) and white pine (*Pinus strobus*) were found 350 m higher on mountains than they are today (Davis 1983).

Because mountain peaks are smaller than bases, as species shift upward in response to warming, they typically occupy smaller and smaller areas, have smaller populations, and may thus become more vulnerable to genetic and environmental pressures (Murphy and Weiss 1990). Species originally situated near mountaintops might have no habitat to move up to and may be entirely replaced by the relatively thermophilous species moving up from below (Fig. 6.2). Examples of past extinctions attributed to upward shifting include alpine plants once living on mountains in Central and South America, where vegetation zones have shifted upward by 1,000–1,500 m since the last glacial maximum (Flenley 1979, Heusser 1974).

Magnitude of Projected Latitudinal Shifts

If the proposed CO_2-induced warming occurs, species shifts similar to those in the Pleistocene would occur and vegetation belts would move hundreds of kilometers toward the poles (Davis and Zabinski 1990, Frye 1983, Peters and Darling 1985). A 300-km shift in the temperate zone is a reasonable minimum

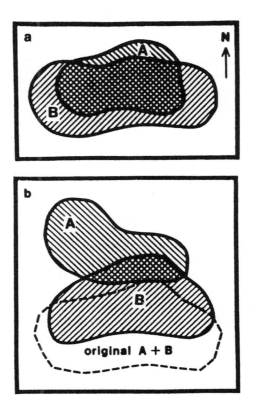

Fig. 6.1. (a) Initial distribution of two species, A and B, whose ranges largely overlap. (b) In response to climate change, latitudinal shifting occurs at species-specific rates and the ranges disassociate.

estimate for a 3°C warming, based on the positions of vegetation zones during analogous warming periods in the past (Dorf 1976, Furley et al. 1983).

Additional confirmation that shifts of this magnitude or greater may occur comes from attempts to project future range shifts for some species by looking at their ecological requirements. For example, the forest industry is concerned about the future of commercially valuable North American species, like the loblolly pine (*Pinus taeda*). This species is limited on its southern border by moisture stress on seedlings. Based on the physiologic requirements for temperature and moisture of *P. taeda*, Miller et al. (1987) projected that the southern range limit of the species would shift approximately 350 km northward in response to a global warming of 3°C. Davis and Zabinski (1990) have projected possible

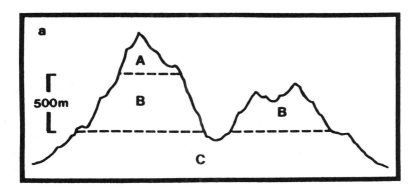

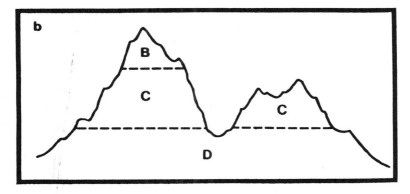

Fig. 6.2. (a) Present altitudinal distribution of three species, A, B, and C. (b) Species distribution after a 500-m shift in altitude in response to a 3°C rise in temperature (based on Hopkin's bioclimatic law, MacArthur 1972). Species A becomes locally extinct. Species B shifts upward and the total area it occupies decreases. Species C becomes fragmented and restricted to a smaller area, and species D successfully colonizes the lowest altitude habitats.

northward range withdrawals among several North American tree species, including sugar maple (*Acer saccharum*) and beech (*Fagus grandifolia*), from 600 km to as much as 2,000 km in response to the warming caused by a doubled-CO_2 concentration. Beech would be most responsive, withdrawing from its present southern extent along the Gulf Coast and retreating into Canada.

Mechanisms Underlying Range Shifts

The range shifts described above are the sum of many local processes of extinction and colonization that occur in response to climate-caused changes in suitability of habitats. These changes in habitat suitability are determined by both direct climate effects on physiology, including temperature and precipitation, and indirect effects secondarily caused by other species, themselves affected by temperature.

There are numerous examples of climate directly influencing survival and thereby distribution. In animals, the direct range-limiting effects of excessive warmth include lethality, as in corals (Glynn 1984), and interference with reproduction, as in the large blue butterfly, *Maculinea arion* (Ford 1982). In plants, excessive heat and associated decreases in soil moisture may decrease survival and reproduction. Coniferous seedlings, for example, are injured by soil temperatures greater than 45°C, although other types of plants can tolerate much higher temperatures (see Daubenmire 1962). Many plants have their northern limits determined by minimum temperature isotherms below which some key physiologic process does not occur. For instance, the grey hair grass (*Corynephorus canescens*) is largely unsuccessful at germinating seeds below 15°C and is bounded to the north by the 15°C July mean isotherm (Marshall 1978). Moisture extremes exceeding physiologic tolerances also determine species' distributions. Thus, the European range of the beech tree (*Fagus sylvatica*) ends to the south where rainfall is less than 600 mm annually (Seddon 1971), and dog's mercury (*Mercurialis perennis*), an herb restricted to well-drained sites in Britain, cannot survive in soil where the water table reaches as high as 10 cm below the soil surface (Ford 1982).

The physiological adaptations of most species to climate are conservative, and it is unlikely that most species could evolve significantly new tolerances in the time allotted to them by the coming warming trend. Indeed, the evolutionary conservatism in thermal tolerance of many plant and animal species, beetles, for example (Coope 1977), is the underlying assumption that allows us to infer past climates from faunal and plant assemblages.

Interspecific interactions altered by climate change will have a major role in determining new species distribution. Temperature can influence predation rates (Rand 1964), parasitism (Aho et al. 1976), and competitive interactions (Beauchamp and Ullyott 1932). Climate-induced changes in the ranges of tree pathogens and parasites may be important in determining future tree distributions (Winget 1988). Soil moisture is a critical factor in mediating competitive interactions among plants, as is the case where the dog's mercury (*Mercurialis perennis*) excludes oxlip (*Primula elatior*) from dry sites (Ford 1982).

Given the new associations of species that occur as climate changes, many species will face "exotic" competitors for the first time. Local extinctions may occur as climate change causes increased frequencies of droughts and fires, favoring invading species. One species that might spread, given such conditions is *Melaleuca quinquenervia*, a bamboo-like Australian eucalypt. This species has already invaded the Florida Everglades, forming dense monotypic stands where drainage and frequent fires have dried the natural marsh community (Courtenay 1978, Myers 1983).

The preceding effects, both direct and indirect, may act in synergy, as when drought makes a tree more vulnerable to attack by insect pests.

Dispersal Rates and Barriers

The ability of species to adapt to changing conditions will depend to a large extent upon their ability to track shifting climatic optima by dispersing colonists. In the case of warming, a North American species, for example, would most likely need to establish colonies to the north or at higher elevations. Survival of plant and animal species would therefore depend either on long-distance dispersal of colonists, such as seeds or migrating animals, or on rapid iterative colonization of nearby habitat until long-distance shifting results. A plant's intrinsic ability to colonize will depend upon its ecological characteristics, including fecundity, viability, and growth characteristics of seeds, nature of the dispersal mechanism, and ability to tolerate selfing and inbreeding upon colonization. If a species' intrinsic colonization ability is low or if barriers to dispersal are present, extinction may result if all of its present habitat becomes unsuitable.

There are many cases where complete or local extinction has occurred because species were unable to disperse rapidly enough when climate changed. For example, a large, diverse group of plant genera, including water-shield (*Brassenia*), sweet gum (*Liquidambar*), tulip tree (*Liriodendron*), magnolia (*Magnolia*), moonseed (*Menispermum*), hemlock (*Tsuga*), arbor vitae (*Thuja*), and white cedar (*Chamaecyparis*), had a circumpolar distribution in the Tertiary (Tralau 1973). But during the Pleistocene ice ages, all went extinct in Europe while surviving in North America. Presumably, the east-west orientation of such barriers as the Pyrennes, Alps, and the Mediterranean, which blocked southward migration, was partly responsible for their extinction (Tralau 1973).

Other species of plants and animals thrived in Europe during the cold periods, but could not survive conditions in postglacial forests. One such previously widespread dung beetle, *Aphodius hodereri* is now extinct throughout the world except in the high Tibetan plateau where conditions remain cold enough for its survival (Cox and Moore 1985). Other species, like the Norwegian mugwort (*Artemisia novegica*) and the springtail (*Tetracanthella arctica*), now live primarily in the boreal zone but also survive in a few cold, mountaintop refuges in temperate Europe (Cox and Moore 1985).

These natural changes were extremely slow compared to predicted changes in the near future. Change to warmer conditions at the end of the last ice age spanned several thousand years yet is considered rapid by geologic standards (Davis 1983). We can deduce that, if such a slow change was too fast for many species to adapt, the projected warming—possibly 40 times faster—will have more severe consequences. For widespread, abundant species, like the loblolly pine (modeled by Miller et al. 1987), even substantial range retraction might not threaten extinction; but rare, localized species, whose entire ranges might become unsuitable, would be threatened unless dispersal and colonization were successful. Even for widespread species, major loss of important ecotypes and associated germplasm is likely (see Davis and Zabinski 1990).

A key question is whether the dispersal capabilities of most species prepare them to cope with the coming rapid warming? If the climatic optima of temperate zone species do shift hundreds of kilometers toward the poles within the next 100 years, then these species would have to colonize new areas rapidly. To survive, a localized species, whose present range all becomes unsuitable, might have to shift poleward at several hundred kilometers or faster per century. Although some species, such as plants propagated by spores or "dust" seeds, may be able to match these rates (Perring 1965), many species could not disperse fast enough to compensate for the expected climatic change without human assistance (Rapoport 1982), particularly given the presence of dispersal barriers. Even wind-assisted dispersal may fall short of the mark for many species. In the case of the Engelmann spruce (*Picea engelmannii*), a tree with light, wind-dispersed seeds, fewer than 5% of seeds travel even 200 m downwind, leading to an estimated migration rate of 1–20 km per century (Seddon 1971); this reconciles well with rates derived from fossil evidence for North American trees of between 10 and 45 km per century (Davis and Zabinski 1990, Roberts 1989). As described in the next section, many migration routes will likely be blocked by human habitation, cities, roads, and fields that replace natural habitats.

Although many *animals* may be physically capable of great mobility, the distribution of some is limited by the distributions of particular plants, that is, suitable habitat; their dispersal rates therefore may be largely determined by those of cooccurring plants. Behavior may also restrict dispersal even of animals physically capable of large movements. Dispersal rates below 2.0 km/year have been measured for several species of deer (Rapoport 1982), and many tropical deep-forest birds simply do not cross even very small unforested areas (Diamond 1975). On the other hand, some highly mobile animals may shift rapidly, as have some European birds (Edgell 1984).

Even if animals can disperse efficiently, suitable habitat may be reduced under changing climatic conditions. For example, it has been suggested that tundra nesting habitat for migratory shore birds might be reduced by high-arctic warming (Myers 1988, Lester and Myers, this volume).

Synergy of Habitat Destruction and Climate Change

We know that even slow, natural climate change caused species to become extinct. What is likely to happen given the environmental conditions of the coming century?

Some clear implications for conservation follow from the preceding discussion of dispersal rates. Any factor decreasing the probability that a species could successfully colonize new habitat would increase the probability of extinction.

Thus, as previously described, species are more likely to become extinct if there are physical barriers to colonization, such as oceans, mountains, and cities. Furthermore, species are more likely to become extinct if their remaining populations are small. Smaller populations mean fewer colonists can be sent out, and the probability of successful colonization is smaller.

Species are more likely to become extinct if they occupy a small geographic range. It is less likely that some part will remain suitable when climate changes than if the ranges were larger. Also, if a species has lost much of its range because of some other factor, like clearing of the richer and moister soils for agriculture, it is possible that remaining populations are located in poor habitat and are therefore more susceptible to new stresses.

For many species, all of these conditions will be met by human-caused habitat destruction, which, as discussed in the beginning of this paper, increasingly confines the natural biota to small patches of original habitat, patches isolated by vast areas of human-dominated urban or agricultural lands.

Habitat destruction in conjunction with climate change sets the stage for an even larger wave of extinction than previously imagined, based upon consideration of human encroachment alone. Small, remnant populations of most species, surrounded by cities, roads, reservoirs, and farm land, would have little chance of reaching new habitat if climate change makes the old unsuitable. Few animals or plants would be able to cross Los Angeles on the way to new habitat. Figure 6.3 illustrates the combined effects of habitat loss and warming on a hypothetical reserve.

Amelioration and Mitigation

Conservationists and reserve managers, because of difficulty in predicting regional and local changes, must deal with increased uncertainty in making long-range plans. However, even given imprecise regional projections, informed guesses can be made at least about the general direction of change. Specifically most areas will tend to be hotter and continental interiors in particular are likely to experience decreased soil moisture. How might the threats posed by climatic change to natural communities be mitigated? One basic truth is that the less populations are reduced by development now, the more resilient they will be to climate change. Thus, sound conservation now, in which we try to conserve more than just the minimum number of individuals of a species necessary for present survival, would be an excellent way to start planning for climate change.

In terms of responses specifically directed at the effects of climate change, the most environmentally conservative response would be to halt or slow global warming by cutting back on production of fossil fuels, methane, and chlorofluorocarbons. Extensive planting of trees to capture carbon dioxide could help slow the rise in carbon dioxide concentrations (Houghton, this volume, Sedjo 1989). Nonetheless, even were the production of all greenhouse gases stopped today, it is very likely that

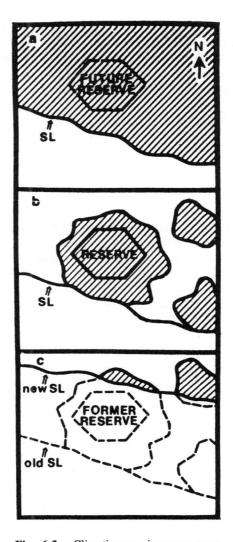

Fig. 6.3. Climatic warming may cause
species within biological reserves to disappear. Hatching indicates (a) species distribution before either human habitation or
climate change (SL indicates southern limit
of species range); (b) fragmented species
distribution after human habitation but before climate change; (c) species distribution
after human habitation and climate change.

there are now high enough concentrations in the air to cause ecologically significant warming (Rind 1989). Therefore, those concerned with the conservation of biological diversity must begin to plan mitigation activities now.

To make intelligent plans for siting and managing reserves, we need more knowledge. We must refine our ability to predict future conditions in reserves. We also need to know more about how temperature, precipitation, CO_2 concentrations, and interspecific interactions determine range limits (e.g., Picton 1984, Randall 1982) and, most important, how they can cause local extinctions.

Reserves that suffer from the stresses of altered climatic regimes will require carefully planned and increasingly intensive management to minimize species loss. For example, modifying conditions within reserves may be necessary to preserve some species; depending on new moisture patterns, irrigation or drainage may be needed (Hayes, this volume). Because of changes in interspecific interactions, competitors and predators may need to be controlled and invading species weeded out. The goal would be to maintain suitable conditions for desired species or species assemblages, much as the habitat of Kirtland's warbler is periodically burned to maintain pine woods (Leopold 1978). On the other hand, if native species die out because of physiological intolerance to climate change, despite management efforts, then some invading species might actually be encouraged as ecological replacements of those that have disappeared.

In attempting to understand how climatically stressed communities may respond and how they might be managed to prevent the gradual depauperization of their constituents, restoration studies, or more properly, "community creation" experiments can help. Communities may be created outside their normal climatic ranges to mimic the effects of climate change. One such "out of place" community is the Leopold Pines, at the University of Wisconsin Arboretum in Madison, where there is periodically less rainfall than in the normal pine range several hundred kilometers to the north (Jordan 1985, 1988). Researchers have found that although the pines themselves do fairly well once established at the Madison site, many of the other species that would normally occur in a pine forest, especially the small shrubs and herbs such as *Trientalis borealis,* the northern star flower, have not flourished, despite several attempts to introduce them.

If management measures are unsuccessful and old reserves do not retain necessary thermal or moisture characteristics, individuals of disappearing species might be transferred to new reserves. For example, warmth-intolerant ecotypes or subspecies might be transplanted to reserves nearer the poles. Other species may have to be periodically reintroduced in reserves that experience occasional climate extremes severe enough to cause extinction, but where the climate would ordinarily allow the species to survive with minimal management. Such transplantations and reintroductions, particularly involving complexes of species, will often be difficult. Many plants, for example, have their flowering times determined by photoperiod, and in such species southern strains flower later in the year than northern ones (McMillan 1959). A southern strain transplanted to the north therefore might flower too late in the season for successful reproduction. Despite such difficulties applicable restoration technologies are being developed for many species (Botkin 1977, Jordan et al. 1988, Lovejoy 1985).

To the extent that we can still establish reserves, pertinent information about changing climate and subsequent ecological response should be used in deciding how to design and locate them to minimize the effects of changing temperature and moisture. One implication is that more reserves may be needed. The existence of multiple reserves for a given species or community type increases the probability that, if one reserve becomes unsuitable for climatic reasons, the organisms may still be represented in another reserve.

Reserves should be heterogeneous with respect to topography and soil types, so that even given climatic change, remnant populations may be able to survive in suitable microclimatic areas. Species may survive better in reserves with wide variations in altitude, since, from a climatic point of view, a small altitudinal shift corresponds to a large latitudinal one. Thus, to compensate for a 2°C rise in temperature, a northern hemisphere species can achieve almost the same result by increasing its altitude only some 500 meters as it would by moving 300 km to the north (MacArthur 1972).

Corridors between reserves, important for other conservation reasons, would allow some natural migration of species to track climate shifting. Corridors along altitudinal gradients are likely to be most practical, because they can be relatively short compared with the longer distances necessary to accommodate latitudinal shifting.

As climatic models become more refined, pertinent information should be taken into consideration in making decisions about where to site reserves to minimize the effects of temperature and moisture changes. In the northern hemisphere, for example, where a northward shift in climatic zones is likely, it makes sense to locate reserves as near the northern limit of a species' or community's range as possible, rather than farther south, where conditions are likely to become unsuitable more rapidly.

Maximizing the size of reserves will increase long-term persistance of species by increasing the probability that suitable microclimates exist, by increasing the probability of altitudinal variation, and by increasing the latitudinal distance available to shifting populations.

Flexible zoning around reserves may allow us to actually move reserves in the future to track climatic optima, as, for example, by trading present range land for reserve land. The success of this strategy, however, would depend on a highly developed restoration technology, capable of guaranteeing, in effect, the portability of species and whole communities.

Summary

In the geologic past, natural climate changes have caused large-scale geographic shifts in species' ranges, changes in species composition of biological communities, and species extinctions. If the widely predicted greenhouse effect occurs, natural ecosystems will respond in ways similar to the ways they did in the past, but the response must be more extreme because of the very rapid rate of the projected change. Moreover, population reduction and habitat destruction due to human activities will prevent many species from colonizing new habitat when their old habitat becomes unsuitable. The synergy between climate change and habitat destruction would threaten many more species than either factor alone.

These effects would be pronounced in temperate and arctic regions, where temperature increases are projected to be relatively large. It is unclear how affected the tropical biota would be by the relatively small temperature increases projected for the lower latitudes, because relatively little is known about the physiological tolerances of tropical species, but substantial disruption may occur due to precipitation changes. Throughout the world, geographically restricted species might face extinction, whereas widespread species are likely to survive in some parts of their range. In the northern mid- and high latitudes, new northward habitat will become suitable even as die-offs occur to the south. However, it may be difficult for many species to take advantage of this new habitat because dispersal rates for many species are slow relative to the rate of warming, and therefore ranges of even many widespread species are likely to show a net decrease during the next century. Range retractions will be proximally caused by temperature and precipitation changes, increases in fires, changes in the ranges and severity of pests and pathogens, changes in competitive interactions, and additional effects of nonclimatic stresses like acid rain (Wyman, this volume) and low-level ozone.

The best solutions to the ecological upheaval resulting from climatic change are not yet clear. In fact, little attention has been paid to the problem. What is clear, however, is that the climatological changes would have tremendous impact on communities and populations isolated by development and, by the middle of the next century, may dwarf any other consideration in planning for reserve management. The problem may seem overwhelming. One thing, however, is worth keeping in mind: If populations are fragmented and small, they are more vulnerable to the new stresses brought about by climate change. Thus, one of the best things that can be done in the short-term is to minimize further encroachment of development upon existing natural ecosystems. Furthermore, we must refine climatologic predictions and increase understanding of how climate affects species, both individually and in their interactions with each other. Such studies may allow us to identify those areas where communities will be most stressed, as well as alternate areas where they might best be saved. Meanwhile, efforts to improve techniques for managing communities and ecosystems under stress, and also for restoring them when necessary, must be carried forward energetically.

Acknowledgments

The bulk of the text on global warming was previously published as an article in *Forest Ecology and Management,* in a special 1989 volume containing the proceedings of the symposium on Conservation of Diversity in Forest Ecosystems, University of California at Davis, July 25, 1988. It draws heavily on other previously published versions, including those in *Endangered Species Update* 5:1–8 and *Preparing for Climate Change: Proceedings of the First North American Conference on Preparing for Climate Change: A Cooperative Approach,* J. C. Topping, ed. Many of the ideas and all the figures derive from a paper by Peters and Darling, published in *Bioscience,* December, 1985. Please see Peters and Darling (1985) for a complete list of acknowledgments for help with this work.

References

Aho, J. M., J. W. Gibbons, G. W. Esch. 1976. Relationship between thermal loading and parasitism in the mosquitofish. In *Thermal Ecology II,* G. W. Esch and R. W. McFarlane (eds), pp. 213–218. Technical Information Center, Energy Research and Development Administration, Springfield, VA.

Baker, R. G. 1983. Holocene vegetational history of the western United States. *Late-Quaternary Environments of the United States, Vol. 2, The Holocene,* H. E. Wright, Jr. (ed.), pp. 109–125. University of Minnesota Press, Minneapolis, MN.

Barron, E. J. 1985. Explanations of the Tertiary global cooling trend. *Palaeogeogr. Palaeoclimatol. Palaeoecol.* 50:17–40.

Beauchamp, R. S. A. and P. Ullyott. 1932. Competitive relationships between certain species of fresh-water triclads. *J. Ecol.* 20:200–208.

Bernabo, J. C. and T. Webb III. 1977. Changing patterns in the Holocene pollen record of northeastern North America: A mapped summary. *Quat. Res.* 8:64–96.

Botkin, D. B. 1977. Strategies for the reintroduction of species into damaged ecosystems. In *Recovery and Restoration of Damaged Ecosystems,* J. Cairns, Jr., K. L. Dickson, and E. E. Herricks (eds.), pp. 241–260. University Press of Virginia, Charlottesville.

Butzer, K. W. 1980. Adaptation to global environmental change. *Prof. Geogr.* 32:269–278.

Caufield, C. 1985. *In the Rainforest.* Knopf, New York.

Coope, G. R. 1977. Fossil coleopteran assemblages as sensitive indicators of climatic changes during the Devensian (Last) cold stage. *Philos. Trans. R. Soc. Lond.* 280:313–340.

Courtenay, W. R. Jr. 1978. The introduction of exotic organisms. In *Wildlife and America,* H. P. Brokaw (ed.), pp. 237–252. Council on Environmental Quality, US Government Printing Office, Washington, DC.

Cox, B. C. and P. D. Moore. 1985. *Biogeography: An Ecological and Evolutionary Approach.* Blackwell Scientific Publications, Oxford.

Critchfield, W. B. 1980. Origins of the eastern deciduous forest. In *Proceedings, Dendrology in the Eastern Deciduous Forest Biome,* held September 11–13, 1979, at Virginia Polytechnic Institute and State University School of Forestry and Wildlife Resources, Publ. Fish and Wildlife Service, Washington, DC FWS-2-80, pp. 1–14.

Daubenmire, R. F. 1962. *Plants and Environment: A Textbook of Plant Autecology.* John Wiley, New York.

Davis, M. B. 1983. Holocene vegetational history of the eastern United States. In *Late-Quaternary Environments of the United States, Vol. 2, The Holocene,* H. E. Wright, Jr. (ed.), pp. 166–181. University of Minnesota Press, Minneapolis.

Davis, M. B. and C. Zabinski. 1990. Changes in geographical range resulting from greenhouse warming effects on biodiversity in forests. In *Proceedings of the World Wildlife Fund Conference on Consequences of Greenhouse Effect for Biological Diversity*, R. L. Peters and T. E. Lovejoy (eds.), Yale University Press, New Haven, CN. In press.

Diamond, J. M. 1975. The island dilemma: lessons of modern biogeographic studies for the design of natural preserves. *Biol. Conserv.* 7:129–146.

Dorf, E. 1976. Climatic changes of the past and present. *Paleobiogeography: Benchmark Papers in Geology*, No. 31, C. A. Ross (ed.), pp. 384–412. Dowden, Hutchinson, and Ross, Stroudsburg, PA.

Duffy, D. C. 1983. Environmental uncertainty and commercial fishing: effects on Peruvian guano birds. *Biol. Conserv.* 26:227–238.

Edgell, M. C. R. 1984. Trans-hemispheric movements of Holarctic Anatidae: the Eurasian wigeon (*Anas penelope L.*) in North America. *J. Biogeogr.* 11:27–39.

Edlund, S. A. 1987. Effects of climate change on diversity of vegetation in arctic Canada. In *Preparing for Climate Change: Proceedings of the First North American Conference on Preparing for Climate Change: A Cooperative Approach*, J. C. Topping Jr. (ed.), pp. 186–193. Government Institutes, Washington, DC.

Ehrlich, P. R. and H. A. Mooney. 1983. Extinction, substitution, and ecosystem services. *Bioscience* 33:248–254.

Emanuel, W. R., H. H. Shugart, and M. P. Stevenson. 1985. Response to comment: "Climatic change and the broad-scale distribution of terrestrial ecosystem complexes" *Clim. Change* 7:457–460.

Environmental Protection Agency (EPA). 1988. *The Potential Effects of Global Climate Change on the United States*, Draft Report to Congress, Vol. 1. EPA, Washington, DC.

Flenley, J. R. 1979. *The Equatorial Rain Forest*. Buttersworths, London.

Flohn, H. 1979. Can climate history repeat itself? Possible climatic warming and the case of paleoclimatic warm phases. In *Man's Impact on Climate*, W. Bach, J. Pankrath, and W. W. Kellogg (eds.), pp. 15–28. Elsevier Scientific Publishing, Amsterdam.

Ford, M. J. 1982. *The Changing Climate*. George Allen and Unwin, London.

Franklin, J. F. 1990. Effects of global climatic change on forests in North Western North America. In *Proceedings of the Conference on Consequences of Greenhouse Effect for Biological Diversity*, R. L. Peters and T. E. Lovejoy (eds.), Yale University Press, New Haven, CN, in press.

Frye, R. 1983. Climatic change and fisheries management. *Natural Resources J.* 23:77–96.

Furley, P. A., W. W. Newey, R. P. Kirby, and J. McG. Hotson. 1983. *Geography of the Biosphere*. Buttersworths, London.

Gleick, P. H., L. Mearns, and S. H. Schneider. 1990. Climate-change scenarios for impact assessment. In *Proceedings of the World Wildlife Fund Conference on Consequences of the Greenhouse Effect for Biological Diversity*, R. L. Peters and T. E. Lovejoy (eds.), Yale University Press, New Haven, CN, in press.

Glynn, P. 1984. Widespread coral mortality and the 1982–83 El Nino warming event. *Environ. Conserv.* 11:133–146.

Graham, R. W. 1986. Plant-animal interactions and Pleistocene extinctions. In *Dynamics of Extinction*, D. K. Elliott (ed.), pp. 131–154. Wiley and Sons, Somerset, NJ.

Hamburg, S. P. and C. V. Cogbill. 1988. Historical decline of red spruce populations and climatic warming. *Nature* 331:428–431.

Hansen, J., I. Fung, A. Lacis, S. Lebedeff, D. Rind, R. Ruedy, G. Russell. 1988a. Prediction of near-term climate evolution: What can we tell decision-makers now? In *Preparing for Climate Change: Proceedings of the First North American Conference on Preparing for Climate Change: A Cooperative Approach*, pp. 35–47. Government Institutes, Washington, DC.

Hansen, J., I. Fung, A. Lacis, D. Rind, S. Lebedeff, R. Ruedy, and G. Russell. 1988b. Global climate changes as forecast by Goddard Institute for Space Studies three-dimensional model. *J. Geophys. Res.* 93:9341–9364.

Hansen, J., A. Lacis, D. Rind, G. Russell, I. Fung, S. Lebedeff. 1987. Evidence for future warming: How large and when. In *The Greenhouse Effect, Climate Change, and U.S. Forests*, W. E. Shands and J. S. Hoffman (eds.). Conservation Foundation, Washington, DC.

Harte, J., M. Torn, and D. Jensen. 1990. The nature and consequences of indirect linkages between climate change and biological diversity. In *Proceedings of the World Wildlife Fund Conference on Consequences of Greenhouse Effect for Biological Diversity*, R. L. Peters and T. E. Lovejoy (eds.), Yale University Press, New Haven, CT, in press.

Heusser, C. J. 1974. Vegetation and climate of the southern Chilean lake district during and since the last interglaciation. *Quat. Res.* 4:290–315.

Hoffman, J. S., D. Keyes, and J. G. Titus. 1983. *Projecting Future Sea Level Rise*. US Environmental Protection Agency, Washington, DC.

Jordan, W. R. III. 1985. Personal Communication. University of Wisconsin, Madison.

Jordan, W. R. III. 1988. Ecological restoration: Reflections on a half-century of experience at the University of Wisconsin-Madison Arboretum. In *Biodiversity*, E. O. Wilson (ed.), pp. 311–316. National Academy Press, Washington, DC.

Jordan, W. R. III, R. L. Peters, and E. B. Allen. 1988. Ecological restoration as a strategy for conserving biological diversity. *Environ. Management* 12:55–72.

Kellison, R. C. and R. J. Weir. 1987. Selection and breeding strategies in tree improvement programs for elevated atmospheric carbon dioxide levels. In *The Greenhouse Effect, Climate Change, and U.S. Forests*, W. E. Shands and J. S. Hoffman (eds.), Conservation Foundation, Washington, DC.

Kellogg, W. W. and R. Schware. 1981. *Climate Change and Society: Consequences of Increasing Atmospheric Carbon Dioxide*. Westview Press, Boulder, CO.

Knopf, F. L. and J. A. Sedgwick. 1987. Latent population responses of summer birds to a catastrophic, climatological event. *Condor* 89:869–873.

Kullman, L. 1983. Past and present tree lines of different species in the Handolan Valley, Central Sweden. In *Tree Line Ecology*, P. Morisset and S. Payette (eds.), pp. 25–42. Centre d'etudes nordiques de l'Universite Laval, Quebec.

Lashof, D. A. 1989. The dynamic greenhouse: Feedback processes that may influence future concentrations of atmospheric trace gases and climatic change. *Clim. Change* 14:213–242.

Leopold, A. S. 1978. Wildlife and forest practice. In *Wildlife and America*, H. P. Brokaw (ed.), pp. 108–120. Council on Environmental Quality, US Government Printing Office, Washington, DC.

Lovejoy, T. E. 1985. *Rehabilitation of degraded tropical rainforest lands*, Commission on Ecology Occasioned Paper 5. International Union for the Conservation of Nature and Natural Resources, Gland, Switzerland.

MacArthur, R. H. 1972. *Geographical Ecology*. Harper & Row, New York.

McMillan, C. 1959. The role of ecotypic variation in the distribution of the central grassland of North America. *Ecol. Monog.* 29:285–305.

Manabe, S., R. T. Wetherald, and R. J. Stouffer. 1981. Summer dryness due to an increase of atmospheric CO_2 concentration. *Clim. Change* 3:347–386.

Marshall, J. K. 1978. Factors limiting the survival of *Corynephorus canescens* (L) Beauv. in Great Britain at the northern edge of its distribution. *Oikos* 19:206–216.

Miller, W. F., P. M. Dougherty, and G. L. Switzer. 1987. Rising CO_2 and changing climate: major southern forest management implications. *The Greenhouse Effect, Climate Change, and U.S. Forests.* Conservation Foundation, Washington, DC.

Muller, H. 1979. Climatic changes during the last three interglacials. In *Man's Impact on Climate,* W. Bach, J. Pankrath, and W. W. Kellogg (eds.), pp. 29–41. Elsevier Scientific Publishing, Amsterdam.

Murphy, D. D. and S. B. Weiss. 1990. The effects of climate change on biological diversity in western North America: species losses and mechanisms. In *Proceedings of the World Wildlife Fund Conference on the Consequences of the Greenhouse Effect for Biological Diversity,* R. L. Peters and T. E. Lovejoy (eds.), Yale University Press, New Haven, CT.

Myers, J. P. 1988. The likely impact of climate change on migratory birds in the arctic. Presentation at the Seminar on Impact of Climate Change on Wildlife, January 21–22, 1988; Climate Institute, Washington, D.C.

Myers, R. L. 1983. Site susceptibility to invasion by the exotic tree *Melaleuca quinquenervia* in southern Florida. *J. Appl. Ecol.* 20:645–658.

National Academy of Sciences (NAS). 1987. *Current Issues in Atmospheric Change.* National Academy Press, Washington, DC.

National Research Council (NRC). 1983. *Changing Climate.* National Academy Press, Washington, DC.

Ono, R. D., J. D. Williams, and A. Wagner. 1983. *Vanishing Fishes of North America.* Stone Wall Press, Washington, DC.

Perring, F. H. 1965. The advance and retreat of the British flora. In *The Biological Significance of Climatic Changes in Britain,* C. J. Johnson and L. P. Smith (eds.), pp. 51–59. Academic Press, London.

Peters, R. L. and J. D. Darling. 1985. The greenhouse effect and nature reserves. *BioScience* 35:707–717.

Picton, H. D. 1984. Climate and the prediction of reproduction of three ungulate species. *J. Appl. Ecol.* 21:869–879.

Rand, A. S. 1964. Inverse relationship between temperature and shyness in the lizard *Anolis lineatopus. Ecology* 45:863–864.

Randall, M. G. M. 1982. The dynamics of an insect population throughout its altitudinal distribution: *Coleophora alticolella* (Lepidoptera) in northern England. *J. Anim. Ecol.* 51:993–1016.

Rapoport, E. H. 1982. *Areography: Geographical Strategies of Species.* Pergamon Press, New York.

Rind, D. 1989. A character sketch of greenhouse. *EPA J.* 15:4–7.

Roberts, L. 1989. How fast can trees migrate? *Science* 243:735–737.

Schneider, S. H. 1988. The greenhouse effect: What we can or should do about it. In *Preparing for Climate Change: Proceedings of the First North American Conference on Preparing for Climate Change: A Cooperative Approach,* pp. 19–34. Government Institutes, Washington, DC.

Schneider, S. H. and R. Londer. 1984. *The Coevolution of Climate and Life.* Sierra Club Books, San Francisco.

Schlesinger, M. E. 1990. Model projections of the climatic changes induced by increased atmospheric CO_2. In *Climate and Geosciences,* J. C. Duplessy, A. Berger, and S. H. Schneider (eds.). Kluwer Academic Publishing, Dordrecht, in press.

Seddon, B. 1971. *Introduction to Biogeography.* Barnes and Noble, New York.

Sedjo, R. A. 1989. Forests: A tool to moderate global warming? *Environment* 31:14–20.

Strain, B. R. and F. A. Bazzaz. 1983. Terrestrial plant communities. In *CO₂ and Plants,* E. R. Lemon (ed.), pp. 177–222. Westview Press, Boulder, CO.

Titus, J. G., T. R. Henderson, and J. M. Teal. 1984. Sea level rise and wetlands loss in the United States. *Nat. Wetlands Newslett.* 6:3–6.

Tralau, H. 1973. Some quaternary plants. In *Atlas of Paleobiogeography,* A. Hallam (ed.), pp. 499–503. Elsevier Scientific Publishing, Amsterdam.

Van Devender, T. R. and W. G. Spaulding. 1979. Development of vegetation and climate in the southwestern United States. *Science* 204:701–710.

Webb, T., III. 1990. Past Changes in Vegetation and Climate: Lessons for the Future. In *Proceedings of the World Wildlife Fund Conference on Consequences of the Greenhouse Effect for Biological Diversity,* R. L. Peters and T. E. Lovejoy (eds.), Yale University Press, New Haven, CT, in press.

Winget, C. H. 1988. Forest management strategies to address climate change. In *Preparing for Climate Change: Proceedings of the First North American Conference on Preparing for Climate Change: A Cooperative Approach,* pp. 328–333. Government Institutes, Rockville, MD.

Woodward, F. I. 1990. Review of the effects of climate on vegetation: ranges, competition and composition. In *Proceedings of the World Wildlife Fund Conference on Consequences of the Greenhouse Effect for Biological Diversity,* R. L. Peters and T. E. Lovejoy (eds.), Yale University Press, New Haven, CT, in press.

World Meteorological Organization. 1982. *Report of the JSC/CAS: A Meeting of Experts on Detection of Possible Climate Change,* Moscow, October 1982, Report WCP29, Geneva Switzerland.

Wright, H. E., Jr. 1971. Late Quaternary vegetational history of North America. In *The Late Cenozoic Glacial Ages,* K. K. Turekian (ed.), pp. 425–464. Yale Univ. Press, New Haven.

7

Double Jeopardy for Migrating Wildlife

Robert T. Lester and
J. Peter Myers

Introduction

Global warming promises to transform the natural world. Unable to keep pace with changing climates, many animal and plant populations will decline and species already at risk will be pushed to extinction (Lester and Myers 1989, Peters and Darling 1985). The size of coastal wetlands, boreal forests, and arctic and alpine communities will diminish (Emanuel et al. 1985a, b, Environmental Protection Agency 1988).

These are some of the more obvious biotic consequences of global warming and climatic change. Other ecological effects of global warming will be much more subtle, yet no less profound in their impacts on wildlife and wildlife habitat. For example, changes in the seasonality of temperature, precipitation, and other climatologic parameters will have important consequences for many biological phenomena such as flowering, breeding, and migration.

Many animals migrate long distances to exploit food and other resources that are unevenly distributed in space and time. Seasonal changes in weather patterns generally control the availability of these resources, and, thus, the timing of these seasonal changes is of critical importance to migratory animals. Global warming threatens to alter many of the fundamental phenologic relationships that have driven the evolution of migration itself. The double jeopardy for migratory animals lies in their reliance upon the precise timing of resource availabilities and their dependence upon habitats that are themselves especially sensitive to changes in climate.

Shorebirds (Aves: Charidii), because of the specific characteristics of their migratory system and life histories, provide an especially good illustration of how migratory animals could be affected by climate change. Shorebirds will be affected most by global warming due to changes in the timing of migrations and the availability of food resources along their migratory pathways. These changes could lead to serious population declines in some species.

By comparing shorebird migrations with the migration of ungulates on the Serengeti Plain in East Africa, we are better able to understand how climatic changes could affect different types of migratory systems. The annual migration of ungulates from dry- to wet-season ranges is less constrained in time and space than the long-distance, latitudinal migrations of shorebirds. However, the complexity of biotic interactions associated with this system could leave it equally vulnerable to the climatic changes wrought by global warming. In both cases, global warming will present an unprecedented challenge to the conservation of migratory species.

Classification of Animal Migratory Systems

Migration is one of several important relationships that will be affected by changes in the seasonality of weather patterns. Other important biological processes such as the flowering and fruiting of plants and the reproduction of animals will also be influenced by changes in seasonality. Phenologic changes of this sort are important for many migratory species because they influence the availability and abundance of food resources. We define migration rather broadly as "the seasonal movement of animals in response to critical resources that are unequally distributed in space and time" (Aidley 1981). Many animal groups such as shorebirds, songbirds, whales, fishes, and insects are highly migratory. A number of these animals are of great economic significance because of their commercial value (e.g., herring, cod, and pollock) or because of their importance as agricultural pests (e.g., locusts).

The reasons for migrating vary from species to species, but in general, the regular movement from place to place allows animals to exploit resources or habitats that could not be exploited on a continual basis. Arctic winters, for example, are too severe for shorebirds or even whales to survive, but the short arctic summer provides an abundant supply of food for those animals able to take advantage of it. Migration, then, confers a selective advantage on animals that allows them to produce more offspring than their nonmigrating counterparts. This selective advantage outweighs the tremendous expenditures of time and energy involved in travelling over such great distances. Global warming, however, could make migration a maladaptive behavior, and in any case, it is certain to present an added challenge to conservation.

Migratory animals can be classified according to the degree to which migratory behavior is essential to survival of the species. They can be placed somewhere along a continuum between facultative and obligate migrators. Facultative migratory systems, such as the migration of Serengeti ungulates, are more opportunistic and flexible, whereas obligate systems, such as that of shorebirds, are more tightly constrained in time and space and therefore less flexible.

The value of this simplistic distinction lies in its use as a guide for thinking about how different migratory systems will respond to changes in climatic means and seasonality. To evaluate and predict the effects of climatic change on a given migratory system, we must identify where it lies along this continuum. In doing so, we are forced to ask many important questions, for example: What are the cues that trigger migration? How habitat specific is the organism in question? What are the factors that affect the timing of migration? What is the ecological role of the migrating species?

Shorebird Migrations

Climate can affect birds and other animals by regulating food supplies, by changing the quantity and quality of suitable habitat, and by controlling winter mortality and the length of the breeding season. Birds, because of their great mobility, have traditionally responded to climatic changes both quickly and opportunistically. In the last half century, for example, the lapwing (*Vanellus vanellus*), rook (*Corvus frugilegus*), house sparrow (*Passer domesticus*), and starling (*Sturnus vulgaris*) have all expanded their northward range in Europe, because of, in part, warmer temperatures (Williamson 1975).

Climate also plays an important role in controlling the onset of migration and in determining the ranges of many species of birds. The spring arrival of geese for two Hudson Bay outposts has been shown to correlate strongly with the percentage of southerly winds (Ball 1983), and the northern range of a number of different passerines appears to be limited by energy expenditures necessary to compensate for the decreased temperatures encountered at higher latitudes (Root 1988).

Shorebirds migrate long distances in response to the sporadic distribution of food and other resources in space and time. Although birds as a whole have been able to respond to climatic changes opportunistically, shorebirds and other animals that migrate over long distances of latitude may actually be more vulnerable to global warming because of constraints imposed by the specific timing requirements of their migratory cycles.

Shorebirds are highly migratory, and include sandpipers, plovers, and curlews. The majority of the 49 shorebird species that breed in North America travel distances of 12,000–25,000 km on their annual migrations between arctic breeding grounds and wintering sites in tropical and temperate Central and South America (Myers et al. 1987). Shorebirds are thus exposed to many changes in climate during the course of their annual migrations between high and low latitudes.

The major flyways of New World shorebirds are located along the Atlantic and Pacific coasts of North and South America and through the western Gulf of Mexico and the American Great Plains. In eastern North America, the most important staging area for shorebirds is the Delaware Bay, where 500,000–1 million shorebirds stop each year on their northward migrations. The most abundant shorebird species in the Delaware Bay are semi-palmated sandpipers (*Calidris pusilla*), red knots (*Calidris canutus*), ruddy turnstones (*Arenaria interpres*), sanderlings (*Calidris alba*), and dunlins (*Calidris alpina*).

Delaware Bay is an excellent example of several ways that migration is related to climate. Shorebirds begin arriving in early May, completely drained of their energy reserves after 40–60 hours of nonstop flying from the Caribbean and Central and South America. At the same time, thousands of horseshoe crabs (*Limulus polyphemus*) emerge from the ocean to lay their eggs on the area's many beaches. These eggs are the most important food source for migratory birds, which stay in the bay for approximately 2–3 weeks until they accumulate enough fat for their long flight to their arctic breeding grounds. During this period, it is common for birds to more than double their weight. The time of spawning of the horseshoe crabs appears to be controlled by water temperatures. A cold spring can delay egg-laying by a week or more. The largest numbers of shorebirds arrive within a few days or so of the peak abundance of horseshoe crab eggs.

By mid-June, most shorebirds have arrived at their arctic breeding grounds, where they rely on yet another resource flush—the summer bloom of arctic insects, primarily chirinomids and diptera. Most shorebirds stay in the Arctic for 5–6 weeks, depending upon their species, age, and sex. By the end of August, they begin their journey southward to complete the annual migratory cycle.

Timing is the critical element for migrating shorebirds. To maximize the likelihood of successful migration and breeding, a shorebird must utilize two different resource flushes, both of which are triggered by climate but which are also widely separated in space and time: horseshoe crabs eggs in the Delaware Bay in early May and the summer bloom of arctic insects in mid-June.

If shorebirds were to miss the spawning of horseshoe crabs in the Delaware Bay, they would fail to accumulate sufficient fat reserves to make the last 3,000-km leg of their northward migration. The reproductive success of shorebirds also depends heavily upon the timing of their arrival at their arctic breeding grounds. Chicks must be hatched and mobile on the tundra by early–July in order to feed on the summer bloom of insects. If shorebirds arrive on the breeding grounds too late, chicks will hatch after this critical resource flush. On the other hand, if adults arrive in the Arctic too early, neither the insect nor plant foods on which adults and chicks normally feed will have yet emerged. Shorebirds, then, must make use of two distinct "windows of opportunity," separated by approximately 3,000 km of space and 1 month of time.

Shorebird Migrations and Climate Change

Populations of several shorebird species have declined precipitously during the last 10–15 years. The populations of 10 out of 12 species monitored along the east coast of the United States over the period 1972–1984 declined approximately 44% (Myers et al. unpublished data). During this 12-year period, sanderling populations declined steadily by 80%, more than any other species and one of the worst declines ever observed in any bird population. Similar trends are not discernable in the Eur-African migratory system, and although there are no long-term surveys available for the shorebird guild on the west coast of the United States, data for sanderlings there reveal no systematic pattern.

There is clearly no signal for global warming as measured by worldwide declines of shorebird populations, assuming, of course, that global warming is already underway. This does not, however, negate the possibility that climatic changes (either anthropogenic or natural) might already be affecting shorebird populations in some regions, such as along the east coast of the United States. A number of other factors, such as habitat loss and pollution, could, however, explain the observed decline in shorebirds along the east coast flyway. It seems more likely that some combination of habitat loss, pollution, and climatic change (either anthropogenic or natural) is responsible for the observed declines in this region.

Regardless of whether or not global warming has had an effect on shorebird populations to date, it is very likely to have an important impact in the future. The specific characteristics of their migratory cycle—most notably the precise nature of the timing involved, their reliance on sensitive habitat types, and a number of physiologic and life history traits—make shorebirds especially vulnerable to global warming and climatic change.

Timing, Bottlenecking, and Other Characteristics of the Migratory Cycle

The latitudinal migrations of shorebirds carry them far enough and fast enough to experience the geographic heterogeneity of climate change. Global warming will be greater at higher latitudes than at low latitudes (Wetherald, this volume). Temperature increases in the Arctic are expected to be 1.5–3 times greater than the global average (Ramanathan 1988). For example, given a doubling of carbon dioxide, temperatures in the Arctic are expected to increase by 4–9°C compared with only 1–2°C for the tropics (Schlesinger and Mitchell 1987).

This polar amplification of temperatures will likewise affect the timing of seasons at higher latitudes—when spring begins, when snowmelt takes place, and when plants and animals emerge. In the Arctic, the onset of spring might be advanced by over a month, whereas at the equator seasonal changes in temperature will be negligible or will not occur at all. This differential effect of global warming on the onset of warmer temperatures at different latitudes could prevent shorebirds from utilizing the two resources essential to their survival: horseshoe crab eggs and arctic insects.

Although global warming will advance the onset of warmer spring temperatures in the Delaware Bay, in the Arctic this warming will be even more advanced. Horseshoe crab spawning and the emergence of arctic insects are both controlled by gradually increasing temperatures; thus the onset of both these events would be accelerated, the latter even more than the former. Consequently, the peak arrivals of shorebirds will no longer coincide with peak abundances of their prey,

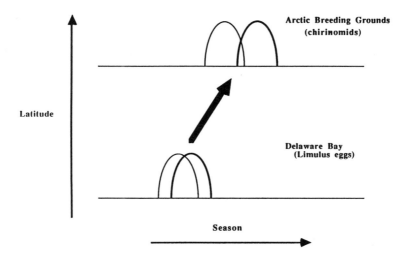

Fig. 7.1. Phase relations of shorebirds (bold line) and their prey. The peak abundance of shorebirds and their prey is increasingly shifted out of phase at higher latitudes due to the enhanced effect of global warming in these regions.

and it would be increasingly shifted out of phase as the birds migrate northward (Fig. 7.1).

Shorebirds, therefore, have essentially two distinct "windows of opportunity": the spawning of horseshoe crabs in the Delaware Bay and the summer bloom of insects on the arctic tundra. The timing of the system is such that shorebirds are currently able to make use of both of these resource flushes (Fig. 7.2A). If, however, global warming causes insects in the Arctic to emerge several weeks earlier, while advancing the spawning of crabs by only a few days, then shorebirds will be unable to make use of both resources sequentially (Fig. 7.2B).

In addition to their dependence upon the precise timing of resource availabilities, shorebirds are vulnerable to global warming because of a number of other characteristics of their migratory cycles. Shorebird staging areas, such as the Delaware Bay are few and far between; they are analogous to small islands in a vast ocean of unsuitable habitat. In many cases there are no alternative habitats, and, even when they do exist, shorebirds exploit existing sites to capacity. Immigrants displaced from other site tend to fare poorly (Myers et al. 1987).

The concentration of shorebirds in small areas results in "bottlenecking" along the migratory pathway. Several sites in North America bring together more than 80% of the flyway. Delaware Bay, for example, plays host to between 50 and 80% of all east coast sanderlings and approximately 50% of all New World semipalmated sandpipers and ruddy turnstones. The fact that such a large fraction of

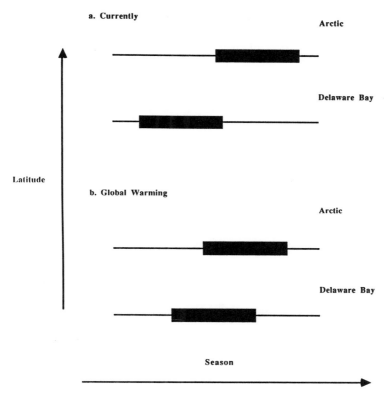

Fig. 7.2. Shorebird "windows of opportunity." Shorebirds are currently able to utilize two distinct resource flushes separated widely in time and space: horseshoe crab eggs in the Delaware Bay and chirinomids in the Arctic (a). Global warming will cause these two windows of opportunity to cooccur (b), thus preventing shorebirds from making optimal use of both these resources.

a given population is concentrated at one site makes many shorebird species especially vulnerable to extinction.

Sensitivity of Shorebird Habitats

Some habitats are more sensitive than others by virtue of their location and the nature of expected changes in climate. Shorebirds rely on two of the most sensitive habitat types: arctic tundra and coastal areas. Global warming will cause warmer weather to come sooner and last longer at higher latitudes, the length of the Arctic growing season is likely to increase. This, in turn, could cause changes in the productivity, structure, and composition of arctic vegetation (Edlund 1986,

Walker 1987). These changes will be important for shorebirds, because plant matter constitutes a major part of their diet during the breeding season and because an increase in taller vegetation types could interfere with the foraging ability of newly hatched chicks.

Alterations in temperature and moisture regimes could likewise affect arctic insect populations with important consequences for shorebirds. Although the biomass of arctic insects is unlikely to change, the composition of species could shift dramatically to favor those that are able to increase the number of generations they produce per year (Mac Butler, personal communication). In some insect taxa such as chirinomids, climatic changes might also favor winged over flightless forms. This could cause a long-term decrease in the availability of certain shorebird prey species. Finally, changes in seasonality at high latitudes could lead to completely novel plant–insect associations with no modern day analogs (Davis 1985). Such changes might lead to a decrease in the insect prey species favored by shorebirds.

Changes in the tundra landscape caused by global warming may also be important for shorebirds. As permafrost melts, it creates surficial depressions, flooding and eventually, severe erosion; this condition is known as thermokarst. The formation of thermokarst is known to alter the mosaic of wet and dry microsites, which are important for shorebirds and waterfowl (Walker et al. 1987).

In addition to causing changes in arctic breeding habitats, global warming will also affect the coastal areas that are critical wintering and staging sites for migrating shorebirds. The rising sea levels expected to accompany global warming will decrease the area of wetlands and barrier beaches available to birds. Sea levels are expected to rise 1–3 m by the year 2100 (Hoffman et al. 1983), and it is projected that the United States will experience a 25–80% net loss of wetlands over the course of this same time period (Environmental Protection Agency 1988).

Global warming may also alter nearshore upwelling and circulation patterns. In some instances, this might lead to a situation similar to El Nino events, with mass mortality, starvation, and breeding failure of many coastal organisms. It is also likely to alter important phenologic relationships, as we have hypothesized for the breeding schedule of horseshoe crabs. Changes in the primary productivity of arctic waters might also have an indirect impact on shorebirds. The immense biological productivity of these waters is maintained by complex upwelling patterns and sea ice. Melting of sea ice would eliminate the habitat essential to algae and other organisms at the base of the arctic marine food chain (Alexander 1989).

Shorebird Physiology and Life History

A number of characteristics of shorebirds' physiology and life history may increase their susceptibility to the climatic changes wrought by global warming

(Myers et al. 1987). Some species of shorebirds such as sanderlings and knots only breed north of the 5°C mean July isotherm. Because global warming will displace this isotherm northward, the amount of suitable breeding habitat for these species would be reduced. In contrast, the short-term physiologic impacts of increased temperatures during the breeding season could be beneficial. A decrease in the frequency of subfreezing weather would lessen the amount of time required for brooding chicks, thereby increasing opportunities for adults and chicks to forage. Global warming is also likely to cause a protracted breeding season with increased opportunities for a second breeding attempt.

Shorebirds have low reproductive rates, with a typical clutch size of four eggs. They also have a high rate of survival among adult birds (approximately 70–95% per year). They are therefore particularly vulnerable to any factor that decreases survivorship away from the breeding grounds (i.e., during migration and wintering). This means that high mortality among adult birds—caused, for example, by the effects of global warming on bird-prey phase relationships—would be especially detrimental to shorebird populations.

Finally, it must be emphasized that the effects of climatic change on shorebird populations will not occur in isolation. Human activities, including attempts to mitigate the effects of climate change such as coastal fortifications and river impoundments, will also continue to have many adverse effects on shorebirds and their habitat.

Addressing the Unknowns

Although our knowledge of the shorebird migratory system is still rather sketchy in many respects, it is clear that it will be vulnerable to the effects of global warming for the reasons discussed above. There is, however, an obvious need for quantitative descriptions of these effects and more precise mechanistic explanations.

A better understanding of this system would begin with climatologic models of higher resolution and an improved capability of predicting the variability and extrema of important climatic parameters such as temperature and precipitation. This would allow for the development of more detailed scenarios of climate change for specific regions, and these, in turn, could be linked to biotic models that attempt to predict the response of animal and plant populations to these altered climatic regimes.

To predict how shorebirds will ultimately be affected by climate change, we need to know a great deal more about the response of arctic plant and insect communities to increased temperatures and changes in moisture. How, for example, will a protracted growing season affect the structure, productivity, and species composition of the arctic plant species that are important to shorebird species as either a source of food or an obstacle to optimal foraging?

How, too, will insect communities respond to altered temperature and moisture regimes? Will they be affected by changes in plant communities? Which insect species will be capable of producing a greater number of generations per year under these new climatic conditions? Finally, can we expect the transition line separating the winged and flightless forms of certain insect species to shift northward?

There are also many unknowns associated with the migratory behaviors of shorebirds themselves. For example, we know almost nothing about the cues that trigger shorebird migrations nor do we know much about the plasticity of migratory behaviors. We are also largely ignorant of the factors that are used in the selection of shorebird breeding ranges. Are competitive interactions or the occurrence of particular plant assemblages more important?

Lastly, the predictive power of ecologists has been universally hampered by the lack of sufficient long-term, baseline data. Without information about actual trends in key species, it is impossible to distinguish between natural population fluctuations and the effects of climate change or other anthropogenic disturbances.

Serengeti Ungulate Migrations

The shorebird migratory system can be contrasted with the annual migration of ungulates on the Serengeti Plain in East Africa. The differences between these two systems offer some clues as to how susceptible each one might be to climatic changes and how management options and responses will vary between the systems.

Each year more than a million wildebeest (*Connochaetes taurinus*) and large populations of zebra (*Equus burchelli*) and Thomson's gazelle (*Gazella thomsoni*) migrate between their wet-season range on the open plains and their dry-season range in the woodlands to the west and north of the plains. The main factor controlling these annual movements is rainfall and it's effect on the grasses that serve as food supply (Maddock 1979).

The migratory populations of ungulates are a large fraction of the total biomass of the Serengeti ecosystem (Maddock 1979). They represent 60% of the total biomass for the region and 90% of the biomass of the plains. Migratory ungulates avoid competition with their nonmigrating counterparts by regularly migrating to and from the Plains, which provide only seasonal grazing.

Although wildebeest, zebra, and gazelle occupy similar areas, they are separated from each other by different food requirements. Thus, rather than competing, they form an interdependent "grazing succession" (Bell 1971). This succession is based upon body size and digestive system (ruminant versus nonruminant). Nonruminants, such as zebra, can tolerate poorer quality forage because they process larger amounts of food through their digestive systems per unit of time. Consequently, they are able to feed on the coarser, less nutritious parts of grasses. Smaller animals generally require food higher in protein because they have higher metabolic rates. They must, therefore, feed on tender new growth that is high in protein.

During the rainy season (November–May), the Serengeti Plains support a diverse assemblage of grazers: wildebeest, zebra, gazelle, topi (*Damaliscus korrigum*), impala (*Aepyceros melampus*), and African buffalo (*Syncerus caffer*). As conditions become drier, the larger species, such as zebra and buffalo, move westward first, followed by topi and wildebeest and finally, gazelle. Zebras initiate the grazing succession by feeding on long grasses of poor quality. Wildebeest are then able to reach parts of the grass with higher protein content, thus stimulating new growth, which has a higher protein content. Gazelle finally move into the area where they eat the highest protein layers of the sward and dicotyledon material.

This annual migration occurs in a clockwise fashion from the Plains (low rainfall and short grasses) to the Western Serengeti (intermediate rainfall and intermediate-sized grass) and finally to the Northern Serengeti (high rainfall and high grass). All ungulates have marked birth peaks on the Plains during the height of the rainy season when the protein content of grasses is at its highest (Maddock 1979). The Plains are able to support such a large biomass due to migration and segregation of animals into different food niches based on the grazing succession described above.

Changes in the seasonality of rainfall are known to have an important effect on animal populations. Animals stay longer on the Plains in years of heavy rainfall and they leave earlier in years of scant rainfall. From 1971 to 1976, the average dry-season rainfall was consistently higher than it had been in the past (total rainfall did not change, however), and this led to much more luxuriant grass growth and burgeoning populations of herbivores (Sinclair 1979).

According to the classification scheme proposed earlier, the migration of Serengeti ungulates lies more toward the facultative end of the spectrum, whereas the migration of shorebirds lies more toward the obligate end. The migratory behavior of Serengeti ungulates is opportunistic, flexible, and less constrained in time and space than that of shorebirds. The emergence of suitable forage (i.e., grasses) is more protracted than the resource flush of horseshoe crab eggs or the emergence of arctic insects. Unlike shorebirds, ungulates in the Serengeti move in a broad front without being restricted to small numbers of suitable sites, widely scattered in space.

However, the complexity of biotic interactions that characterizes the ungulate migratory system could also make it vulnerable to climatic change. The interdependent nature of the grazing succession implies that a climatic change resulting in the reduction or removal of one species would have important repercussions for other species. For example, a climatic change that reduces zebra populations could cause declines in wildebeest and gazelle populations, as well, because they are functionally related through the grazing succession.

Changes in the amount and/or seasonality of rainfall might conceivably alter competitive interactions by causing animals with normally separate feeding niches to overlap. A succession of dry years, for example, might give large, nonruminants (e.g. zebra) a selective advantage over small ruminants (e.g. gazelle) because of the former's ability to utilize a more diverse assemblage of forage (i.e., both old and new grasses). Changes in rainfall might also cause zebra and wildebeest populations to become more sedentary. In this case, predation rather than food availability could become the dominant factor determining population size (Sinclair 1979). Finally, a succession of very dry years might even force certain ungulate populations to disperse into smaller herds, thus altering the social behavior of populations and perhaps their reproductive success (Sinclair 1979).

Conservation and Management of Migratory Species

A comparison of shorebird and ungulate migratory systems highlights some of the problems and opportunities of devising effective management and conservation strategies for migratory animals. The most obvious difference between the two is their geographical coverage. Ungulate migration in the Serengeti takes place over an area about the size of the state of Massachusetts. In contrast, shorebirds commonly migrate latitudinal distances of 12,000–25,000 km.

The management and conservation of shorebirds is complicated by the large number of sovereign states and management jurisdictions involved. Although management of Serengeti ungulates is by no means an easy task, it is made somewhat simpler because the Serengeti ecosystem spans only two countries (Kenya and Tanzania) and three or four management jurisdictions. The geographic extent of these two systems also affects the nature of the projected climatic change. Ungulates will not be affected by the latitudinal heterogeneities associated with global warming, because they migrate over contiguous areas of a relatively small size. The smaller size of the ungulate migratory system also offers more opportunities for successful application of intrusive management techniques, such as translocation, irrigation, and fencing. However, the complexity of biotic interactions involved in the migration of Serengeti ungulates makes it difficult to manipulate the system without running the risk of disturbing some vital but little understood component.

Regardless of the type of migratory system that is being managed, it is clear that it's geographic limits must be linked together in some ecologically meaningful way. This has been the purpose of the Western Hemisphere Shorebird Reserve Network (WHSRN, 550 South Bay Avenue, Islip, NY, USA). WHSRN is a collaboration of government and private organizations started in 1985 through the efforts of the World Wildlife Fund, The International Association of Fish and Wildlife Agencies, and the Academy of Natural Sciences of Philadelphia. The underlying philosophy of the network is that a migratory system can only be as strong as the weakest link in the chain; therefore, piecemeal efforts to protect widely scattered sites are futile. To protect the most vulnerable sites of greatest biological importance (i.e., the "weak links"), it was recognized that an interconnected network transcending political boundaries would be needed.

This is precisely what WHSRN does today. The network now includes five national agencies and 32 state or provincial wildlife agencies from North and South America. It encourages local protection of critical sites, and it focuses international attention on the preservation of these sites, while linking them in a coordinated management and research program.

To be considered for inclusion in the network, sites must fall into one of two categories. For an area to be named a "Hemispheric Site," it must be used by 250,000 or more shorebirds on an annual basis or it must support at least 30% of a flyway population of a given species. A Regional Site is used by more than 20,000 shorebirds or at least 5% of the flyway population. In 1985, the Delaware Bay became the first Hemispheric Site in the network. Thus far, six other wetlands or beaches have entered the network as Hemispheric Reserves and more than 200 Hemispheric or Regional Sites have been identified.

The WHSRN might serve as a valuable model for the conservation of certain migratory species in the face of global climatic change, depending upon the specific life history and migratory characteristics of the species in question (Myers et al. 1987). Some animals, such as cetaceans and raptors, that pass through geographic bottlenecks and use widely scattered discrete sites might successfully be incorporated in such a network. On the other hand, this network approach would be more problematic for animals such as songbirds that travel in broad migratory fronts because of the difficulty in establishing discrete critical sites. Nevertheless, WHSRN still offers a valuable lesson that is relevant to the conservation of all migratory species in the face of climate change: managing migratory species will require an unprecedented degree of international and regional cooperation and a tremendous amount of flexibility and creative thinking.

Humans are often seduced into the folly of trying to control and manage natural systems about which they know very little. This type of tinkering often results in failure because of the unforeseen and detrimental consequences of our actions. In the final analysis, it is rather presumptuous and naive to think that we can control or manage the migrations of shorebirds, ungulates, or other animals to any significant degree. At this point, our efforts are perhaps best directed at improving our understanding of how migratory systems work and conserving habitats we already know to be critical to the sound functioning of these systems. By working to ensure their survival as intact and healthy ecosystems into the future, we maximize the likelihood that these habitats will be able to adapt to global climatic change. This, of course, begs the question about concrete conservation actions that can be taken now to conserve these species. In the case of most migratory systems, we already know enough to start protecting habitats that are critical to the functioning of these systems. However, we must answer many important unknowns before we can link these habitats in a way that will be meaningful as climates change. A concerted attempt to better understand how many of these migratory systems function, while simultaneously protecting critical habitats would put us in a good position over the next 5–10 years to begin making intelligent management recommendations for coping with the preservation of migratory species in the face of climatic change.

References

Aidley, K. J. 1981. Questions about migration. In *Animal Migration*, D. J. Aidley (ed.), pp. 1–8. Cambridge University Press, Cambridge.

Alexander, V. 1989. Arctic marine ecosystems. In *Proceedings of the Conference on the Consequences of the Greenhouse Effect for Biological Diversity*, R. L. Peters and T. E. Lovejoy (eds.), Yale University Press, New Haven, CT.

Ball, T. 1983. The migration of geese as an indicator of climate change in the southern Hudson Bay region between 1715 and 1851. *Clim. Change* 5:85–93.

Bell, R. H. V. 1971. A grazing ecosystem in the Serengeti. *Sci. Am.* 224:86–93.

Davis, M. B. 1985. Climatic instability, time lags, and community disequilibrium. In *Community Ecology*, J. Diamond and T. J. Case (eds.), pp. 269–284. Harper and Row, New York.

Edlund, S. A. 1986. Modern arctic vegetation distribution and it's congruence with summer climate patterns. In *Proceeding of the Impact of Climate Change on the Canadian Arctic*, Orillia, Ontario, Canadian Climate Program, H. M. French (ed.), pp. 84–99. Ottawa, Canada.

Emanuel, W. R., H. H. Shugart, and M. P. Stevenson. 1985a. Climatic change and the broad-scale distribution of terrestrial ecosystem complexes. *Clim. Change* 7:29–43.

Emanuel, W. R., H. H. Shugart, and M. P. Stevenson. 1985b. Response to comment: climatic change and the broad-scale distribution of terrestrial ecosystem complexes. *Clim. Change* 7:457–460.

Environmental Protection Agency. 1988. *The Potential Effects of Global Climate Change on the United States*, Draft Report to Congress. Office of Policy, Planning, and Evaluation and Office of Research and Development. Washington, D.C.

Hoffman, J. S., D. Keyes, and J. G. Titus. 1983. *Projecting Future Sea-Level Rise: Methodology: Estimates to the Year 2100, and Research Needs*. Environmental Protection Agency, Washington, DC.

Lester, R. T. and J. P. Myers. 1989. *The Greenhouse Effect, Climate Disruption and Biological Diversity*. Audubon Wildlife Report, National Audubon Society, New York.

Maddock, L. 1979. The migration and grazing succession. In *Serengeti: Dynamics of an Ecosystem*, A. R. E. Sinclair and M. Norton-Griffiths (eds.), Chapter 5. University of Chicago Press, Chicago.

Myers, J. P., R. I. G. Morrison, P. Z. Antas, B. H. Harrington, T. E. Lovejoy, M. Sallaberry, S. E. Senner, and A. Tarank. 1987. Conservation strategy for migratory species. *BioScience* 75:19–26.

Peters, R. L. and J. D. S. Darling. 1985. The greenhouse effect and nature reserves. *BioScience* 35:707–717.

Ramanthan, V. 1988. The greenhouse theory of climate change: A test by an inadvertent global experiment. *Science* 240: 293–299.

Root, T. 1988. Energy constraints on avian distributions and abundances. *Ecology* 69:330–339.

Schlesinger, M. E. and J. Mitchell. 1987. Climate model simulations of the equilibrium climatic response to increased carbon dioxide. *Rev. Geophys.* 25:760–798.

Sinclair, A. R. E. 1979. Dynamics of the Serengeti ecosystem. In *Serengeti: Dynamics of an*

Ecosystem, A. R. E. Sinclair and M. Norton-Griffiths (eds.), Chapter 1. University of Chicago Press, Chicago.

Walker, D. A. 1987. Height and growth rings of *Salix lanata ssp. richardsonii* along the coastal temperature gradient of northern Alaska. *Can. J. Botany* 65: 988–993.

Walker, D. A., P. J. Webber, E. F. Binnian, K. R. Everett, N. D. Lederer, E. A. Nordstrand, and M. D. Walker. 1987. Cumulative impacts of oil fields on northern Alaskan landscapes. *Science* 238:757–761.

Williamson, K. 1975. Birds and climatic change. *Bird Study* 22:143–164.

8

Multiple Threats to Wildlife: Climate Change, Acid Precipitation, and Habitat Fragmentation

Richard L. Wyman

Introduction

Even with predictions of future air temperatures and soil moisture regimes, researchers have been able to project only a few of the direct effects of global climate change on plant and animal populations. If the concentration of atmospheric greenhouse gases double, the rising sea level will inundate coastal marshes and lowlands and may make millions of people "ecorefugees," forests will have to migrate or they will disappear, birds will arrive at migratory feeding grounds at the wrong time relative to food availability, and potential agricultural production will shift to new areas.

The indirect and synergistic effects are even more difficult or impossible to predict. Synergistic interactions are those in which the effect of two stresses applied at once are more than the additive effect of each stress applied separately. For instance, many animal species show greatly increased sensitivity to heat when water is scarce. Indirect effects occur because unknown or unpredictable interactions arise from the direct effects. For instance, trees dying is a direct effect. Indirect effects would be the loss of insects adapted to exist on those trees and the subsequent loss of birds that feed on these insects. Another indirect effect would be the loss of the modulating effect of the trees on local climate and soil.

Here I present several case studies that illuminate how indirect effects and synergistic interactions may have a more profound effect on natural systems than the direct effects of climate change considered alone. I focus on the amphibians because they are particularly vulnerable to climate change.

Changing Weather Patterns and Community Responses

The sun provides the energy and the spinning tilted Earth provides the momentum that runs the Earth's climatic system. By heating the equatorial regions more than elsewhere, the sun sets into motion large-scale movements of air and the

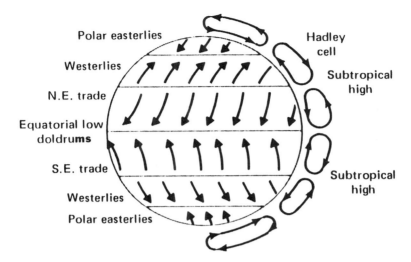

Fig. 8.1. Generalized graphic representation of the circulation of the earth's atmosphere (after Flohn 1969 and Smith 1981). On a rotating Earth, heated air rises at the equator and descends at 30°N and 30°S latitudes. This air flows south and north, respectively, but because of the rotating planet is deflected to the right giving rise to the NE and SE trade winds in low latitudes and westerlies in the midlatitudes. The air mass loses water as it rises over the equator giving rise to moist conditions. The dry air that falls at the 30° latitudes gives rise to desertlike conditions in continental interiors. In the greenhouse world these belts may move further away from the equator.

movement of the Earth causes those air masses to circle the globe (Flohn 1969). These moving tubular air masses, known as Hadley cells, in part control the climatic regimes of the planet (Fig. 8.1). Because the Earth is not uniform, the unequal land and water masses prevent the development of uniform rain belts that correspond to ascending masses of air. However, as a general and simple model of the climate regimes of the Earth, this is a sufficient description (see Smith 1980). For example, the zone closest to the equator is responsible for the warm air that rises at the equator, dropping its moisture as it rises. This dry air falls at latitudes of 30° north and 30° south, causing deserts at these latitudes over many of the continental portions of the planet. The next zone to the north (30–60° north latitude) gives rise in the northern hemisphere to the prevailing westerlies, and regulates, in part, the quantity of precipitation received by the continents. One way to view the predictions of the general circulation models is to imagine that in the greenhouse world these bands of air would move farther away from the equator. That is, warmer and drier conditions would prevail farther north and south than they do at present. Even in regions predicted to have increases in precipitation, the average soil moisture could decrease because of

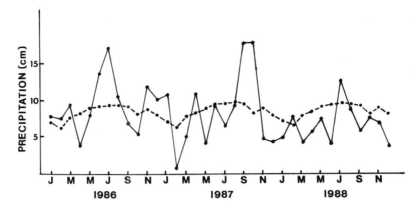

Fig. 8.2. Monthly precipitation for Albany County, New York, from 1986 through 1988 (solid line) compared to the average for 1931 through 1985 (dashed line) (from NOAA weather data for Albany, New York).

increased evapotransporation caused by warmer temperatures. At some higher latitudes, soil moisture regimes would be increased.

General circulation models (GCMs) give only a gross indication of what may happen to precipitation patterns and soil moisture in the future. There are many potential scenarios depending on the characteristics of the particular GCM employed (Hansen et al. 1988, Manabe et al. 1981, Schneider and Londer 1984, Wetherald, this volume) and there are still many phenomena that are not accounted for by the GCMs. All models generally predict that many temperate soils will be drier during the growing season (Hansen 1989), and that most of the precipitation will fall during winter, instead of being spread throughout the year. We may be able to assess some of the potential greenhouse-like changes by examining the effects of recent weather. The 1980s, for example, may provide clues about the future effects of drought. Five of the twelve driest months on record, and six of the ten warmest years since 1855 have occurred during the 1980s (Kerr 1990). The rainfall pattern of 1988 may illustrate what a typical greenhouse year may be like (Fig. 8.2). Only February and July received above-normal precipitation, all the remaining months were far below average. The drought continued until May 1989.

Plant and animal communities are adapted to the environmental conditions in which they exist. Based on this premise, Holdridge (1959) developed a system of classifying the vegetative communities of the world using the average annual temperature, humidity regimes, and evapotranspiration potential (Fig. 8.3). Emanuel et al. (1985) suggested that if climate changed, local conditions to which plant communities are adapted would likewise change, and plant species would have to migrate with climatic conditions or they would disappear. Current projec-

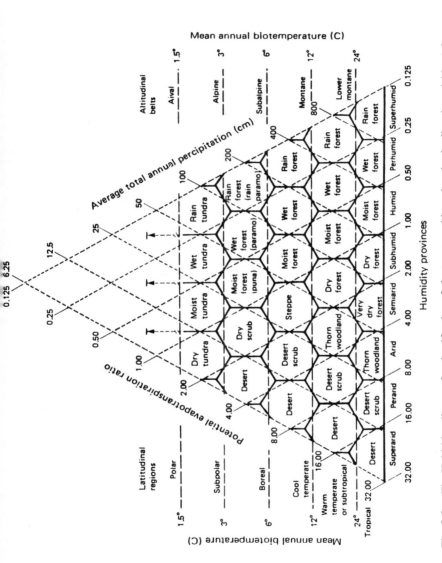

Fig. 8.3. The Holdridge diagram for classification of plant communities using simple climatic variables (after Holdridge 1959). Greenhouse conditions would alter the climatic conditions to which the plant communities have adapted. Reprinted with permission from L. R. Holdridge (1959) and *Science*.

tions suggest that the changes in climate predicted to occur within the next 40–100 years would cause the average climatic conditions to move northward by some 500–1,000 km (Davis 1983, Davis and Zabinski 1990). Even with the fastest rate of forest movement documented to date (200 km/century for spruce), the forests could move only 20–40% of this distance. Many species of animals that depend on forest trees may have an extremely difficult time sustaining their populations.

Effects of Climate Change on Amphibians

I have concentrated on the amphibians, which consist of more than 3,900 living species of frogs, salamanders, and caecilians and occur nearly throughout the world (Duellman and Trueb 1986). They are abundant and diverse in the forests of North, Central, and South America, Asia, Africa, and Australia. Their physiological adaptations, density, distribution, life history characteristics and ecology make them sensitive indicators of the kinds of environmental stress that will be associated with global climate change (Shoemaker 1987, Spight 1967, Spotila and Berman 1976). For example, many of the salamanders of the eastern United States are adapted to exist at higher elevation in cool-moist environments. These environments are likely to change rapidly, and they are isolated from other similar habitats by lower lying habitats, making the migration of the community impossible (Peters, this volume). The relict communities at the southern edge of its component species ranges will probably be the first to show pronounced changes in species composition.

Amphibians may well be the best indicators of climate change because they appear to respond to subtle changes that do not produce effects in larger, more obvious creatures like trees. For example most amphibians require a moist environment. Frogs, toads, and salamanders lack the cornified epithelium possessed by reptiles, birds, and mammals, and they lose water rapidly in dry environments (Spotila and Berman 1976). Their eggs require a moist environment for development. Many spend at least a portion of their life in water, and those that do not require standing water during their life cycle, still require a moist environment. Because most amphibians must maintain a moist epidermis for respiration, they generally cannot exist in areas with frequent droughts without becoming dormant during dry periods. Some have fascinating adaptations to allow them to take advantage of ephemeral puddles or ponds (Duellman and Trueb 1986).

Another reason that amphibians may be good indicators of global climate change is that they are abundant and ubiquitous. In most of the mature forests in New York that I have studied, there is an average of one amphibian in every two meter squares of leaf litter (Wyman 1988, Wyman unpublished) or approximately 5,000 amphibians per hectare. Although many amphibians reproduce in water, most spend the majority of their life in forests. There they prey on a host of invertebrates including isopods, ants, springtails, worms, millipedes, mites, spiders, slugs, and a variety of insect larvae. These invertebrates are consumers of the detritus-based food web. This food web is responsible for decomposition of the leaves, twigs, and logs that end up on the forest floor each year, and the food web recycles nutrients and minerals that are important for tree health and growth. The detritivores themselves are also susceptible to disruption by pollution (Cline and Kaul 1988, Hagvar 1988) and changes in temperature and moisture (Orsborne and Macauley 1988, Taylor and Parkinson 1988). Clark (this volume) suggests that decomposition rates in temperate hardwood forests may show larger responses to changing climatic conditions than production rates because decomposition rates slow with increasing latitude to a greater degree than do production rates. Amphibians, because they are numerous and upper level consumers of the detritus-based food web, are in a position to indicate the changes in that food web.

The yellow-spotted salamander (*Ambystoma maculatum*) is fairly typical of an amphibian that has to migrate to water each year to reproduce. Usually following an intense courtship ritual, eggs are laid in temporary forest ponds. Normally the males migrate to temporary forest ponds following the first rain in the spring after the ground has defrosted. If the rain continues, the females follow in a day or two. Once in the pond, the males begin to lay down a field of spermatophores, small (1–2 mm) jellylike mounds topped with small sperm filled caps. Females appear to be attracted to the field of spermatophores. The males then engage in a mass mating aggregation with many males probing and butting the female. Eventually she follows one male who deposits a fresh spermatophore. The female then removes the sperm cap with the lips of her cloaca to achieve internal fertilization.

I have monitored movements of *A. maculatum* by installing drift-fence, pit-fall trap arrays in several forests in southcentral New York. On the Helderberg Plateau (Albany County) on April 8, 1988, males began to move toward the breeding pond, coincident with the ground defrosting and the first spring rain. The rain lasted only during the night and it did not rain again until May 1–23 days later (Fig. 8.4). The females then began to migrate to the pond, but by then many males had already abandoned that year's breeding effort. Very few yellow-spotted salamander egg masses were produced during 1988. The drought in the northeast United States continued through April 1989, and as a result the 1989 reproductive event of yellow-spotted salamanders was not very productive either. In fact, no salamander larvae were found in 1989 in the pond that was monitored (B. Ybarrondo personal communication).

For animals like amphibians, the absolute quantity of precipitation may not be as important as the timing of precipitation events. Yellow-spotted salamanders need rains in the early spring when they are programmed by natural selection to migrate toward breeding habitats. More frequent droughts at this time of year will interfere with breeding in this species, which may endanger the species survival. The yellow-spotted salamander has already been shown to be sensitive

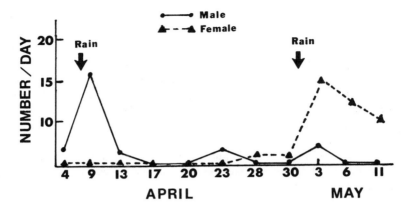

Fig. 8.4. Comparison of the migration of male and female *Ambystoma maculatum* (as determined by numbers of animals caught in a pit-fall trap drift-fence array) during the spring of 1988 on the E. N. Huyck Preserve, Albany County, New York.

to acidification of its temporary breeding ponds (Pough and Wilson 1977), and is currently on New York State's list of species of special concern. In addition, this species is subject to impact by soil acidification, habitat fragmentation, and automobile traffic (see below).

Acid Rain and Climate Change

The combustion of fossil fuels releases a plethora of gases into the atmosphere including greenhouse gases and those that combine with water to form acids. The two dominant acid-forming compounds are oxides of sulfur and nitrogen. Most of the sulfur comes from industries and utilities; most of the nitrogen comes from internal combustion engines and utilities. The term *acid rain* is somewhat misleading because acid may be deposited in rain and snow as well as by dry deposition. Ozone, hydrogen peroxide, long-chain carbon compounds, and heavy metals are also present in the atmosphere and in deposition. At present scientists have not been able to separate out the individual or synergistic effects of this chemical soup (Pitelka and Raynal 1989), although areas with high rates of acidic deposition are likely to be receiving high concentrations of these other pollutants as well. In what follows, I use the term acid deposition, to refer to the suite of chemicals released by human actions that are deposited into habitats. The effects I discuss may be due to acid or to some combination of acid and/or these other pollutants.

Temperate hardwood forest soils acidify with age (Billett et al. 1988, Blank et al. 1988, Krug and Frink 1983, Murach and Ulrich 1988). However, the rate of acidification may be accelerated and the final equilibrium pH lowered in regions receiving acidic deposition over prolonged periods (Murach and Ulrich 1988, Schulze 1989, Van Breeman et al. 1983, 1984). Soils that have already lost a substantial portion of their acid-neutralizing capacity (ANC) or which never contained much ANC will have the lowest pH (Van Breeman et al. 1984). Many high-elevation and high-latitude environments in North America are sensitive to soil acidification because they lie on bedrocks that weather slowly and provide limited ANC to the soil. Organism that are sensitive to soil acidity may show reduced population sizes and reduced ranges in areas sensitive to acidic deposition.

The most abundant amphibian in the forests of the northeastern United States is the red-backed salamander *Plethodon cinereus*. This fully terrestrial species possesses two adaptations that have helped make it so successful: terrestrial reproduction and lunglessness. First, although it still requires high soil moisture to survive, it has been freed from having to return to water to reproduce. The female constructs a small chamber within or under a log or under a rock and attaches her clutch of about nine eggs to the chamber's upper surface. She then wraps her body around the clutch of eggs and remains there until they hatch about a month later. Apparently during this time it is her body moisture and the moisture of the surrounding log or soil that prevent the eggs from dehydrating. If the female is removed the eggs usually die. In these lungless salamanders, all respiration takes place through the epidermis and the lining of the mouth and pharynx. Lunglessness also means that the bones and cartilage that otherwise would protect the opening to the lungs are no longer needed for that purpose. These structures have become modified to form an attachment for the back of the tongue, and as a result, the tongue may be projected from the mouth allowing plethodontid salamanders to catch more mobile prey than can other salamanders with lungs.

It is well documented that acidic conditions affect the aquatic life stages of amphibians (Cook 1983, Freda and Dunson 1985, Pierce 1985, Schlichter 1981). Acidic waters may inhibit sperm mobility, and embryos in acid water fail to develop or are deformed (Freda and Dunson 1985, Gosner and Black 1957, Pough and Wilson 1977). Little research has been conducted, however, on the effects of acidic conditions on terrestrial stages. Recently, Wyman and Hawksley-Lescault (1987) showed that the density and distribution of red-backed salamanders were reduced by soil acidity in the Catskill Plateau region of New York. Salamander density was dramatically reduced when soil pH fell below 3.8 (Fig. 8.5). The average soil pH of the two study sites was 3.9. In a later study in four counties of New York, I found that the pH of quadrats with the American toad (*Bufo americanus*), red-backed salamander, two-lined salamander (*Eurycea bislineata*), dusky salamander (*Desmognathus fuscus*), and yellow-spotted salamander was significantly greater than in quadrats that lacked these species (Table 8.1, see also Wyman 1988).

Although fewer data were available, other amphibians (*Hyla crucifer, Hyla versicolor, Rana clamitans, Rana pipiens, Desmognathus ochrophaeus,* and *Gyrinophilus porphyriticus*) occurred in areas with higher pH than the average

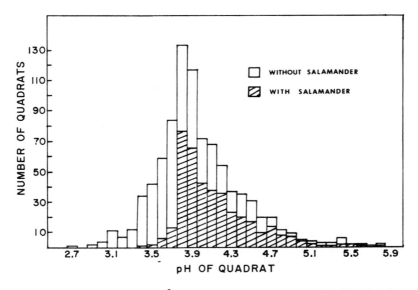

Fig. 8.5. Frequency of 1-m² quadrats with a particular soil pH value for quadrats with or without *Plethodon cinereus* present for two sites in Delaware County, New York, from 1982 through 1985. Reprinted with permission from Wyman and Hawksley-Lescault (1987) and the Ecological Society of America.

of quadrats without amphibians. There is a strong negative correlation between the number of species of amphibians in a habitat and the acidity of the soil (Fig. 8.6) These data suggest that soil acidity affects the composition of amphibian communities and the distribution of at least 10 species. Wyman and Hawksley-Lescault (1987) suggested that a soil pH of 3.7 was the long-term, lower limiting pH for the red-backed salamander. This would mean that in our study areas of New York, approximately 30% of the forest floor is now too acidic to support this species and perhaps the nine other species as well.

Malcolm Frisbie (Eastern Kentucky University) and I proposed that the density of salamanders is decreased on acid soil because of a disruption of the osmotic regulatory apparatus. In amphibian larvae exposed to acidic water, sodium efflux is increased and sodium uptake is reduced. This causes the larvae to die when approximately half of the body sodium is lost (Freda and Dunson 1985). We have found that sodium loss in the red-backed salamander is elevated on low-pH substrates (Fig. 8.7). Species (e.g., red-backed, two-lined, and dusky salamanders) with distributions in the field affected by soil pH lose sodium on acidic substrates faster than salamanders whose field distributions are not affected by soil acidity (red eft of the red-spotted newt, *Notophthalmus viridescens*, Fig. 8.8). Thus it appears that acidic soils alter the basic physiology of sensitive species. This may explain the low density of many amphibians on acidic soils.

Table 8.1. Comparisons of mean soil moisture (numbers in parentheses are standard deviations) and mean soil pH between meter-square quadrats of forest litter containing amphibians* and those without amphibians in four counties of southcentral New York

Order/species	N	Moisture		pH		t value	
		With	Without	With	Without	Moisture	pH
Anura							
Rana sylvatica	57	100 (21)	65 (15)	4.2 (0.2)	4.1 (0.2)	8.33[†]	0.21
Bufo americanus	26	74 (12)	69 (16)	5.7 (0.3)	4.0 (0.3)	0.67	5.44[†]
Caudata							
Plethodon cinereus	686	80 (9)	83 (11)	4.2 (0.1)	3.9 (0.1)	0.45	8.99[†]
Notophthalmus viridescens	83	82 (13)	69 (14)	3.9 (0.3)	4.1 (0.3)	4.67[†]	1.21
Eurycea bislineata	51	126 (14)	88 (15)	5.0 (0.2)	4.2 (0.3)	10.45[†]	9.55[†]
Desmognathus fuscus	46	149 (15)	68 (18)	4.7 (0.3)	4.0 (0.2)	16.78[†]	8.77[†]
Ambystoma maculatum	24	132 (22)	82 (20)	4.2 (0.2)	3.9 (0.2)	14.40[†]	4.56[†]

*Only species with $N > 20$.

[†] $P < 0.05$.

143

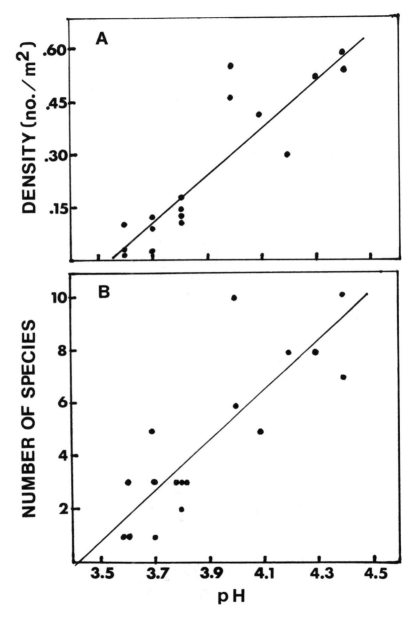

Fig. 8.6. Scatter diagrams of the relationships between the density of individuals (A) or the number of species (B) in amphibian communities and the pH of the soil of the habitat in five counties of New York. The solid lines are the least squares linear regression lines of best fit ($P < 0.05$).

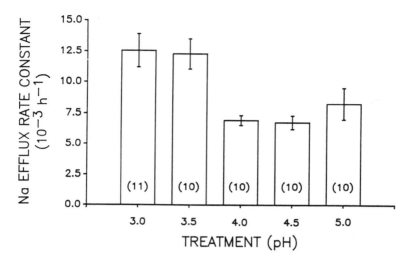

Fig. 8.7. Sodium efflux measured over a 48-hour period for *Plethodon cinereus* confined on substrates of various pHs (Frisbie and Wyman, unpublished). Bars depict means ± 1.0 SE. Sample sizes are in parentheses. Sodium effluxes at pHs 3.0 and 3.5 are significantly greater than effluxes at pHs 4.0, 4.5, and 5.0 ($P < 0.05$).

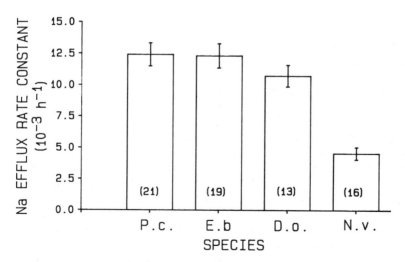

Fig. 8.8. Comparison of the unidirectional loss of sodium (sodium efflux) from four species of salamanders confined on low pH substrates (pH < 3.5). Species are *Plethodon cinereus*, (P.c.), *Eurycea bislineata* (E.b.), *Desmognathus ochrophaeus* (D.o.), and *Notophthalmus viridescens* (N.v.). Effluxes for *N. viridescens* are significantly lower than effluxes for the other species ($P < 0.05$). Bars are means ± 1.0 SE, and sample sizes are in parentheses.

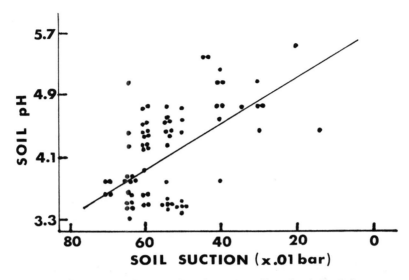

Fig. 8.9. Plot of soil pH and soil moisture (as soil suction in bars) for spruce forests on the E. N. Huyck Preserve, Albany County, New York, during 1988. The solid line represents the least squares linear regression line of best fit between soil pH and moisture ($P < 0.05$).

Since 1975, I have gathered data on the acidity and moisture of soils where amphibians are found. This has allowed me to determine the relationship between soil acidity and moisture. Regression analyses between soil moisture and acidity show that soil acidity increases when conditions become drier. Further analyses by season reveals that in hardwood forests, during a drought (like that of 1988), the average soil pH fell below the limiting soil pH of 3.7, but only during the fall. This effect was particularly pronounced in spruce forests (Fig. 8.9), where soil pH would fall below the critical value regardless of the season in which the drought occurs (Table 8.2). I find very few amphibians in spruce forests. Thus, it appears that one factor influencing the density of amphibians is an interaction between the type of forest and the frequency of droughts. Since droughts occur frequently (e.g., for the Helderberg Plateau during the spring and summer of 1982–83 and 1988–1989), they may be preventing successful reinvasion of spruce stands by most amphibians following their elimination due to reduced soil moisture and increased acidity.

The GCMs project that droughts may occur more frequently and with greater intensity in the greenhouse world. The combination of dryness and increased soil acidity might eliminate from large areas of North America many amphibians that would not be eliminated by one factor alone. Amphibians may also be affected before the forest would show other major adverse effects.

The Environmental Protection Agency (1988) Report to Congress on global

Table 8.2. Summary of soil pH (with standard error and 95% confidence intervals) predicted by solving regressions equations between soil moisture and soil pH for four forest types and for various seasons, with soil moisture as 25% of dry weight of the soil to mimic conditions that would occur during a drought

Forest Type	Season	Predicted Soil pH	Standard Error	Lower Limit	Upper Limit
Hardwood	Spring	3.93	0.04	3.13	4.72
	Summer	4.03	0.08	2.92	5.13
	Fall	3.70	0.08	2.29	5.12
Hemlock	Summer	4.06	0.23	3.30	4.82
	Fall	3.66	0.11	2.87	4.46
Red pine	Fall	3.95	0.08	3.33	4.56
Spruce	All seasons	3.59	0.12	2.52	4.65

climate change predicted that with the warming accompanying a doubling of the concentration of greenhouse gases, electrical use in the United States would increase approximately 15% mainly due to increased air conditioning. Most electricity is produced by fossil fuel combustion; therefore the additional fossil fuel combustion would increase the release of greenhouse and acid-producing gases. An increase in acid-producing gases coupled with a projected increase in frequency and intensity of droughts (Hansen 1989) could mean greatly increased concentration of wet and dry acidic deposition. Soils that lack sufficient ANC will acidify and sensitive communities on those soils may disappear.

In addition to North America, severe acidic deposition is occurring in Europe, Central America, and China. Future research should attempt to determine how amphibian species of these regions are responding.

Habitat Fragmentation

Natural habitats are shrinking, and, as they do, they become more isolated from one another. These small, isolated patches of natural habitat may be thought of as "man-locked" islands. The theory of island biogeography may be useful in helping us understand current species richness patterns and may allow us to predict what species richness may be like in the future.

MacArthur and Wilson (1967) explain why large islands and islands near source areas tend to have more species and higher immigration rates than small islands or islands located at greater distance from source areas. Put simply, the theory suggests that the number of species an island supports is the result of a dynamic equilibrium between the successful invasion of the island by species and the extinction of populations already on the island. Small islands tend to have greater extinction rates than large islands lowering the equilibrium number of species on small islands. This may be because on small islands population sizes

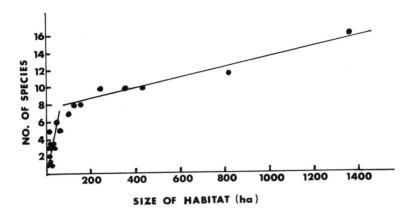

Fig. 8.10. Scatter diagram of the relationship between the size of habitats and the number of amphibian species found in the forests of five counties in New York. The two solid lines are the least squares linear regression lines of best fit for small and large habitats.

are smaller, increasing the probability of extinction or because small islands are likely to contain fewer microhabitats suitable for particular species. Data for plants on islands (MacArthur and Wilson 1967), megavertebrates in western United States parks (EPA 1988), and amphibians in habitats in New York (Fig. 8.10) support the concept that small natural areas and islands have fewer species and higher extinction rates than larger areas. As we continue to shrink the remaining natural world, we can expect the number of species surviving to decrease. In addition, tropical and temperate deforestation not only shrinks and fragments the habitat, it also causes the release of greenhouse and acid forming gases because the wood is often burned and decomposition of organic material held in the soil is accelerated.

Habitats also may become fragmented because within them there are areas that are unsuitable for particular species. From an amphibian's point of view, the forest floor may appear to be quite fragmented even in areas where amphibians may be abundant. My students and I have mapped soil acidity in the forests of New York (Fig. 8.11). Conifer plantations tend to have uniformly high acidity and very low amphibian densities. Beech forests have higher acidity with patches of lower acidity spread throughout. Also, in the beech forest, as you move toward streams, soil acidity decreases. The ANC appears to have been leached from the forest interior and the remaining ANC is held in soils near streams. For amphibians that are sensitive to acid soils and therefore must avoid them, movement from one stream to the next may be precluded by the acidic soils in between. During droughts, areas with soil acidity suitable for amphibians would decrease, further fragmenting the already fragmented habitat.

Geographic information systems represent a valuable tool for addressing prob-

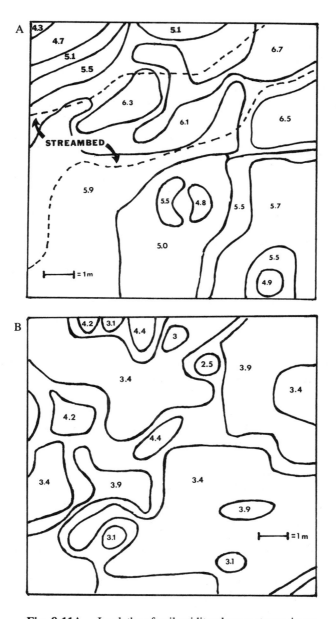

Fig. 8.11A. Isopleths of soil acidity along a stream in an 150-year-old beech stand on the E. N. Huyck Preserve, Albany County, New York, during 1989. B. Isopleths of soil acidity in the central portion of an 150-year-old beech forest (25 m away from the stream shown in A).

lems like the acidification of forest landscapes, because these computerized systems allow the representation and analysis of patterns of spatial heterogeneity in several parameters simultaneously. Many state and federal agencies, ecologists, and planners are now implementing these kinds of systems. This tool could help to bridge the gap between ecologic research and practical policy making, perhaps decreasing confrontations between ecologists and policy makers.

Amphibians that grow to maturity in forests and then migrate to breeding ponds or swamps, face yet another form of fragmentation—roads. In the early spring of 1983, my students and I observed high numbers of amphibians crossing a rural road outside of Oneonta, New York. The road separated a forested mountain side and a swamp. Because of the way the road was constructed, it funneled amphibians into a 30-m-wide corridor. We saw that many amphibians were being killed by traffic in 1983. In 1984 we installed drift-fences and pit-fall traps covering approximately half the migratory corridor to monitor the movement of amphibians and to document the impact of traffic on survival of the species involved.

It was clear that the automobile traffic had a significant impact on the amphibians trying to cross the road. Frogs fared better than salamanders (Table 8.3). Salamanders (red-spotted newts and yellow-spotted salamanders) upon reaching the road surface, stopped and looked around. When a car approached, the salamander crouched closer to the pavement but did not try to run. They were squashed. Frogs, on the other hand, jumped when cars approached.

Preceding the 4th year of the study, the forested mountain was logged. Large log skidders were used to drag out most trees bigger than approximately 25 cm in diameter. The rutted depressions left by the skidders were everywhere in the forest. The next spring very few amphibians emerged from the forest (Table 8.3). Apparently the skidders had either crushed the amphibians or had compacted the soil so that the frost penetrated deeply enough into the soil to kill them. Clearly such operations should be limited to times when the soil is hard enough to prevent compaction.

Many animal and plant populations are maintained over long periods of time by immigration and emigration. That is small populations of plants and animals may periodically become extirpated because of, for instance, a severe winter, drought, and exploitation by man. These lost populations may be replaced by new populations founded by individuals emigrating from areas where the species fared better. These kinds of movements are probably responsible for the long-term maintenance of many species. Habitat fragmentation and the disruption of movement corridors by overt human activity reduces the ease with which animals and plants may move about. This in turn increases the likelihood that populations will not be reestablished. In the long run this leads to loss of species.

Summary

We do not have to look too far or too hard to find examples of the impacts of anthropogenic environmental changes. Amphibians alone provide many exam-

Table 8.3. Amphibians migrating across Route 23 outside Oneonta, New York, and the percentage killed by automobiles during 1984, 1985, and 1986

Species	Common Name	Numbers Observed			Percent Killed		
		1984	1985	1986	1984	1985	1986
Frogs and Toads							
Rana sylvatica	Wood frog	225	312	14	23	41	50
Rana palustris	Pickerel frog	110	89	2	31	38	50
Hyla crucifer	Spring peeper	158	132	18	44	48	60
Bufo americanus	American toad	31	22	0	28	36	—
Salamanders							
Notophthalmus viridescens	Red-spotted newt	111	145	21	58	62	31
Ambystoma maculatum	Yellow-spotted salamander	78	89	2	73	82	50
Plethodon cinereus	Red-backed salamander	3	1	0	100	100	—
Totals		716	790	57	41	50	47

ples. Amphibians are often small and inconspicuous and so escape our attention. They are, however, very abundant and occur in most forested habitats worldwide. They are also important because they consume huge numbers of invertebrates and hence may play a role in structuring the detritus-based food web. They are sensitive to the kinds of changes that are likely to occur as the earth warms in the greenhouse world. They may be among the first groups to show large scale and rapid changes in population sizes and species numbers.

Small changes in overall precipitation or slight changes in timing of precipitation events can spell doom for species that depend on water for survival and reproduction. In one case illustrated here, the yearly chance to reproduce was lost by a species of salamander that already appears to be in peril, when the usual spring rains did not fall.

Acid precipitation and climate change may act together to eliminate amphibians from forests, regardless of logging activities, which are harmful in their own right. Long-term deposition of acid on sensitive forest soils is likely to increase acidification. When soils dry, they become increasingly acidic. Acid soils appear to be affecting the distribution of 10 species of amphibians in New York already. The projected increase in severity and frequency of droughts may eliminate many amphibians because of dryness, increased soil acidity, or the synergistic effects of the two factors.

Fragmentation of habitats by human activity shrinks population sizes and makes them more vulnerable to extinction. Loss of migratory corridors forecloses the opportunity for new individuals to reach empty habitats. Polluting aquatic and terrestrial habitats may make them fragmented to the plants and animals that live there. For example, acid deposition may accelerate soil acidification and fragment the habitats of sensitive amphibians. Roadways may be formidable obstacles to animals that migrate among habitat patches. Deforestation shrinks and fragments habitats and produces greenhouse and acid-forming gases, which further fragments habitats.

There are too many unknowns regarding the degree and extent of changes that will occur to allow for accurate predictions of likely effects of global climate change. But there is virtual unanimity of opinion that detrimental changes are occurring. Now we are faced with a crisis that we must address and solve. The wholesale loss of habitats, due to overt and more subtle kinds of destruction, the loss of species and local populations, and the polluting of our Earth represent the symptoms of the crisis.

The roots of the crisis lie in the ever expanding size of the human population. There are now 5.3 billion people on Earth with an annual increase of 80–90 million. Each person wants clean air, clean water, a place in which to live, food, clothing, and warmth. Each dreams that his/her children's children will live in a world as good or better than the one in which he/she lives. But we have built up a human population that uses both our renewable and nonrenewable resources beyond carrying capacity. Many nonrenewable resources simply are running out, and we can not support our population with the renewable ones alone. Even our once renewable resources, like our forests, do not appear to be quite so renewable any more. The dream appears to be moving out of our reach.

Acknowledgments

I thank the E. N. Huyck Preserve for the financial and other support that allowed me to organize the conference on Global Climate Change and Life on Earth and the New York State Museum for hosting the conference. I would especially like to thank M. E. Sullivan (Director of the New York State Museum) for his encouragement and help. The soil pH maps were prepared by Jeannette Jancola (deceased). I am also grateful for the help provided by my family and the many friends, students, and colleagues who have aided in the field work. N. Elliott, W. Elliott, M. Frisbie, and D. Steadman kindly reviewed and improved this chapter, for which I am thankful. Financial support has been provided by Hartwick College Trustee Research Grants, the E. N. Huyck Preserve, and the National Science Foundation (Grant No. BSR8812788).

References

Billett, M. F., E. A. FitzPatrick, and M. S. Cresser. 1988. Long term changes in soil acidity of forest soils in North-east Scotland. *Soil Use Management* 4:102–107.

Blank, L. W., T. M. Roberts, and R. A. Sheffington. 1988. New perspectives on forest decline. *Nature* 336:27–30.

Cline, G. R. and K. Kaul. 1988. Effects of acidity and aluminum on growth of *Bradyrhizobium iaponicum* in soil extracts. *Commun. Soil Sci. Plant Anal.* 19:933–946.

Cook, R. P. 1983. Effects of acid precipitation on embryonic mortality of *Ambystoma* salamanders in the Connecticut Valley of Massachusetts. *Biol. Conserv.* 27:77–88.

Davis, M. B. 1983. Holocene vegetational history of the eastern United States. In *Late-Quaternary Environments of the United States, Vol. 2, The Holocene*, H. E. Wright, Jr. (ed.), pp. 161–181. University of Minnesota Press, Minneapolis.

Davis, M. B. and C. Zabinski. 1990. Changes in geographical range resulting from greenhouse warming effects on biodiversity in forests. In *Proceedings of World Wildlife Fund's Conference on Consequences of the Greenhouse Effect for Biological Diversity*, R. L. Peters and T. E. Lovejoy (eds.), Yale University Press, New Haven, CT.

Duellman, W. E. and L. Trueb. 1986. *The Biology of Amphibians*. McGraw-Hill, New York.

Emanuel, W. R., H. H. Shugart, and M. P. Stevenson. 1985. Climate change and the broad-scale distribution of terrestrial ecosystem complexes. *Clim. Change* 7:29–43.

Environmental Protection Agency (EPA). 1988. *The Potential Effects of Global Climate Change on the United States*, Draft Report to Congress. Office of Policy, Planning, and Evaluation and Office of Research and Development. Washington, DC.

Flohn, H. 1969. *Climate and Weather*. McGraw-Hill, New York.

Freda, J. and W. A. Dunson. 1985. Field and laboratory studies of ion balance and growth rates of Ranid tadpoles chronically exposed to low pH. *Copeia* 1985:415–423.

Gosner, K. L. and I. H. Black. 1957. The effects of acidity on the development and hatching of New Jersey frogs. *Ecology* 38:256–262.

Hagvar, S. 1988. Decomposition studies in an easily-constructed microcosm: effects of microarthropods and varying soil pH. *Paedobiologia* 31:293–303.

Hansen, J. E. 1989. The Greenhouse effect: impacts on current global temperature and regional heat waves. In *The Challenge of Global Warming*, D. E. Abrahamson (ed.), pp. 35–43. Island Press, Washington, DC.

Hansen, J., I. Fung, A. Lacis, D. Rind, S. Lebedeff, R. Ruedy, and G. Russell. 1988. Global climate changes as forecast by Goddard Institute for Space Studies three-dimensional model. *J. Geophys. Res.* 93:9341–9364.

Holdridge, L. R. 1959. Determinations of world plant formations from simple climatic data. *Science* 130:572.

Keer, R. A. 1990. Global warming continues in 1989. *Science* 247:521.

Krug, E. C. and C. R. Frink. 1983. Acid rain on acid soil—a new perspective. *Science* 221:520–525.

MacArthur, R. A. and E. O. Wilson. 1967. *The Theory of Island Biogeography*. Princeton University Press, Princeton, NJ.

Manabe, S., R. T. Wetherald, and R. J. Stouffer. 1981. Summer dryness due to an increase of atmospheric CO_2 concentration. *Clim. Change* 3:347–386.

Murach, D. and B. Ulrich. 1988. Destabilization of forest ecosystems by acid deposition. *GeoJournal* 17:253–260.

Orsborne, J. L. and B. J. Macauley. 1988. Decomposition of *Eucalyptus* leaf litter: Influence of seasonal variation in temperature and moisture conditions. *Soil Biol. Biochem.* 20:369–375.

Pierce, T. K. 1985. Acid tolerance in amphibians. *BioScience* 35:239–243.

Pitelka, L. F. and D. J. Raynal. 1989. Forest decline and acidic deposition. *Ecology* 70:2–10.

Pough, F. H. and R. E. Wilson. 1977. Acid precipitation and reproductive success of *Ambystoma* salamanders. *J. Water Air Soil Pollution* 7:531–544.

Schlichter, L. 1981. Low pH effects the fertilization and development of *Rana pipiens* eggs. *Can J. Zool.* 59:1693–1699.

Schneider, S. H. and R. Londer. 1984. *The Coevolution of Climate and Life*. Sierra Club Books, San Francisco.

Schulze, E. -D. 1989. Air pollution and forest decline in a spruce (*Picea abies*) forest. *Science* 244:776–783.

Shoemaker, V. H. 1987. Osmoregulation in amphibians. In *Comparative Physiology: Life in Water and on Land*, P. Dejours, L. Bolis, C. R. Taylor, E. R. Weibel (eds.), pp. 109–120. Liviana Press, Padova.

Smith, R. L. 1980. *Ecology and Field Biology*, p. 43. Harper and Row, New York.

Spight, T. M. 1967. The water economy of salamanders: exchange of water with soil. *Biol. Bull.* 132:126–132.

Spotila, J. R. and B. H. Berman. 1976. Determination of skin resistance and the role of the skin in controlling water loss in amphibians and reptiles. *Comp. Biochem. Physiol.* 55:407–411.

Taylor, B. R. and D. Parkinson. 1988. Does repeated freezing and thawing accelerate decay of leaf litter? *Soil Biol. Biochem.* 20:657–665.

Van Breeman, N., J. Mulder, and C. T. Driscoll. 1983. Acidification and alkalinization of soils. *Plant Soil* 75:283–308.

Van Breeman, N., C. Driscoll, and J. Mulder. 1984. Acidic deposition and internal proton sources in acidification of soils and water. *Nature* 307:599–604.

Wyman, R. L. 1988. Soil acidity and moisture and the distribution of amphibians in five forests of Southcentral New York. *Copeia* 1988:394–399.

Wyman, R. L. and D. Hawksley-Lescault. 1987. Soil acidity affects distribution, behavior and physiology of the salamander *Plethodon cinereus*. *Ecology* 68:1819–1827.

9

Extinction of Species:
Past, Present, and Future

David W. Steadman

Introduction

Today a large percentage of the world's roughly 10 million species of plants and animals are faced with extinction. Because most of the species becoming extinct are tropical plants and invertebrates about which we know almost nothing, their losses go unlamented by the public. Three years ago, Peter Raven (1988) estimated that several species of plants or animals were becoming extinct every day, a rate predicted to increase into the hundreds within two or three decades (Wolf 1987). At current rates of deforestation, roughly 5–10% of all tropical forest species are expected to become extinct in each of the next five decades (Reid and Miller 1989). This would mean annual rates of extinction measured in the tens or even hundreds of thousands of species, resulting in an environmental, evolutionary, and socioeconomic crisis greater than any other in history. Even if human impact on the environment were halted today, species would continue to become extinct for decades because of the environmental damage that already has occurred.

These predictions and facts, like so many other aspects of extinction, are very sobering. Yet, I do not believe that the overall situation is beyond repair. If we act now in a vigorous, responsible, and international manner, we can begin to solve many of the environmental problems that are causing the extinctions. Chief among these problems is the loss and alteration of natural habitats, although overharvesting, pollution of all sorts, and introduced species also play important roles in extinction. If we ignore these problems, or continue to fight them half-heartedly, the Earth will experience a wave of extinction during the next 50 years more pervasive than that which accompanied the loss of the dinosaurs 65 million years ago.

Because reptiles, birds, and mammals are relatively large and conspicuous, as well as being the organisms that I study, they will provide most of my examples of extinct or endangered species. This approach is hardly representative of global biodiversity, for these three groups of vertebrates together make up less than 2% of known species. To make one more disclaimer, this short chapter is not meant to be a comprehensive review of the extinction crisis. I refer the reader to Collar and Andrew (1988), Ehrlich and Ehrlich (1981), Gradwohl and Greenberg (1988), Norton (1986), Reid and Miller (1989), Wilson (1988), and Wolf (1987) for a sample of the diverse and abundant literature on extinct and endangered species. Rather than only repeat what these and other authors have already said, much of this chapter will be a personal perspective on the extinction of species.

Attitudes and Policies

The world's rapidly growing human population and its insatiable demand for food and space have placed greater stresses on populations of plants and animals than ever before. All peoples have a significant impact on the natural environment, regardless of religious beliefs, moral values, economic status, level of technology, or any other cultural trait. Per capita environmental impact is much greater, however, in the "developed" countries than in the "developing" nations. Fueled by the selfish (and ultimately, self-destructive) notion that "more is better," per capita consumption of natural resources is alarmingly high in some countries, such as the United States and Japan. If similar rates of consumption occurred worldwide, the environmental degradation of the Earth would accelerate beyond its current rate by perhaps tenfold or more, with catastrophic impacts for humans and most other organisms. A variety of social, political, financial, climatic, and ecologic conditions make it impossible for the entire world to attain such consumption rates. Nevertheless, as the world's human population grows beyond its current level of 5.3 billion, even minimal per capita consumption rates of natural resources might be more than the Earth's soils, fresh water, and air can support in the long run.

Globally, there are more people alive today than ever before who are oblivious to or apathetic about environmental problems, such as the extinction of species. On the bright side, there are also more people than ever before who are concerned about these problems. This is particularly true in developed countries, where environmental issues received unprecedented publicity in 1988 and 1989 (Brown et al. 1989). For example, a graph on the front page of *The New York Times* on Sunday, July 2, 1989, showed that 79% of 1497 adult Americans surveyed on June 20–25, 1989 agreed with this statement: "Protecting the environment is so important that requirements and standards cannot be too high, and continuing environmental improvements must be made regardless of cost." By comparison, agreement with this statement was about 45% in September 1981, and about 65% as late as July 1988.

To be effective environmentally, this important change in attitude must be accompanied by similar changes in private and public policy. Even though the major oil spills of 1989 and early 1990 (Alaska, Antarctica, California, Delaware, New Jersey, New York, Rhode Island, Texas) have angered many people, it remains to be seen if these same people actually decrease their consumption of petroleum products. The world's economic communities, regardless of size, must begin to recognize that many short-term financial gains have been, and continue to be, more than offset by long-term environmental, social, and financial problems. The business world, designed to be concerned with quarterly and yearly profits, is out of synch with the natural world, where evolutionary adaptations generally are measured on time scales ranging from centuries to hundreds of millenia.

Along with population control, our global challenge is to swing the balance in favor of an environmental awareness that directly affects our lifestyle, regardless of who we are or where we live. Private individuals must begin to lead their lives in ways that are more environmentally sensitive. This has been difficult to achieve in a society such as ours that promotes consumption and where urban and suburban lifestyles can result in a detachment from nature rather than a practical genuine concern about the environment in our day-to-day routines. There is hope that this detachment is decreasing as people are exposed to more and more environmental information.

Essential in the process of environmental awareness is active participation and cooperation by governments at all levels (local, state, national, and international). A promising development is the growing strength in Europe of environmentally oriented Green parties. As we enter the 1990s, the public is putting more pressure on elected officials to be environmentally aware. Much of the environmental disregard of the Reagan administration (Meese 1989) is no longer politically expedient. Today it is difficult to find a politician who does not claim to be an environmentalist. Ironically, it is still a struggle to enact environmentally sound legislation.

Unfortunately, legislative solutions to the loss of species (and other conservation issues) have been implemented in much the same way as many of the other serious issues that face our country, such as civil rights, the national debt, or the drug problem. In the beginning, the seriousness of the problem is recognized by relatively few persons, who are ignored or ridiculed. Once general recognition of the problem is attained, the problem is found to be much larger and more serious than most people had imagined. Rather than being attacked comprehensively and quickly at its source, the problem is patched up here and there after long delays, with much of the allocated funds spent on bureaucratic red tape. [Donnelly (1989) provides a detailed example of governmental red tape on an environmental problem (drowning of sea turtles in shrimp nets) that could have had a simple solution.] Finally, the potential or real solutions to the problem usually are not accompanied by the changes in human attitude that would be needed to guarantee a long-term solution.

We can no longer afford to allow politicians to use the "imperfect state of knowledge" as an excuse for environmental inaction, particularly since poor funding is the primary factor that limits the knowledge. Although environmental issues are a major concern of the scientific community (Koshland 1990), funding for the natural sciences still lags far behind that of medical and molecular sciences, and colleges and universities continue the trend of the past two decades of phasing out natural history professorships, courses, collections, and libraries. Many of today's graduating biology majors know quite a bit about DNA but cannot distinguish a salamander from a lizard and have no clue that cashews and poison ivy belong to the same plant family. If environmentalists compete successfully in the next decade for a share of the money anticipated to be saved by a reduced military budget (the "peace dividend"), much of the new funding will be needed to rebuild educational programs, so that enough new scientists can be trained to deal with future environmental problems, including the extinction crisis.

Lessons from the Past

Human impact on the environment is not new. During the tens of thousands of years that mankind has existed, we have modified habitats and preyed upon innumerable species of animals. For example, a significant increase in extinctions and range contractions of large mammals (and presumably other species not yet studied) followed the evolutionary development of "anatomically modern" humans in Africa about 40,000 years ago (Klein 1987). Some 30,000 years later, the development of agriculture led to human population increases and greater modifications of habitats.

The North American fauna was far from pristine when the first Europeans arrived nearly 500 years ago. Hunting activities of the Paleo-Indians 11,000 years ago have been implicated in the loss at that time of more than 40 species of large mammals (Martin 1984), such as ground sloths, mammoths, mastodons, horses, camels, and sabertooth cats. The effects of changing climates and habitats have also been implicated in these losses (see Graham and Lundelius 1984), although no one has ever explained why the large mammals were able to endure all of the previous glacial-interglacial climatic transitions only to succumb exactly when people first appeared in the New World. Not surprisingly, the loss of so many large mammals resulted in the disappearance of species dependent upon them, such as scavenging birds that fed upon their carcasses. For example, the critically endangered California condor, a scavenger currently confined to captivity, once ranged far from its final retreat on the West Coast. Late Pleistocene bones of the condor have been found with those of large extinct mammals in New Mexico, Texas, Nuevo Leon, Florida, and even New York (Steadman and Miller 1987).

Scattered across much of the South Pacific are the hundreds of islands that make up Polynesia. The scenic beauty of these islands, however, belies their environmental history. To accommodate Polynesian agriculture, the indigenous island forests have been reduced (see Fig. 9.1) or eliminated during the past several thousand years by cutting, burning, and the introduction of nonnative plants (Kirch 1983). These habitat changes, as well as hunting and the introduction of nonnative mammals by prehistoric Polynesian peoples have extinguished many more species of birds than survive in the region today (James et al. 1987,

Fig. 9.1. A rain forest recently cleared on Eua Island, Tonga. The field supports only one species of bird, whereas the forest, which supports eight species of birds today, was inhabited by about 25 species of birds when the first Polynesians arrived 3,000 years ago. Photograph by J. G. Stull.

Steadman 1989). Thousands of populations, perhaps even thousands of full species, of Polynesian birds were already gone when Captain Cook explored the islands more than 200 years ago. Every Polynesian island that has been thoroughly explored for prehistoric bird bones has yielded the remains of two or three endemic species of flightless rails that have been unable to survive in the company of humans. Considering that approximately 800 islands in Oceania are inhabitable by people and presumably by flightless rails as well, the rails alone may account for about 2,000 species of birds that would exist today if not for human activities. Thus the number of modern species of birds in the world, usually cited as about 8,600 (based upon Mayr 1946), might actually be at least 10,600, if not for human activities in the Pacific.

Aside from rails, the heaviest losses of birds in Polynesia have been among various species of petrels, shearwaters, pigeons, parrots, and songbirds. From the Marquesan island of Ua Huka, for example, the bones recovered from a single archaeological locality (the Hane Site) provide a dramatic example of the decline in Polynesian birdlife in the first 1,000 years after the arrival of people (Table 9.1). Approximately 90% of the bird bones from the Hane Site are from petrels and shearwaters that are easily plucked from their underground nesting burrows. Of the 16 species of landbirds recorded from the Hane Site, 14 no longer live on Ua Huka, including 5 of the 6 pigeons and doves and all 3 species of parrots, the latter relished by Polynesians for their colorful feathers as well as their tasty flesh.

Table 9.1. Resident birds of Ua Huka, Marquesas Islands*

	Bones from the Hane Site	Exists today on Ua Huka
SEABIRDS		
Wedge-tailed shearwater (*Puffinus pacificus*)	x	x
Christmas shearwater (*Puffinus nativitatis*)	x	—
Audubon's shearwater (*Puffinus lherminieri*)	x	—
Bulwer's petrel (*Bulweria* cf. *bulwerii*)	x	x
Tahiti petrel (*Pterodroma rostrata*)	x	—
Phoenix petrel (*Pterodroma* cf. *alba*)	x	—
Unknown petrel (*Pterodroma* small sp.)	x	—
Polynesian storm-petrel (*Nesofregetta fuliginosa*)	x	x
White-bellied storm-petrel (*Fregetta grallaria*)	x	—
White-tailed tropicbird (*Phaethon lepturus*)	x	x
Red-footed booby (*Sula sula*)	x	x
Brown booby (*Sula leucogaster*)	x	x
Masked booby (*Sula dactylatra*)	x	—
†Abbott's booby (*Papasula abbotti costelloi*)	x	—
Great frigatebird (*Fregata minor*)	x	x
Lesser frigatebird (*Fregata ariel*)	x	x
Gray-backed tern (*Sterna lunata*)	—	x
Sooty tern (*Sterna fuscata*)	x	x
Brown noddy (*Anous stolidus*)	x	x
Black noddy (*Anous minutus*)	x	x
Blue-gray noddy (*Procelsterna cerulea*)	—	x
Marquesas fairy-tern (*Gygis microrhyncha*)	x	x
LANDBIRDS		
Pacific reef-heron (*Egretta sacra*)	x	x
†Tuamotu sandpiper (*Prosobonia* cf. *cancellata*)	x	—
†Undescribed crake (*Porzana* new sp.)	x	—
†Undescribed rail (*Gallirallus* new sp.)	x	—
Marquesas ground-dove (*Gallicolumba rubescens*)	x	—
†Giant ground-dove (*Gallicolumba* new sp.)	x	—
Red-moustached fruit-dove (*Ptilinopus mercierii*)	x	—
White-capped fruit-dove (*Ptil. dupetithouarsii*)	x	x
Nuku Hiva pigeon (*Ducula galeata*)	x	—
†Undescribed cuckoo-dove (*Macropygia* new sp.)	x	—
Marquesas lorikeet (*Vini ultramarina*)	x	—
†Conquered lorikeet (*Vini vidivici*)	x	—
†Sinoto's lorikeet (*Vini sinotoi*)	x	—
Marquesas swiftlet (*Collocalia ocista*)	—	x
Marquesas kingfisher (*Halcyon godeffroyi*)	x	—
†Undescribed flycatcher (cf. *Myiagra* new sp.)	x	—
Iphis monarch (*Pomarea iphis*)	—	x
Marquesas reed-warbler (*Acrocephalus mendanae*)	—	x
†Undescribed starling (*Aplonis* new sp.)	x	—
Total species of seabirds	20	14
Total species of landbirds	16	5
Total species	36	19

*Over 95% of the more than 11,000 bird bones from the Hane Archaeological Site are from the two lowest cultural strata, which are from 800 to 2,000 years old.

†Extinct species or subspecies.

To make matters worse, many of the birds that survived the impact of prehistoric Polynesians have not been able to withstand the new problems brought by Europeans, Americans, and Japanese, such as nonnative predators (especially cats and black rats), innumerable exotic plants, metal tools and machinery to facilitate forest clearing, and a world war. More than half of the species of Polynesian landbirds that still exist are endangered (i.e., total populations in the tens or hundreds). Island birds have been, and still are, more vulnerable to human activities than continental species because of their relatively small population sizes, confinement to small land areas, low resistance to disease, and poorly developed behavioral responses to nonnative predators.

Quite appropriately, islands have been regarded by scientists as wonderful "natural laboratories" where evolutionary and ecological processes can be studied in ecosystems much less complex than those of continents. The natural simplicity of islands, however, has been exacerbated by human activity to the point where many island ecosystems have little left to lose. Unless vigorous programs are implemented to protect a large number of islands, these showcases of evolution soon will be lost, representing a major loss not only of biological diversity, but also of any opportunity to study and understand the fascinating natural history of islands. The establishment of an extensive series of Pacific island nature reserves should be a priority of the international conservation movement. In many ways we are lucky that anything natural is left to protect on these islands. The future of low-lying atolls is particularly perilous, for their very existence is threatened by the rising sea level accompanying global warming (Brookfield 1989, Ward 1989).

Understanding the Present, Looking to the Future

Protecting large tracts of suitable habitat is the key to preservation of biodiversity. Although the original reasons for setting aside wilderness areas in the United States were "largely spiritual, esthetic and ethical" (Shabecoff 1989), contemporary reasons are related more to long-term survival of species. Private nonprofit land trust groups in the United States also play an important role in protecting land (Staimer 1989), a subject traditionally regarded more as a governmental responsibility.

Monospecific conservation programs are important and often enjoy popular appeal, especially for large reptiles, birds, or mammals. Many species of turtles, snakes, crocodiles, parrots, primates, elephants, rhinoceroses, and whales, among others, have conservation problems related as much to specific human uses (hunting, pet trade, etc.) as to loss of habitat. Nevertheless, there is little hope in the near future that specific "recovery plans" can be formulated and implemented for more than a small fraction of all endangered species. For example, as of April 1989, recovery plans had been approved for only 242 of 1041 species listed as endangered or threatened by the United States Fish and

Wildlife Service (Anonymous 1989a). By August 1989, five more recovery plans had been approved while 29 more species had been listed (Anonymous 1989b). In the 4 months that the five recovery plans were approved, perhaps 400 to 1,000 species of plants and animals became extinct. Thus it is widely recognized that protection of entire natural ecosystems, with their interdependent assemblages of plants and animals, is the only effective way to preserve a major portion of the remaining biodiversity. The Office of Endangered Species is beginning to emphasize geographic areas or ecosystems rather than single species in its listing efforts (S. M. Chambers, personal communication). Captive breeding programs are essential to preserve the remaining genetic stock of many highly endangered species; however, such programs will have no effect on wild populations if natural habitats cannot be reoccupied because of human impact.

The changes in temperature and precipitation regimes associated with global warming are expected to cause major changes in the location, extent, and species composition of many habitats. Unless extremely large parcels of land are preserved in a natural state, many plants and animals may not be able to adapt to these changes. Particularly in the eastern two-thirds of our country, the entire system of national wildlife refuges, parks, and forests represents "islands" of potential natural habitat rather than the "corridors" needed to promote natural movements. Only approximately 70 of the hundreds of endangered or threatened species in the United States are protected in existing national wildlife refuges (Meese 1989).

Major northward and southward migrations of forest trees have occurred in eastern North America by seed and fruit dispersal during the glacial-interglacial cycles of the past two million years. Thus, one might expect that the dispersal capabilities of these trees could accommodate the northward range changes predicted to occur during the next century of global warming. There are, however, at least three obstacles to these future movements. First, the modern forests are fragmented into habitat islands by human activities that may prevent the intervening nonforested land from sustaining new forest growth. Second, the reproductive and dispersal abilities of many trees may be stressed today by acid precipitation, air pollution, and introduced insect and fungal pests (MacKenzie and El-Ashry 1988, and Mello 1987). Third, the populations of many animals that are effective agents of dispersal are reduced or gone. Particularly important is the loss, early this century, of the passenger pigeon (Fig. 9.2), a mast-eating species that formerly blanketed the deciduous and mixed forests in the billions. More than any other species, the passenger pigeon dispersed seeds of beeches, oaks, hickories, and chestnuts through eastern North America until its extinction at the turn of the century. It remains to be seen if the turkeys, grouse, blue jays, squirrels, and black bears that remain will be able to disperse propagules of these forest trees at the rates dictated by future climatic changes.

Tropical rainforests are spectacular showcases of evolution and natural beauty (Australian Heritage Commission 1986) that sustain most of the world's species

Fig. 9.2. The passenger pigeon. Now extinct, it was the most abundant bird in the eastern United States until the late 19th century. New York State Museum catalogue number 391. Photograph by C. Supkis and M. C. Zarriello.

of plants and animals (Raven 1988). Because deforestation is most intense in the tropics (Burley and Hazlewood 1985, Gradwohl and Greenberg 1988, Houghton this volume), it is here that most of the current extinction is taking place. The biotic diversity of tropical forests is staggering. In 1 ha (2.5 acres) of Amazonian lowland rainforest in Peru, entomologist Terry Erwin found 41,000 species of insects, more than 25% of which were beetles (Wolf 1987). Recent research by Erwin and colleagues suggests that there may be as many as 10 to 30 million species of insects alone, with the overwhelming majority confined to tropical forests.

More than 30 years ago, the eminent tropical botanist F. R. Fosberg (1958) stated,

". . . expeditions [to the tropics] have been relatively few. The tropical regions are large and tropical faunas and floras are enormous. Growth continues the year around. The accessibility of many tropical areas has been limited and difficult. Expeditions are frightfully expensive, and most scientists are poor. Therefore our knowledge of even the basic facts—the very geography of the tropical parts of the earth and such elementary things as what animals and plants live together—is very imperfect. Full understanding can scarcely be based on inadequate knowledge."

Travel to the tropics is much easier and cheaper today than in 1958, but in spite of the admirable efforts of many dedicated scientists, our current knowledge of the systematics, distribution, community structure, general ecology, and chemical properties of tropical plants remains incomplete (Campbell and Hammond 1989, Daly 1989). For example, only approximately 5,000 of the world's 250,000 to 300,000 species of plants have been studied thoroughly for possible medical uses (Abelson 1990), with the majority of the unstudied species growing in tropical forests.

At the current rate of logging, less than 10% of the world's tropical forests will remain standing in 20 years. Yet Peter Raven estimates that only about $50 to $75 million were spent *worldwide* on research in tropical biology in 1986 (Wolf 1987). The minuscule nature of this allocation can be appreciated by comparisons with defense spending, where the price of individual aircraft or ships may exceed $1 billion. While conservationists plead with Brazil and other equatorial nations to reduce deforestation, the United States (1) clear cuts large tracts of our own old-growth forests, especially in the Pacific Northwest (Lemonick 1989); (2) contributes to the financing of tropical deforestation through huge multinational loans; and (3) provides markets for tropical hardwoods.

Current human impact on tropical forests is a situation that includes a bewildering array of cultural, social, economic, political, and environmental issues (Denslow and Padoch 1988, Gradwohl and Greenberg 1988). The environmental issues can and should be compatible with the others, but this will require realization by governments of the long-term socioeconomic benefits of protecting the forests, as well as declines in human populations. The recent "debt-for-nature swaps" in Brazil, Bolivia, Ecuador, Costa Rica, Zambia, Madagascar, and the Philippines hold great promise for setting aside areas of natural habitat. Under these programs, countries can exchange a portion of their financial indebtedness to developed countries for protecting large tracts of land. Similar deals are being negotiated now in Peru, Guatemala, and Jamaica. Debt-for-nature swaps should be pursued in any highly indebted developing country.

Many temperate and polar species are also endangered or have already become extinct within the past few centuries. Aside from the passenger pigeon already mentioned, the irreversible casualties include the Labrador duck, crested shelduck, heath hen, great auk, Carolina parakeet, Tasmanian wolf, sea mink, and Steller's sea cow. The nearly or possibly extinct species include the California condor, whooping crane, eskimo curlew, ivory-billed woodpecker, Algerian nuthatch, Bachman's warbler, and black-footed ferret. Thousands of other species of North American, Eurasian, and Australian organisms have undergone major range contractions during this same period, often resulting in losses of genetically distinct subspecies. Extrapolating these range contractions into the future suggests massive extinctions during the next century or two.

As a first step in planning habitat-oriented conservation programs, many states are surveying their remaining natural areas. Much of this is done through the Natural Heritage Program, which is implemented cooperatively by The Nature Conservancy and state agencies. Critically endangered North American habitats include a variety of forests, prairies, deserts, wetlands, and combinations thereof. The next two decades will be crucial. All levels of government must be willing to face the problem of habitat preservation and do their best to solve it.

Most riparian forests in the southwestern United States have been damaged or destroyed during the past century (Rea 1983), resulting in local losses of many species of plants and animals. From state to state, only tiny fractions of prairie habitat remain unaltered by agriculture. In the northeastern United States, there are diseases of unknown long-term impact in many important forest trees, such as beech, sugar maple, ash, hemlock, and spruce. Will the damage to these species be as widespread and lethal as that in the American elm and American chestnut? If so, the composition of eastern forests will change significantly, with unknown impact on the other plants and animals that live there. In New York, the native vegetation of many wetlands is being replaced by a nonnative weed called purple loosestrife, creating vast tracts of marsh now devoid of the least bitterns, marsh wrens, swamp sparrows, muskrats, and mink that lived there only a few years ago.

North American songbirds that migrate to the neotropics (especially flycatchers, thrushes, vireos, and warblers) are adversely affected by habitat losses on temperate breeding grounds as well as their tropical wintering grounds (Morton and Greenberg 1989). Although systematically collected long-term data are scarce (Baird 1990, Marshall 1988), anyone who regularly watches or surveys songbirds has noticed recent scarcities of migratory forest species, even where the temperate forests have not been disturbed (Terborgh 1989). Many amphibian populations are declining in regions as diverse as New York, Colorado, Mexico, Costa Rica, Brazil, and Australia (Barinaga 1990, Wyman this volume). Reason for these declines are often uncertain, although acid precipitation seems to be involved in at least the temperate species. Although our environmental information remains inadequate in many specific instances, there is no longer any doubt among scientists that the overall picture regarding biological diversity is alarming and is getting worse.

Summary

Throughout the world, species are being lost at a higher rate than ever before. In destroying these products of billions of years of organic evolution, we threaten the existence of all natural communities including human communities. In spite of our attempts to live apart from nature, humans require adequate supplies of air, water, and food just like any other animal. Our struggles to attain these supplies have been at the expense of natural communities. Reduction of the world's human population is essential if we are to preserve any respectable portion of the current diversity of plants and animals. In order to be implemented effectively, population reduction and all other environmental efforts must have popular and governmental support at the local, state, national, and international levels. Although one country's problem may have a clear impact on other nations, international cooperation is facilitated today by the technological advances in communication and transportation that are homogenizing human cultures.

The environmental damage being done today in the tropics, particularly the clearing of tropical forests, is the single largest factor contributing to the loss of species. Although such forest clearing provides short-term sustenance for humans, it also guarantees long-term environmental degradation that eventually will limit human populations as well. Particularly in the past decade, many tropical countries have begun to realize the importance of preserving large tracts of forest. Still today there is a net loss of tropical forest. Recent innovative financial programs such as "debt-for-nature swaps" are helping to save some tropical habitats. These programs should be supported vigorously by those of us who can afford it.

As citizens of the developed world, there are a number of simple, practical things we can do to alleviate the loss of species. Although these and many other actions are outlined in some detail elsewhere (Wyman et al. this volume), a few deserve mention here as well, such as having fewer babies, reducing per capita consumption of natural resources, becoming knowledgeable and active in local environmental issues (particularly involving habitat loss), joining conservation groups, doing a nature-oriented trip to the tropics, planting native species of plants to support indigenous wildlife, and not buying products made from tropical hardwoods or from rare or endangered species of animals.

A close look at the past 40,000 years shows that we already live in a world much impoverished by human activity. Rather than accept the extinctions of plants and animals that have already occurred as an excuse to continue these exploitations, our challenge today is to learn lessons from these losses as we plan for the future.

Acknowledgments

Much of the research for this paper was supported by the National Science Foundation (grant BSR–8607535) and the National Geographic Society (grants 2088, 2482–82, 3359–86, 4001–89). For comments on the manuscript, I thank N. G. Miller and R. L. Wyman. This is contribution number 639 of the New York State Museum and Science Service.

References

Abelson, P. H. 1990. Medicine from plants. *Science* 247:513.

Anonymous. 1989a. Box score of listings and recovery plans. *Endangered Species Tech. Bull.* 14:8.

Anonymous. 1989b. Box score of listings and recovery plans. *Endangered Species Tech. Bull.* 14:12.

Australian Heritage Commission. 1986. *Tropical Rainforests of North Queensland: Their Conservation Significance,* Special Australian Heritage Publication Series No. 3. Australian Government Publishing Service, Canberra.

Baird, T. H. 1990. Changes in breeding bird populations between 1930 and 1985 in the Quaker Run Valley of Allegheny State Park, New York. *N.Y. State Museum Bull.* 477:1–42.

Barinaga, M. 1990. Where have all the froggies gone? *Science* 247: 1033–1034.

Brookfield, H. 1989. Global change and the Pacific: problems for the coming half-century. *Contemp. Pacific* 1:1–17.

Brown, L. R., C. Flavin, and S. Postel. 1989. A world at risk. In *State of the World,* L. R. Brown et al. (eds.), pp. 3–20. Norton, New York.

Burley, F. W. and P. T. Hazlewood. 1985. *Tropical Forests: A Call for Action, Part 1, The plan; Part 2, Case Studies; Part 3, Country Investment Profiles.* World Resources Institute, Washington, DC.

Campbell, D. G. and H. D. Hammond (eds.). 1989. *Floristic Inventory of Tropical Forests.* New York Botanical Garden, New York.

Collar, N. J. and P. Andrew. 1988. *Birds to Watch: The ICBP Checklist of Threatened Birds.* International Council for Bird Preservation, Technical Publication No. 8.

Daly, D. 1989. Pressing plants, monographing, and networking: tropical systematic botany in the 1990s. *Endangered Species UPDATE* 6:1–4.

Denslow, J. S. and C. Padoch (eds.). 1988. *People of the Tropical Rain Forest.* University of California Press, Berkley.

Donnelly, M. 1989. The history and politics of turtle excluder device regulations. *Endangered Species UPDATE* 6:1–5.

Ehrlich, P. and A. Ehrlich. 1981. *Extinction: The Causes and Consequences of the Disappearance of Species.* Random House, New York.

Fosberg, F. R. 1958. Climate, vegetation, and rational land utilization in the humid tropics. Proc. *Pacific Science Congress* 20:1–3.

Gradwohl, J. and R. Greenberg. 1988. *Saving the Tropical Forests.* Island Press, Washington, DC.

Graham, R. W. and E. L. Lundelius, Jr. 1984. Coevolutionary disequilibrium and Pleistocene extinctions. In *Quaternary Extinctions,* P. S. Martin and R. G. Klein (eds.), pp. 223–249. University of Arizona Press, Tucson.

James, H. F., T. W. Stafford, Jr., D. W. Steadman, S. L. Olson, P. S. Martin, A. J. T. Jull, and

P. C. McCoy. 1987. Radiocarbon dates on bones of extinct birds from Hawaii. *Proc. Nat. Acad. Sci.* USA 84:2350–2354.

Kirch, P. V. 1983. Man's role in modifying tropical and subtropical Polynesian ecosystems. *Archaeol. Oceania* 18:26–31

Klein, R. G. 1987. Reconstructing how early people exploited animals: Problems and prospects. In *The Evolution of Human Hunting,* M. H. Nitecki and D. V. Nitecki (eds.), pp. 11–45. Plenum Press, New York.

Koshland, D. E., Jr. 1990. Priority one: Rescue the environment. *Science* 247:777.

Lemonick, M. D. 1989. What can Americans do? *Time* 134:85.

MacKensie, J. J. and M. T. El-Ashry. 1988. *Ill Winds.* World Resources Institute, Washington, DC.

Marshall, J. T. 1988. Birds lost from a giant sequoia forest during fifty years. *Condor* 90: 359–372.

Martin, P. S. 1984. Pleistocene overkill: The global model. In *Quaternary Extinctions,* P. S. Martin and R. G. Klein (eds.), pp. 354–403. University of Arizona Press, Tucson.

Mayr, E. 1946. The number of species of birds. *Auk* 63:64–69.

Meese, G. M. 1989. Saving endangered species: Implementing the endangered species act. In *In Defense of Wildlife: Preserving Communities and Corridors,* G. Mackintosh (ed.), pp. 47–62. Defenders of Wildlife, Washington, DC.

Mello, R. A. 1987. *Last Stand of the Red Spruce.* Island Press, Washington, DC.

Morton, E. S. and R. Greenburg. 1989. The outlook for migratory songbirds: "Future shock" for birders. *Am. Birds* 43:178–183.

Norton, B. G. 1986. *The Preservation of Species.* Princeton University Press, Princeton, NJ.

Raven, P. H. 1988. Our diminishing tropical forests. In *Biodiversity,* E. O. Wilson (ed.), pp. 119–122. National Academy Press, Washington, DC.

Rea, A. M. 1983. *Once a River.* University of Arizona Press, Tucson, Arizona.

Reid, W. V. and K. R. Miller, 1989. *Keeping Options Alive: The Scientific Basis for Conserving Biodiversity.* World Resources Institute, Washington, DC.

Shabecoff, P. 1989. A rising American impulse to leave the land alone. *New York Times* June 11, 1989: E6.

Staimer, M. 1989. Protecting the land. *USA Today* June 20, 1989:1.

Steadman, D. W. 1989. Extinction of birds in Eastern Polynesia: A review of the record, and comparisons with other Pacific island groups. *J. Archaeol. Sci.* 16:177–205.

Steadman, D. W. and N. G. Miller. 1987. California condor associated with spruce-jack pine woodland in the late Pleistocene of New York. *Quat. Res.* 28:415–426.

Terborgh, J. 1989. *Where Have All the Birds Gone?* Princeton University Press, Princeton, NJ.

Ward, R. G. 1989. Earth's empty quarter? The Pacific islands in a Pacific century. *Geographical J.* 155:235–246.

Wilson, E. O. 1988. *Biodiversity.* National Academy Press, Washington, DC.

Wolf, E. C. 1987. *On the Brink of Extinction: Conserving the Diversity of Life,* Worldwatch Paper 78, Worldwatch Institute, Washington, DC.

10

Impact of Climate-induced Sea Level Rise on Coastal Areas

Stephen P. Leatherman

Introduction

A significant portion of the world's population lives within the coastal zone, with many buildings and facilities built at elevations less than 3 m above sea level. Presently, many of these structures are not adequately above existing water levels or located far enough landward to ensure their survival and the safety of residents during major storm activity. This hazard has grown increasingly apparent and serious along much of the United States East and Gulf coasts, particularly the highly urbanized sandy barrier islands, as relative sea levels for eastern North America have risen at an average rate of 1.0–1.5 mm per year during most of the 20th century (Braatz and Aubrey 1987).

Changing sea levels have moved the position of shorelines over geologic time. Tens of millions of years ago, the seas had advanced 100–200 km farther inland than where they are today along the eastern coast of the United States. These old shorelines are marked by the "falls" in the river systems. Many of the major cities and state capitals were established by the colonists at these locations (e.g., Raleigh, North Carolina; Richmond, Virginia; Washington, DC; Baltimore, Maryland; Philadelphia, Pennsylvania) because this was as far upstream as the rivers were navigable. This fall line also represents the landward edge of the coastal plain. Sea levels could rise dramatically again if all the water tied up in the world's glaciers and ice caps were to melt. Sea levels would rise over 70 m, which would be devastating on a global basis. Fortunately, this prospect is unlikely and (based on the geologic record) could only occur over a time span of millions of years.

Sea levels have been much lower in the "recent" geologic past, approaching 100 m below present levels approximately 15,000 years ago. Resort areas, like Ocean City, Maryland, would have been over 165 km landward of the shoreline as the seas receded to the shelf edge, exposing the wide continental shelf. The Chesapeake Bay and associated marshes did not exist at this time because the Susquehanna River was rapidly down-cutting its bed. With the retreat of the glaciers, the water incorporated in these huge ice sheets, which had extended as far south as northern New Jersey, was released to again start filling up the oceans' basins.

The general effect of sea-level rise on coastal lowlands is to induce landward retreat—beaches erode and marshes are lost. Most sandy shorelines worldwide have experienced recession during the past century (Bird 1985). Such has also been the case along the United States coasts; historical data indicate that about 90 percent of our sandy beaches are eroding (Leatherman 1989). In Louisiana, where the rate of sea-level rise is very high due to local subsidence, there is also a high rate of marsh loss (Wells and Coleman 1987). Accelerated sea-level rise, through the thermal expansion of the surface layer of the oceans and the melting of alpine glaciers due to greenhouse-induced global warming, will only increase erosion rates and exacerbate the present shoreline problems. Furthermore, coastal marshlands will be lost at ever-increasing rates, with the nation's marshes perhaps disappearing in the coming decades at the high rates of loss presently experienced in Louisiana.

Causes And Estimates Of Sea-Level Rise

Changes in eustatic sea level, on a short time scale of decades to a century, are caused by changes in ice mass on land and changes in ocean water temperature. These processes are sensitive to climate changes. A warmer atmosphere will warm the ocean water, induce the water molecules to expand and cause the actual volume of water to expand, thereby raising the level of the oceans. A warmed atmosphere will also cause land-based ice to melt, thereby adding fresh water to the volume of the oceans.

Average surface temperatures in the Northern Hemisphere have risen approximately 1°C in the last century (Jones et al. 1986). Current projections estimate an increase in global average surface temperature of 3–5°C by the year 2050 (Meier 1990) and warming of the Earth's atmosphere due to the greenhouse effect from increased atmospheric greenhouse gases. It is unclear exactly how this accelerated warming will translate into sea-level rise, because the dynamics between the atmosphere and the ocean are not well understood. However, global average surface temperatures have risen approximately 1°C during the last century, and global average sea-level has risen approximately 10 cm during the past century (Gornitz and Lebedeff 1987). Projections of future sea-level rise range from 0.3 m (Meier, 1990) to 3.5 m by the year 2100 (Hoffman et al. 1983). Even the less dramatic estimates of sea-level rise will result in social, economic, and environmental problems in coastal areas.

Impacts Of Sea-Level Rise

The physical impacts of sea-level rise include inundation of low-lying areas, erosion, saltwater intrusion, higher water tables, and increased storm damage and flooding. Depending on geomorphology, energy conditions, elevations, sediment

Fig. 10.1. High-density real estate at Miami Beach, Florida.

type, tectonic activity, and the rate of relative sea-level rise in a particular area, the effects of any one, or a combination, of these impacts will vary.

Inundation is simply the submergence of land lying below the raised sea level. In the United States, the Atlantic and Gulf coasts are low-lying and relatively flat and hence, are highly vulnerable to inundation. Low-lying island nations, such as the Maldives, which are currently only a few meters above sea-level, are susceptible to total inundation.

Any area that is not hard rock is subject to erosion. As sea level rises even small amounts, it can cause a dramatic retreat of the shore (e.g., a 1-m rise of sea level can cause up to 100 m of beach recession). Erosion rates will not be as problematic in areas where there is an ample supply of sediment to the beach, where tectonic uplift counters the rate of sea-level rise, and where there are not high-density economically valuable real estate developments (Fig. 10.1).

Saltwater intrusion occurs as higher sea levels push saline water farther upstream in bays and rivers. This could cause saltwater contamination of drinking water supplies of some coastal cities, such as Philadelphia, Pennsylvania. Saltwater intrusion is also a concern for coastal farmers whose crops and fields lie just above the water table. These crops would be damaged or killed if saltwater reached their roots.

In some places, such as islands, water tables will rise up to nearly the land surface as the sea level rises. This is especially important on low-lying islands and atolls where a fresh water lens lies on top of the saltwater below. A higher sea level will reduce the depth of the fresh water lens, thereby killing non salt-tolerant vegetation and rendering the groundwater undrinkable. Thus, in addition to the threat of inundation, these small island communities may lose their drinking water supplies due to rising sea level.

Higher sea-level will allow storm waves and surges to overtop existing seawalls and dikes as presently constructed. Thus, cities such as Galveston, Texas, which are completely protected by a seawall, would have to rethink their present engineering structures. In addition, island overwash during storms will occur more frequently, which would pose a problem for low-lying developed barrier islands such as the Outer Banks of North Carolina. Also, storm surges will be able to reach farther inland.

Impacts On Wetlands

Coastal wetlands account for much of the land less than 1 m above sea level. These extensive marshes, swamps, and mangrove forests fringe most of the coastline of the United States, particularly along the Atlantic and Gulf coasts. These areas are vital to our fisheries industry since many economically important species such as bluefish, flounder, shrimp, crabs, oysters, and clams are supported by the sheltered, biologically rich environment provided by the marshes. In addition, wetlands act to filter and process agricultural and industrial runoff from the land, thereby maintaining water quality in the adjacent water body.

Salt marshes exist in a delicate balance with water levels. A change in controlling factors, such as sea level, water salinity or tidal and wave energy, will cause a displacement in marsh zonation. Since the distribution of plants in a marsh is partially based on their elevation above sea level (Redfield 1972), a rise in sea level will shift the distribution of plant species proportionately landward. With gradual sea-level rise (due to local subsidence or worldwide changes in sea level), marshes can naturally keep pace by trapping sediments in the water column and through accumulation of their own organic material (dead stems and leaves). However, an imbalance can develop if sea-level rises significantly faster than the deposition on the marsh surface, eventually resulting in waterlogging and loss (Orson et al. 1985).

Land loss in most wetlands results from a combination of mechanisms, with shoreline erosion at the seaward edge of the marsh being the most obvious process. This factor can be expected to accelerate with increased water levels, but probably accounts for only a small percent of all marsh losses annually. Most marshes will be long since submerged before extensive shoreline erosion occurs.

A more probable catastrophic mechanism of marsh loss with a significant increase in sea levels (e.g., 1 m) will be the formation of extensive interior marsh ponds allied with general tidal creek bank erosion and headward growth as tidal prisms increase. These shallow-water bodies enlarge and coalesce at the expense of marsh vegetation in response to rapid coastal submergence (Orson et al. 1985). The magnitude of such losses can be quite extensive, as shown by studies in the

Mississippi delta (DeLaune et al. 1983), and in the Chesapeake Bay, Maryland and Louisiana (Stevenson et al. 1986). The physiologic mechanism behind the development of interior ponds is believed to be anoxia and ultimate death of marsh plants, as sea level outpaces the ability of the marsh to maintain elevation (Fig. 10.2).

In addition to naturally occurring marsh loss, wetlands have historically been impacted by man's activities via filling, dredging, draining, and flood control measures. Although salt marshes are protected by federal legislation, major losses of estuarine marshes can be anticipated in the future because of bulkheading along bay shores. Holocene sea level-rise has naturally translated these marshes landward through time. With the construction of landward-flanking bulkheads, which are prevalent along the mainland bay shores of many coastal states, these marshes will be precluded from migrating landward, and will literally be squeezed out of existence with sea level-rise. Thus, the combined impacts of man's past activities and the likelihood of rapid sea level-rise result in a limited future for wetlands.

Impacts On Beaches and Coastal Barriers

Most sandy shorelines worldwide have retreated during the past century (Bird 1985). Accreting coasts have been restricted to areas where excess sediment is supplied by river sources or where the land is being elevated due to tectonic uplift or isostatic rebound. Human interference cannot be considered a primary cause of erosion since retreat also occurs on sparsely populated and little-developed sandy coasts (Bird 1976). Such recession could result from an increase in storminess, but this trend would have to be almost worldwide to account for erosion on geographically dispersed sandy shorelines. Therefore, in view of the demonstrated general relative rise of sea level along the United States shoreline during the past century (Gornitz and Lebedeff 1989), the link between shore retreat and sea-level rise is based on more than circumstantial evidence; it can be stated that the relationship is causal in nature. Rising relative sea level causes shoreline recession, except where this trend is offset by an influx of sediment.

In some areas, it is clear that human modifications to the nearshore have caused substantial erosion pressures. Undoubtedly the principal problem has been construction of jettied inlets and deepening of channel entrances for navigation. Along shorelines with high rates of longshore sediment transport, these constructed features trap sediment at the jetty on the updrift side of the inlet. If material dredged from the navigation channel is not placed on the beaches downdreft of the inlet, the jetty system can cause an amount of erosion equal to the reduction in transport of sand along the beach. Ocean City, Maryland (Fig. 10.3) is a good example of this situation (Leatherman 1984). At some Florida entrances, tens of millions of cubic meters of dredged material have been dumped offshore and thus are permanently removed from the beach. This has resulted in very high erosion concentrated downdreft of tidal inlet entrances.

The effect of rising sea level is to establish the potential for shore retreat, but storms provide the wave energy needed to cause this erosion. A net erosional change of 1 m or more per year is often difficult to measure when the beach width naturally fluctuates by 16 m or more seasonally, thus confusing the casual observer. However, measured over decades to centuries with accurate means of shoreline mapping (Leatherman 1983), the trends become apparent and rates of beach erosion can be quantified for particular areas along the coast.

Possible Responses

Humans can generally respond in three ways to accelerated shoreline erosion: (1) retreat from the shore, (2) armor the coast, or (3) nourish the beach. The choice of a response strategy will depend on a number of factors, including socioeconomic and environmental conditions. The decisions reached will likely be site-specific so that each area or community must be evaluated separately.

For highly urbanized areas, such as Miami Beach, Florida (Fig. 10.1) or Ocean City, Maryland (Fig. 10.3), the abandonment option is not realistic. The value of such beachfront property with high-density and high-rise structures often approaches $100 million per mile, making beach restoration the most attractive alternative. Elsewhere, seawalls have been constructed to stabilize the shore and protect coastal communities from the ravages of major hurricanes, as in Galveston, Texas (Leatherman 1984). For eroding shorelines that are less developed, the decision becomes more difficult. Therefore, the costs and benefits of protection must be weighed against those of retreating from the shoreline.

Summary

The general response of low-lying lands to sea-level rise is retreat via beach erosion and wetland loss. Already extensive coastal marshes are being lost in Louisiana and in the Chesapeake Bay (Stevenson et al. 1986), because the marshes are not able to keep pace with relative sea-level rise and are presently being drowned in place. The prospect for coastal wetlands is bleak in light of existing conditions and projected changes in climate. It is likely that there will be substantial losses of coastal marshes in the future.

Approximately 90% of the nation's sandy beaches are experiencing erosion (Leatherman 1989). Historical shoreline studies indicate a wide range in erosion rates (May et al. 1983). The Atlantic coast average is between 0.6 and 1 m of beach erosion per year. The Gulf coast exceeds 1.6 m per year due mostly to local subsidence. The Pacific coast is stable on average due to local tectonic uplift. These spatial variations in erosion rates are due to site-specific conditions

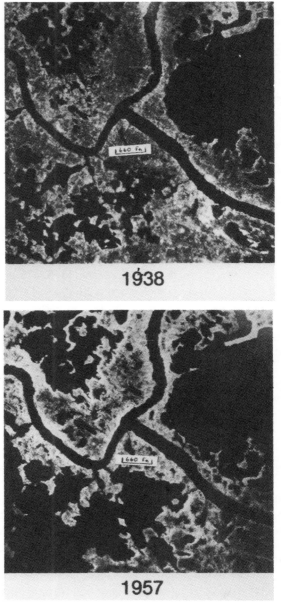

Fig. 10.2. Juncture of Big and Little Blackwater Rivers, Dorchester County, Maryland. Successive marsh loss in the Chesapeake Bay, Cambridge, Maryland (courtesy of Dr. C. Stevenson).

1964

1972

Fig. 10.2. Continued

177

Fig. 10.3. Beach erosion at Ocean City, Maryland draws the buildings closer to the water's edge.

such as energy conditions, sediment types, tectonic activity, and rates of relative sea-level rise.

Three general categories of human responses to shoreline recession are to retreat from the shore, armor the coast, or nourish the beach. The proper response is site-specific depending on a number of socioeconomic and environmental factors. Costs and benefits of stabilization or retreat must be carefully considered because the cost in either case is likely to be quite high.

The apparent national desire to live in the coastal zone has long-term and expensive consequences. The federally insured flood program is already burdened with billions of dollars of insured properties close to the water's edge. Accelerated sea-level rise due to the greenhouse effect will further jeopardize these vulnerable properties, eventually resulting in massive destruction (without ameliorating action) during future major storms at great expense to the American taxpayer.

Acknowledgments

This research was supported by the U.S Environmental Protection Agency. Ms. Rachel Donham utilized the author's earlier work and added some additional material to constitute this chapter. Her assistance is greatly appreciated.

References

Bird, E. C. F. 1976. Shoreline changes during the past century. In *Proceedings of the 23rd International Geographical Congress, Moscow*. Pergamon, Elmsford, NY.

Bird, E. C. F. 1985. *Coastline Changes—A Global Review*. Wiley–Interscience, New York.

Braatz, B. V. and D. G. Aubrey. 1987. Recent relative sea-level change in eastern North America. In *Sea Level Fluctuation and Coastal Evolution*, Special Publication No. 41, D. Nummedal, O. Pilkey, and J. Howard (eds.), pp. 29–26. The Society of Economic Paleontologists and Mineralogists, Tulsa, OK.

DeLaune, R. D., R. H. Baumann, and J. G. Gosselink. 1983. Relationships among vertical accretion, coastal submergence, and erosion in a Louisiana Gulf Coast marsh. *J. Sedimentary Petrol.* 53:147–157.

Hoffman, J. S., D. Keyes, and J. G. Titus. 1983. *Projecting Future Sea-Level Rise: Methodology, Estimates to the Year 2100, and Research Needs*. Environmental Protection Agency, Washington, DC.

Gornitz, V. and S. Lebedeff. 1987. Global sea level changes during the past century. In *Sea Level Fluctuation and Coastal Evolution*, Special Publication No. 41, D. Nummedal, O. Pilkey, and J. Howard (eds.), pp. 3–16. The Society of Economic Paleontologists and Mineralogists, Tulsa, OK.

Jones, P. D., S. C. B. Raper, R. S. Bradley, H. F. Diaz, P. M. Kelley, and T. M. L. Wigley. 1986. Northern Hemisphere surface air temperature variations 1851–1984. *J. Climate Appl. Meteorol.* 10:12–19.

Leatherman, S. P. 1983. Shoreline mapping: A comparison of techniques. *Shore Beach* 51:28–33.

Leatherman, S. P. 1984. Shoreline evolution of North Assateague Island, Maryland. *Shore Beach* 52:3–10.

Leatherman, S. P. 1989. Impact of accelerated sea-level rise on beaches and coastal wetlands. In *Global Climate Change Linkages*, J. C. White (ed.), pp. 43–57. Elsevier Science Publishing, New York.

May, S. K., R. Dolan, and B. P. Hayden. 1983. Erosion of U.S. shorelines. *EOS* 64:551–552.

Meier, M. F. 1990. Reduced rise in sea level. *Nature* 343:115–116.

Orson, R., W. Penageotou, and S. P. Leatherman. 1985. Response of tidal salt marshes of the U.S. Atlantic and Gulf coasts to rising sea levels. *J. Coastal Res.* 1:29–37.

Redfield, A. C. 1972. Development of a New England salt marsh. *Ecol. Monogr.* 42:201–237.

Stevenson, J. C., L. G. Ward, and M. S. Kearney. 1986. Vertical accretion in marshes with varying rates of sea-level rise. In *Estuarine Variability*, D. A. Wolfe (ed.), pp. 241–260. Academic Press, New York.

Wells, J. T. and J. M. Coleman. 1987. Wetland loss and the subdelta life cycle. *Estuarine Coastal Shelf Sci.* 25:111–125.

11

The Nexus of Agriculture, Environment, and the Economy Under Climate Change

Daniel J. Dudek

Introduction

Agriculture is a critical part of most nations' economies. It is also the economic sector most directly affected by climate and weather. Poor harvests in 1987 and 1988, due in part to severe regional droughts, have slimmed global grain stocks, raised prices, and raised fears about increasing world hunger. These events validate the focus of many studies of the impact of climate change on agricultural systems (e.g., Parry et al. 1988).

However, little attention has been focused on the interface between agricultural and natural resource systems under a changing climate. Agriculture, because it is a primary extractive industry transforming mineral and biological resources into food and fiber, directly affects both the quantity and quality of land, water, biological, and atmospheric resources. Of particular concern are impacts on water resources and wildlife habitat.

I address resource-use conflicts against the background of expected agricultural responses to a changing climate. The intent is to present the interrelationships between agriculture, the environment, and the economy (Fig. 11.1). I begin with a discussion of the effects of environmental factors on agriculture and of agricultural operations on environmental systems. Land development and the pollution produced from agricultural operations typify this set of interactions. Beyond the farmgate, the success of agriculture is important for the performance of most economies. How may changes in agriculture driven by a changing climate reverberate throughout the economy? Lastly, changes in the economic system at large will also feedback to the agricultural sector. Recent experiences in the United States with inflation and farm debt are potent reminders of the power of such forces. The effects of industrial pollution, tropospheric ozone for example, are also important for agriculture and complete the circle.

How the Environment Affects Agriculture

The impacts of a changing climate on agricultural systems have been described by Decker et al. (1986) and Warrick et al. (1986). These impacts range from the

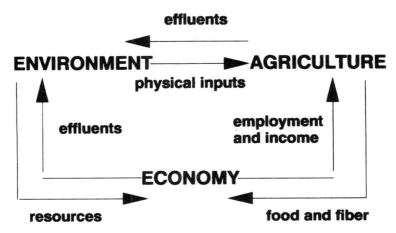

Fig. 11.1. Interrelationships among agriculture, the environment, and the economy.

well-publicized fertilization effect of increased atmospheric CO_2 concentrations, to increased temperature stress, to changes in soil moisture (Manabe and Wetherald 1986), changes in annual as well as seasonal precipitation patterns, and altered pest conditions. Each of these physical impacts can be translated into expected yield effects and farm income changes. Whereas the specific impacts vary by location and crop, there are several general possibilities for adjustment by farmers in response to these climate-driven changes: substitute crop varieties, substitute crop enterprises, use additional inputs, and change location.

Each of these options will affect income. By arraying the changes in the relative profitability of combinations of crops and resources, we can assess the likely nature and direction of response. In nations with abundant land and water resources and with market-oriented economies, the tendency over time will be to change regional cropping patterns and resource-use patterns.

In market-based economies, agriculture is a highly competitive industry where all producers vie for a share of the market. Productivity, cost, and profitability changes affect supply response, that is, the quantity of output produced for market under any expected price. For any given demand, aggregated to include both domestic and foreign buyers, changes in supply result in changes in equilibrium prices, which in turn affect revenues and profitability. Production decisions in the next crop year are then affected by these price changes because they affect farmer's expectations about the future. Finally, these yearly production decisions, in turn, affect the use of land, water, and environmental resources. These decisions drive spatial cropping changes within the many regional agricultural optimization models typically used to assess the impacts of exogenous shocks. As such, the analytic approach is a direct conceptual extension of Parry's work (1985) on agricultural margins to simultaneously consider the impact and effect on all production regions' margins.

A recent example of the application of one such model is a study of climate change implications for western United States agriculture (Adams et al. 1988). Overall, the study found that crop production under $2 \times CO_2$ climate conditions was generally lower, whereas prices were higher. However, substantial additional land and water resources were required to produce this reduced level of agricultural output. Within the southern United States over 3 million additional acres were brought into production, a 4% increase. Another 1.8 million acre-feet of water was required for irrigation, a 13% increase. The spatial shifts of production and resource use among the individual regions were more dramatic than the aggregate results reveal. Figure 11.2 illustrates the degree of regional variation in terms of estimated changes in irrigation water use.

Depending upon future technologic advances, export market conditions, and the nature of adaptive responses, actual costs to the agricultural sector could be significantly different. For example, if water-marketing institutions evolve, then the economic and environmental damages associated with increased competition for water supplies will be modulated (Dudek 1988). If biotechnology significantly alters the productive potential of crops, then significantly fewer resources will be required to meet demand. However, since the transient path of the economic system to that doubled CO_2 condition is not known, it is not possible to estimate the average annual cost to agriculture from a changing climate. Nonetheless, simulations of system responses under sets of assumptions about the future, that is, alternative scenarios, will remain one of the primary methodologies for evaluating possible impacts. A recent compendium of such studies is included in the EPA report to Congress on the effects of climate change (Smith and Tirpak 1988).

Other than directly competing for soil and water resources that would otherwise be used by natural ecosystems, agricultural operations also generate significant pollution. Primary examples are chemical residues from pesticide, herbicide, or fertilizer applications and erosion and sedimentation. Recent examples of the powerful effects such discharges can have on natural systems include the waterfowl and fish poisoning incidents at the Kesterson and Stillwater National Wildlife Refuges in California and Nevada, respectively (Harris and Morris 1985). In each of these regions, agricultural water carrying chemical residues and trace elements leached from the soil profile were collected for use as waterfowl habitat during periods of high flow. In justifying this project, the United States Bureau of Reclamation claimed that Kesterson would provide waterfowl habitat. Unbeknownst to the facility designers, selenium in the drain waters caused reproductive failure in the ducks.

As agriculture adjusts spatially to a changing climate, land and water resources will be developed and environmental costs incurred. Regions not currently profitable for exploitation may come under the plow. These regions will be subjected

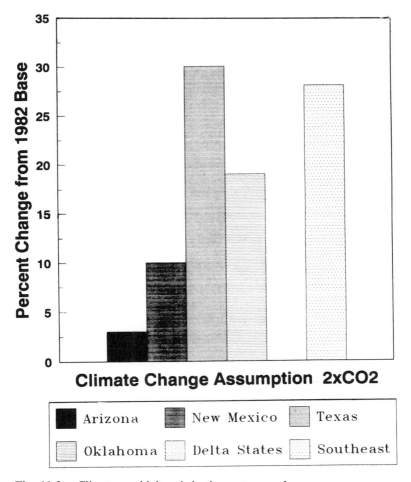

Fig. 11.2. Climate sensitivity—irrigation water use changes.

to agricultural pollution with resulting degradation and/or destruction of adjacent natural ecosystems. Thus, climate change will exacerbate the existing public demand for increased environmental expenditures to compensate for increased resource degradation (impaired or reduced productivity). The result can be more draconian control of the economy by regulators. For example, the initial government reaction to discovery of the Kesterson contamination was to refuse additional agricultural drainage discharges, effectively shutting down irrigated agricultural operations. In turn, this can produce increased stress for agricultural production systems and a drag on the economy. In general, adjustments will be expensive and run counter to the efforts to remove agricultural subsidies. Agriculture is a large and entrenched constituency whose traditional response to increased costs has been to demand public funds.

Adjustments in agricultural systems caused by climate change will reverberate back into the economy creating a set of indirect effects. In developing economies relying upon an agricultural base to fuel economic development, these linkages are critical. Climate changes in these circumstances have the capacity to transform surpluses into deficits.

Atmospheric Pollutants

The resource endowment of a region, its soils, climate, and water, are primary determinants of the success of any agricultural endeavor. Much of the existing climate impact literature focuses on the effects of temperature, precipitation, and CO_2 changes on crop productivity (Rosenzweig 1986). However, these are not likely to be the only changes occurring. For example, the problem of acid deposition has forced us to recognize that pollutants can cause damages over wide regions. Ozone, acid deposition, and its precursors each affect crop productivity. Since each of these pollutants is linked with fossil fuel use, the intensity of their respective loadings is likely to vary with factors influencing fossil fuel use, including policies that may be instituted to manage climate change.

Analyzing the response of a dynamic agricultural economy to a changing climate also requires an understanding of how the total environment will change. Will fossil fuel use and availability increase or decrease? Where? When will acid deposition be controlled? To what extent? Failure to control environmental problems of this type will mean yield losses to agriculture. However, yield losses do not always translate into income losses for agricultural producers. The critical relationship is that between the reduction in output and the increase in product price due to reduced supply. In a recent review of pollution impact studies for agriculture, Adams and Crocker (1987) pointed out that increasing air pollution causes increasing reductions in economic welfare, but that most of these costs are borne by consumers who face higher food and fiber prices. One important and counterintuitive result they describe is that competition for scarce land and water resources can lead to reductions in the acreages of pollution-tolerant crops, if they are less profitable than pollution-sensitive types.

Any source of productivity loss, particularly uncompensated losses due to industrial pollution, intensifies the demand for environmental resources for agricultural production. However, it is critical to remember that these changes may be highly different spatially. There will be regional gainers and losers. If, for example, agricultural operations are profitable, but productivity declines due to pollution, then more land and water resources will be brought into production. Such land-use changes necessarily involve environmental resources, either directly as raw inputs or indirectly when used as a waste repository. To the extent that agricultural adjustment to a changing climate involves either relocation or the development of additional resources, these adjustments will be exacerbated by the negative effects of air pollution.

Other global problems, such as stratospheric ozone depletion from the release of chlorofluorocarbons into the atmosphere, will also worsen the damage from climate change. Although field data are scanty, Teramura (1986) has estimated that a 25% ozone depletion (simulated by increasing damaging UV-B radiation in his experiment; UV-B is that portion of the U.V. spectrum that causes tissue damage) resulted in up to 20% yield declines. Even though Teramura's three season experiment involved only a single variety of soybeans, over two-thirds of the crop cultivars tested have exhibited UV-B sensitivity. In addition, this research indicates that subtle changes involving the quality of yield are also occurring. Reductions in both oil and protein content were noted during these field trials. Qualitative yield changes are important since they affect pricing. Using the dose-response relations developed by Heck et al. (1983), Dudek (1986) estimated yield reductions for corn, wheat, cotton, and soybeans under alternative stratospheric ozone changes. For total column ozone depletions of roughly 5%, yield declines ranged from approximately 1% for wheat to over 3% for cotton. Differential sensitivity could also affect the competitive balance between crop and new species with implications for chemical use, productivity, and profitability.

Gery and Whitten (unpublished manuscript) focused on the role of increased UV-B in the photochemistry of tropospheric ozone production. In a computer simulation, the temperature increases resulted in linear increases in ozone and hydrogen peroxide and decreases in peroxyacetyl nitrates. Increased ultraviolet irradiance would stimulate photochemical oxidation with the result that ozone concentrations would peak earlier in the day and be dispersed over a wider distance. However, these effects are not limited to urban areas. To date some of the most significant damages associated with increasing ambient ozone concentrations have occurred in rural agricultural areas. As described by Garcia et al. (1986), yield reductions have already produced economic damage estimated between $700 million and $2 billion annually. Increases in the ambient concentration of ozone in rural areas would obviously increase the extent of these damages.

Climate Change Effects on Agriculture

The dependence of agriculture upon water resource supplies is obvious in arid regions; however, this linkage is equally critical in dryland farming systems. Midcontinental reductions in soil moisture have been predicted by most simulations of future climates. One possible response to such reductions is the increased use of supplemental irrigation, an increasingly common practice in many humid agricultural regions in the United States. Currently, supplemental irrigation demands are satisfied by direct withdrawals or by groundwater pumping. Increasing the levels of such withdrawals or the construction of dams to increase supplies will alter the in-stream flow patterns, quantities, and temperatures upon which aquatic ecosystems depend. It is well known that relatively small changes in precipitation can have major consequences for streamflow (Karl and Riebsame unpublished data). In the extreme, a 10% reduction in precipitation can reduce streamflow by 50%. Precipitation and run-off changes also have major implications for groundwater recharge and overdraft.

For existing irrigation projects, the impact of changes in precipitation and run-off can be severe. Dracup (1987) has observed that, in the United States, planning for climate change among water-resource managers is nonexistent. As with most long-term planning, the future is imagined to be a perfect clone of the past. Introducing scenarios of climate change into water resource planning is no environmental panacea, however. As Dracup notes, climate change considerations in water-resources planning would likely be manifested as an increase in uncertainty. This increased uncertainty could result in increasing the safety margins for project designs, thus increasing the size of projects and their environmental impact (Klemes 1983). The impact of climate change upon water resources will be a key determinant of the nature and direction of agricultural adjustments. However, substantial evidence has accumulated that large-scale water-resource development projects inherently involve substantial environmental trade-offs (Krutilla and Fisher 1975). Many contemporary environmental conflicts involve the operations of agencies like the United States Bureau of Reclamation in regions where the remaining natural ecosystems are scarce or irreplaceable. Competition for water is likely to increase and in-stream uses will likely suffer.

Crop pests are also important determinants of agricultural profitability, and they greatly impact the environment. Little research has been conducted on the significance of climate change for important pest populations. In one example, Muller and Tucker (1982) discussed field experiments designed to explain corn earworm moth migration across the southwestern United States. This particular pest causes hundreds of millions of dollars of damages annually. They discovered that increased air temperatures are more conducive to moth flight, thus increasing the size of the affected crop region.

Climate changes can be expected to affect the normally strong interaction between climate, pest appearance, and crop damages. Examples of this interaction include the mildew responsible for the Irish potato famine, the southern corn leaf blight, and locusts and grasshoppers (Waggoner 1983). Other possible implications of climate change for pest populations include expanded high-latitude ranges for those pests currently limited by cold temperatures, changes in distribution of wind-borne pests with changes in atmospheric circulation patterns, and potential increases in the number of reproductive cycles. If any of these changes result in increased crop losses, all other negative agricultural impacts will be exacerbated. Of particular importance would be the increased demand for land and water resources to compensate for any widespread losses and the increased use of agricultural chemicals, a primary source of environmental degradation.

Concern with the environmental impacts of agricultural operations has prompted many governments to adopt policies to limit such impacts. Frequently, these policies restrict the choice of production practice, limit the use of particular inputs, or control the timing of operations. Common examples include pesticide restrictions, manure disposal regulations, and erosion control policies. Depending upon the policy chosen, crop productivity and/or profitability is often negatively affected. As with many policies, there are trade-offs between competing objectives. For example, the no till policy was developed to reduce the amount of land lost to soil erosion; however it has increased agricultural chemical use and therefore the impacts on groundwater and other environmental resources. As environmental problems are worsened by a changing climate, we can expect a tightening of rules controlling agricultural operations. Increased environmental regulation will also change the location, amount, and intensity of resource use and pollutant loadings.

Agricultural Impacts on Natural Ecosystems

Agriculture is not only a victim, but a primary contributor to environmental stresses. Methane from livestock and rice paddies, carbon dioxide from fossil fuel use and deforestation, nitrous oxide from fertilizer use and land conversion, chlorofluorocarbons used in food storage and processing all contribute to global atmospheric change. More commonly studied are the direct effects of agricultural operations on local or regional terrestrial and aquatic ecosystems. Ironically, some of the government programs designed to reduce these environmental impacts may exacerbate concerns for the adequacy of food supplies under a changed climate. For example, the United States has embarked on an ambitious program to retire approximately 10% of its cropland from production in an effort to reduce soil erosion. Dudek (1988b) has suggested that the Conservation Reserve Program could be used to increase the uptake of CO_2, if incentives for tree planting were strengthened.

Nonpoint Source Pollution

Agricultural impacts on natural ecosystems result both from the exploitation of land and water resources for agricultural operations and from the discharge of pollutants. Of particular concern are the contributions of agriculture to groundwater contamination, lake eutrophication, estuarine pollution, and sedimentation. Nonpoint source (NPS) pollution from agricultural production has long been recognized as a significant source of water pollution within the United States (US General Accounting Office 1978). It is widely acknowledged that further progress in improving surface water quality will depend upon the success of efforts to manage nonpoint sources of pollution (Smith et al. 1987). Humenik et al. (1987) declare that

"NPS pollution is often the limiting factor in improving or maintaining water quality, thus point source control without corresponding NPS pollution control generally will be insufficient. Agricultural pollution is clearly identified as the principal NPS concern nationwide."

Initial regulatory efforts, most notably the mid-1970s Rural Clean Water Program, attempted to overlay the technology-based control approach favored for point sources on agricultural production practices. Regulators would prescribe a set of "best management practices," which farmers would be induced to employ through direct subsidies and cross-compliance requirements (i.e., farm operator cannot receive government support payments of any kind unless they comply by adopting pollution-control methods).

The regulatory approach to nonpoint pollution control has not produced dramatic success. In large measure, the failure of this policy is rooted in the institutions developed to manage resources important to agriculture as much as in the fallacy that remote bureaucrats can divine production techniques that are economically viable for diverse agricultural enterprises. For example, in arid regions, the rules governing water allocation and use are the most important determinant of the extent of NPS pollution. In much of the western United States, water is allocated via long-term contracts featuring subsidized costs. The result is that contract holders have no incentive to use water efficiently. In general, water markets do not exist to provide growers with the alternative opportunity of selling or leasing their water entitlement to a user willing to pay more than the grower could earn by irrigating. Effectively, then, the grower's decision is one of "use it or lose it" since a normal requirement of maintaining the legal water entitlement is beneficial use. Most of the pollution generated by irrigated agricultural operations is transported by return flows; thus the efficiency of water use and management is critical. Dudek and Horner (1982) have estimated that irrigation return flows could be reduced by over 30% with the profitable adoption of existing technology such as tailwater-recycling systems and irrigation scheduling.

Sediment and Erosion. Nonpoint source pollution encompasses a wide spectrum of chemicals, processes, and effects. Common examples are erosion and sedimentation, salinity, pesticide and herbicide residues, nutrients, trace elements, and rising water tables. Erosion and sedimentation, particularly from dryland agriculture, are a major source of water-quality problems. Sedimentation destroys fertile anadromous fish spawning beds, reduces the useful capacity of water impoundments, and provides a vehicle for the transport of agricultural chemical residues. The process of erosion raises questions about long-term productivity of soils and sustainability of agricultural operations. Only recently has agricultural productivity research attempted to estimate the effect of erosion upon crop productivity (Williams and Renard 1985).

Estimates of the magnitude of sediment and related chemical damages to aquatic ecosystems are hampered by the lack of consistent and reliable economic methodologies. However, Clark et al. (1985), believed that the hydrologic impacts of soil erosion and related nutrients is as high as $3.5 billion annually in the United States. Surveys of aquatic ecosystems indicate that fish communities in 81% of rivers and streams are already affected. Most of these effects are due to NPS pollution (Judy et al. 1984). Agricultural run-off is estimated to chronically affect approximately 30% of the nation's stream miles.

The magnitude of environmental impacts of sediment and erosion under a changing climate will depend upon the extent of spatial adjustment by agriculture, the nature of the soils that are in production, any differences in the intensity of rainfall, and the mix of production practices employed. As with many physical processes, erosion and sedimentation may not exhibit linear responses to control actions or changes in agricultural production intensity. One confounding effect is the sediment balance in individual rivers and streams. Upstream sediment discharges from farms may decline, but downstream delivery may be constant due to the pickup of previously stored sediments in streambeds. Thus, as agricultural spatially adjusts, the spatial distribution of sediment loads will also shift, but it will shift more slowly. In the transition, the net effect could be substantial increases in erosion and resulting sediment loads.

As previously indicated, policy responses to these environmental problems will also affect their future magnitude. For example, the United States is currently pursuing a Conservation Reserve Program under its national farm legislation, which provides direct payments to growers willing to retire highly erodible soils. A total of 40–45 million acres are expected to be retired under the 10-year program. In part, the future success of such programs will depend upon their ability to retain the land resources targeted as agriculture adjusts under changing climatic conditions.

Nutrients. Nutrient-induced algal growth is one of the most severe water-quality impacts associated with agricultural operations. Algal blooms affect the distribution of sunlight and contribute significantly to reductions in dissolved oxygen and changes in the quantity and quality of aquatic species present. Nitrates and phosphates also cause lake eutrophication. Nitrate contamination of groundwater is a separate concern for infants, because high concentrations interfere with the oxygen carrying capacity of red blood cells.

Since agricultural chemicals occur in run-off, management has been an adjunct of the more traditional concern of soil conservation. Focusing on soil loss rather than on chemical loading can result in increases of soluble chemical deliveries to streams even though soil loss is substantially reduced. Thus, conservation tillage programs may make no contribution to solving the eutrophication problem since soluble phosphorous loads can be increased. Therefore, as sediment loads and turbidity decline, algal growths may increase with resulting damage to aquatic ecosystems and valuable fisheries. Also, if rainfall intensity is high after the application of chemicals, losses and concentrations of chemical residues in runoff would be increased (Hallberg 1986). Many of the practices to reduce runoff involve techniques to increase rainfall infiltration into the soil profile; therefore the risk of chemical contaminant transport into groundwater is increased.

The pattern of total phosphorous loadings for the nation followed the pattern of sediment loads (Smith et al. 1987). Significantly correlated with these patterns were fertilized acreage and livestock population density. This same evaluation found total nitrate deliveries to Atlantic coast estuaries, the Great Lakes, and the Gulf of Mexico to have increased by 20–50% in the last two decades. The pattern of nitrate changes were strongly associated with the percentage area fertilized within a hydrologic basin, livestock density, and feedlot activities.

Studies of shallow freshwater aquifers reported by Hallberg indicated that unfertilized conditions showed approximately 2 mg/1 of NO_3-N, whereas, in aquifers underlying agricultural operations, 5 mg/1 is common and observations have ranged over 100 mg/1. In the United States, the Environmental Protection Agency has set the maximum contaminant level for NO_3-N as 10 mg/1. Some areas, Nebraska, for example, have exhibited increases of 1.1 mg/1 per year in NO_3-N concentrations in groundwater under fertilized and irrigated areas (Exner and Spaulding 1985). Dudek and Horner (1982) modeled the interrelationship between crop production decisions and groundwater quality over time in the Central Valley of California. They found that changes in location, intensity, and management were important determinants of mass loading as well as spatial distribution. Other researchers (Carey and Lloyd, 1985) have pointed out the potential for long lags in aquifer response to decisions on land use. For example, in England, NO_3 concentrations in groundwater have been increasing for the last 10–20 years. For some regions, these increases are projected to continue for over 40 years due to the slow transit time to the aquifer. The implication is that any spatial adjustments by agriculture to changing climatic conditions will alter the spatial distribution of nutrient loadings. Further, concentrations in currently polluted regions are likely to continue according to the lag in transit time.

Pesticides and Herbicides.   There are over 50,000 pesticide formulations on the market today. Over 661 million lb. of pesticide active ingredients are used in American agriculture each year, of which more than 11 million lb are estimated to run off into surface or groundwater (Gianessi et al. 1986). Both direct toxicity, bioconcentration, and biomagnification are important impacts upon aquatic ecosystems. However, biogeochemical pathways are not as well understood as those that are purely geochemical. Nonetheless, there is a clear implication that pesticide residues in the hydrologic system are on the increase, certainly in terms of persistence, if not concentration as well. We may be seeing the beginning of a trend of ever-increasing occurrence of residues in groundwater in response to prolonged and widespread use, perhaps analogous to the rise of NO_3 a decade ago! (Hallberg, 1986). Chemical applications on corn and soybeans account for over 80% of the herbicides and nearly 60% of the insecticides used on row crops, small grains, and forages in the United States (US Dept. of Agriculture, 1986). Corn will benefit substantially less from the increased atmospheric concentration of CO_2, because it uses the less productive C_4 photosynthetic pathway. In my study of the implications of a doubled CO_2 climate on southern United States agriculture, corn acreage increases ranged from 4% in the Delta States region to 23% in Appalachia. Under the assumption of similar production technologies, such acreage changes would imply large increases in chemical applications and subsequent nonpoint loadings (Dudek 1987).

Salinity and Subsurface Drainage. Salinity and subsurface drainage are ancient problems associated with irrigated agriculture. These problems are believed to have severely afflicted the Tigris and Euphrates river basin over 2000 years ago (Jacobsen and Adams 1958). In arid irrigated regions underlain with impermeable clay strata, irrigation water percolating beyond the root zone accumulates below the surface. When water in this unconfined aquifer eventually rises into the root zone, the water table must be lowered by means of subsurface collector drains to prevent yield losses. It is this collected drain water stored in facilities like Kesterson that has caused damage to migratory birds.

Irrigation water contains dissolved salts, usually positive ions of sodium, calcium, and magnesium and negative ions of chloride and sulfate. The salinity of water is governed by the geologic character of the stratum through which the water flows and by the extent of consumptive processes, such as transpiration and evaporation, which increase concentration. In arid regions, high evapotranspiration rates and limited natural leaching by rainfall result in salinization or the deposition of salts in soil. Management of salinity on farms typically involves the application of additional irrigation water to flush the critical root zone of salts. Irrigation for leaching adds to the extent of the subsurface drainage problem as well.

Salinity damages plants by increasing the osmotic pressure component of total soil moisture stress. Toxic reactions involving specific ions and plants may also occur. Soil salinization of irrigated lands when the salt balance is not maintained results in high salt soil solutions, which reduce yields. Salinity problems require additional irrigation water, drainage, and treatment facilities to sustain long-term agricultural development. To the extent that climate changes increase temperatures and evapotranspiration and alter rainfall patterns, salinity problems will be exacerbated, reducing the quality of downstream habitats and the quantity of undiverted upstream flows. In the extreme, agricultural regions prone to salinity and drainage problems may prove to be uneconomic in the face of such changes.

As agriculture adjusts spatially, new regions will become polluted as more groundwater resources are exposed to contamination. Contaminated groundwater supplies will in turn create additional demand for the development of alternative supplies. Remaining undeveloped surface supply sites will be appropriated with

concomitant reductions in allocations to in-stream uses and the resulting degradation of aquatic habitats. The interconnections in the hydrologic cycle are such
that polluted groundwater may discharge into streams degrading the quality of
surface water supplies as well.

Trace Elements. Trace elements in both surface and groundwater systems
have been of longstanding concern. The recent analysis of trends in water quality
in the United States has identified increasing trends in arsenic and cadmium, two
potentially toxic trace elements, from sources that include atmospheric deposition
from fossil fuel combustion and water-borne pesticide, herbicide, and phosphate
residues from agriculture. Trace and heavy metal contamination of estuarine
systems is receiving increasing attention and is one cause of closure of coastal
shell fisheries (Rader 1988).

Selenium has been found in the subsurface drainage water collected and stored
at Kesterson Reservoir in California. From 1983 to 1985, at least 1,000 migratory
birds died from feeding on the selenium-contaminated food chain at Kesterson.
Reproductive failure among waterfowl at Kesterson triggered nationwide research
into the distribution and effects of selenium contamination throughout the irrigated
West. The United States Department of Interior has initiated a multiyear study
of western national wildlife refuges that will survey wildlife and water for trace
elements and locally important agrichemicals. Initial results indicate selenium levels in San Francisco Bay surf scoters seven times higher than those of more northerly
control groups (US Bureau of Reclamation 1986). Results from experimental feeding of mallards indicate that, even at dose levels below those currently occurring in
food organisms found in Kesterson, selenium interfered with reproduction.

The complete extent of selenium contamination in irrigated regions is not
known, but serious contamination episodes at Stillwater National Wildlife Refuge
in Nevada and at Ouray National Wildlife Refuge in Utah indicate a widespread
problem. Solutions involve treating the drain water from affected soils, immobi-
lizing the existing selenium-laden waters and sediments, and hazing waterfowl
to prevent further damage. Impacts of climate change on agriculture, water
resources, and waterfowl populations will complicate management efforts to
restore the habitats at the Kesterson, Stillwater, and Ouray facilities. Each of
these facilities was specifically constructed to provide habitat in compensation
for loses of natural systems elsewhere. The problems at these refuges should give
us pause when we consider the effectiveness of mitigation for environmental
losses.

Land and Water Resource Development

Fish and wildlife resources are directly affected by the effluents from agricultural operations discharged into the remaining habitat, and the intensity of land
and water resource development to support agriculture primarily determines the

size of that remaining habitat. Consider for example the wetland resources of the United States. In 1850, there were more than 50 million ha of wetlands. By 1980, the National Academy of Sciences (1982) estimated that only 30 million ha remained and that annual losses were 120–240 thousand ha. However, some argue that wildlife stocks in the United States have improved dramatically for many species since the turn of the century (Harrington 1987). Contributing factors include the reforestation of the northeast as agriculture shifted westward and management regulations and public investment in refuges now totaling some 32 million ha. Nonetheless, annual waterfowl harvest limits are determined by the United States Fish and Wildlife Service on the basis of the areal extent of potholes available for breeding in the prairie pothole and Parklands region, an area subject to agricultural development.

Waterfowl provide an excellent case study of the interactions between agriculture and natural ecosystems. The recent results of the joint United States and Canadian 5-year study of the relationships between duck populations and duck hunting regulations provide important insights into the potential effects of interactions between agriculture and waterfowl. During the 5-year period ending with the 1984–1985 season, hunting regulations governing season length and limits were held constant at 1979–1980 levels. Some of the findings from this study were (US Dept. of the Interior 1987):

1. Drought has a strong effect in limiting production
2. Deterioration of habitat quality has reduced population recovery response
3. Increased pond availability does not increase duck use
4. Increased predator losses due to loss of nesting habitat and the concentration of ducks and predators in preserved "islands"

Competition for land and water resources between wildlife and agriculture underlies many of the effects described by this study. Continued irrigation development particularly in the Missouri Basin has fueled conflict between environmentalists, national resource development authorities, and regional economic interests over the fate of the productive prairie pothole breeding region. The Garrison Diversion in North Dakota exemplifies this type of resource use conflict. The scale of the facility and the ultimate number of irrigated acres to be served determine the magnitude of impact upon breeding areas. Under a changing climate, waterfowl could be hard pressed as a result of the possible shifting of the corn and wheat belts into major breeding areas in the Canadian prairies and the "overheating" of areas now used as winter concentration sites (Dudek 1988b). Land use change, water competition, and degraded water quality would all negatively affect waterfowl.

Wild plant and animal species depend on protected areas (e.g., national parks and national wildlife refuges) and may be severely disrupted as climate change causes ecologic change within protected areas and land-use patterns outside those areas prevent "retreat" to other suitable habitats. Reduced rainfall, altered distribution, or changed mix between rain and snow in already arid regions could create pressures for still more water storage to sustain irrigated agriculture. The result would be reduced stream flows and increased damage to the remaining aquatic ecosystems. Regions currently subjected to periodic drought, defined as 1 in 20 years, include California, Arizona, New Mexico, Utah, Nevada, and Texas. Regions that can be expected to become increasingly drought-prone or to suffer potential shortages as a result of overallocation include the Missouri Basin states of Montana, Wyoming, North Dakota, South Dakota, Nebraska, Kansas, Colorado, Minnesota, and Iowa. Expected future increases in demand should raise the relative values of in-stream allocations and thus the magnitude of the damages incurred. Both existing natural systems and the substantial investments made in conservation areas are at risk from climate change.

The resource trade-offs described above are only one limited example of the effects of development upon biological diversity. Other examples include, at one extreme, the reduction in soil microbial activity associated with fertilizer applications and, at the other, tropical deforestation. Cultivar diversity decline around the world prompts concerns about the increased vulnerability of contemporary agricultural production, but the ultimate land development and biodiversity problem is occurring in tropical rainforests.

The mid-to-high latitude regions contain many of the world's developed economies, which act as bankers to the world economy. These developed economies finance the economic development of the less developed countries, the main repositories of the world's tropical forest resources. Interest rate increases, oil price shocks, and other commodity price shifts against a backdrop of poor economic performance in the world economy coupled with questionable loan practices by the developed nations have created circumstances under which debtor nations find that they can no longer service their obligations. This has threatened the solvency of major banking institutions in the developed world, created additional pressure for quick payoff resource exploitation, and prevented more orderly investment in economic development.

There is a possible mutuality of interest between developed and less developed nations that could focus on tropical forests as the nexus between the climate change and debt problems. The first step is to assess the role of tropical forests in the carbon budget of the biosphere. The contribution of tropical forest maintenance to delaying the climate warming could be determined and translated into an economic value to measure the magnitude of damages avoided. These estimates could be compared with the debt service obligations of those nations with significant forest resources. Payment schedules and amounts could be recomputed on the basis of the values of forests to the developed nations. It is not expected that the values estimated will be large enough to offset all outstanding debt obligations. However, it is hoped that they would be sufficiently great to stimulate interest in debt for forest swaps. This kind of intermediate exchange experience could help to lay the foundation for wider trading between nations for the purpose of managing global atmospheric environmental problems.

Interrelations Between Agriculture and the Economy

Direct Effects of Economic Activity on Agriculture

No matter the form of economic system employed by a nation, the fundamental interaction between the economy and agriculture is expressed in prices, in free or black markets, for agricultural produce. Relatively bountiful years lower food bills, whereas a poor harvest can spell disaster and hardship. As indicated earlier, it is this automatic weighing of supply and demand that induces changes in the pattern of agricultural investments and engenders all succeeding impacts.

However, other sectors within the economy are important determinants of the health of the agricultural system. For example, in the rural-urban fringe, the overall level of economic activity determines the demand for land for residential and commercial uses. The conversion of land from agricultural to urban uses is a permanent reduction in the land resource base available for agriculture. To the extent that climate change induces changes in settlement patterns particularly in the densely populated coastal regions from sea level rise, these changes may have negative consequences for the quality of land resources for agriculture. For nations less well-endowed with land than the United States, this could be a serious problem, if not compensated by technologic advances in food production.

International trade is another key ingredient in assessing the impact of climate change. For the United States, modest changes in export demand have the capacity to dramatically alter the quantities of resources employed in agriculture (Horner et al. 1985). From this vantage, export markets have a greater capacity to influence agricultural adjustments and their environmental consequences than climate change. However, the net global effect of climate change on agriculture has not been estimated. Consequently, it is not possible to predict whether the United States and the other developed nations will be net gainers or losers in their agricultural accounts.

International trade in agricultural inputs is also an important source of environmental damages. Chemicals that have been banned in the United States often find markets in nations where environmental protection is lax. Increasingly, successful and environmentally safe pest management involves substantial knowledge and intervention by the grower. Restrictions on pesticide use often involve soils, crop types, timing, and weather conditions. Any of these restrictions may or may not be effectively implemented.

To the extent that the agricultural policies of the developed nations continue to tie agricultural subsidies to the production of commodities, research and development will continue to emphasize more chemically intensive production methods. The potential exists for greater environmental damage from agricultural operations globally as these trends continue. Technologic change is one hallmark of 20th century agriculture, which we can easily assume will continue. Recent developments in the field of biotechnology indicate the potential for radical changes in yield limits, but increasing reliance upon chemical inputs. Achieving the promise of these developments without increasing the level of environmental insult must await both commercialization and field experience. In less developed countries, research into appropriate technology geared to the resources and means of the particular agricultural region may be more significant than capital-intensive production methods.

Throughout this chapter, the role of institutions has been emphasized. The effect of rules governing property, for example, have been described as one source of the environmental damages caused by irrigated agriculture in the western United States. Specifically, irrigators do not currently have the incentive to reduce water use, because their water rates are low and they have no market for the otherwise unused resource. The absence of water markets results in inefficient and environmentally damaging use of resources, including the use of environmental resources as waste repositories. Resource-management institutions, therefore, as they function to measure the "true worth" of a resource, have much to do with the actual realized impact from any climate change. Water is a classic case in point. Agricultural policies are another. In general, policies in the more developed nations have promoted overinvestment in agriculture and consequently overproduction of environmental damage. In the absence of institutional change, climate change impacts will be exacerbated by the defective incentives produced by current institutions.

The crowding out of investment opportunities or other macroeconomic effects are also likely as individual nations adopt expensive policies to mitigate climate change effects. The best analog for this effect is the economic response to the formation of the Organization of Petroleum Exporting Countries (OPEC) and the resulting price shocks. Preventing climate change will mean large new outlays in energy production and pollution control. In the OPEC situation, increased expenditures for oil resulted in a large one-time transfer of wealth between oil consumers and OPEC members, which was subsequently reflected in generally reduced economic activity. Such large economic stresses reverberate throughout the economy, reducing demand and placing great pressure on public treasuries to fund mitigation projects. Public funds for agricultural subsidies will come under increased scrutiny.

Agriculture's Effects on Economic Growth

The economic importance of the agricultural sector to each nation's economy varies. The recent agricultural financial crisis in the United States and its ramifications for rural regions illustrates that even highly diversified economies can feel the effects of agricultural shocks. One significant determinant of the size of national effect is the strategy for and state of economic development. Agricultural and food policies are central features of many development programs. The agricultural sector is frequently called upon to provide an economic surplus, which can be used to fuel more capital-intensive projects, a labor force to man those capital projects, and cheap food to feed growing urban populations. Contemporary manifestations of these development strategies and others are readily seen in the tropical deforestation of Brazil and Indonesia. Climate changes will affect all of these relationships.

As population growth continues, agricultural productivity through technical progress, trade, or increased resource use must keep pace. Each of these choices has liabilities, but most critical in context of environmental concerns is resource development. One of the fastest ways to increase agricultural output in irrigated regions is to increase land under irrigation. Frequently such expansion occurs through the mining of groundwater resources, that is, pumping at levels greater than the rate of aquifer recharge. The usual result of this practice, if sustained, is groundwater overdraft and the loss of scarce water-storage capacity. Many aquifers collapse as they are dewatered with significant reductions in their storage potential. Replacing this lost subsurface capacity with surface projects to support the new increased acreage base is enormously expensive, if feasible. The environmental and health damages associated with large-scale water-resource development projects are sufficiently well-known that they do not bear repeating here. Desertification is another major environmental problem caused by poor resource-management practices, which can be worsened by climate changes.

Issues involving the relationships between resource exploitation and economic development always beg questions concerning intergenerational effects. What kind and quality of resource endowment is being bequeathed to future generations? What is the nature and size of the capital stock? Is the economy healthy or plagued by poor prior decisions? Do contemporary decisions automatically commit future generations to higher levels of environmental expenditures because past generations were unwilling to invest in prevention? Until very recently, one of the arguments used to justify resource-development investments with very long-term benefits involved the use of below-market interest rates. These rates were justified on the grounds that the projects involved were sufficiently meritorious in building long-lived capital that they should be undertaken to improve the quality of bequest to future generations. Only recently have we recognized that the argument is only valid when resource supplies are vast and easily substitutable and when the climate is not changing. For example, as population increases with time, we can expect the demand for outdoor recreation opportunities to expand. Resource-development strategies operate to reduce the diversity of recreational opportunities as well as to reduce their availability. Thus, demand may be rising at the same time that supplies are limited. This may not be the best way to enhance the welfare of future generations.

Summary

This chapter has attempted to portray the diverse interrelationships between agriculture, the environment, and the economy. A particular emphasis has been placed upon describing how climate change might affect each sector and how some of these effects might spill over and cause secondary effects. A central thesis of the paper has been that such secondary effects are crucial to an understanding of the potential consequences of a changing climate and may themselves be enormous. Furthermore, because our knowledge of the current environmental damages from agricultural pollution is so limited, a premium is placed on highlighting these limited implications for natural ecosystems. As always though, policy development must be approached holistically with a view to the entire functioning system if it is to be effective.

References

Adams, R. M. and Crocker, T. D. 1987. The impact of pollution from other sources on agriculture: An assessment and review of the economics. Paper presented for the OECD workshop on the Integration of Environmental Policies with Agricultural Policies, May 11–13, Paris, France.

Adams, R. M., B. A. McCarl, and D. J. Dudek. 1988. Implications of global climate change for western agriculture. *Western J. Agric. Econo.* 13:348–356.

Carey, M. A. and J. W. Lloyd. 1985. Modeling nonpoint sources of nitrate pollution of groundwater in the Great Ouse Chalk, *U. K. J. Hydrol.* 78:83–106.

Clark, E. H. II, J. A. Haverkamp, and W. Chapman. 1985. *Eroding Soils: The Off-Farm Impacts.* The Conservation Foundation, Washington, DC.

Decker, W. L., V. K. Jones, and R. Achutuni. 1986. *The Impact of Climate Change from Increased Atmospheric Carbon Dioxide on American Agriculture.* University of Missouri, Report No. DOE/NBB–0077, St. Louis.

Dracup, A. 1987. Climate change impacts on water resources: Issues and options. Paper presented at the Symposium on Climate Change in the Southern United States: Future Impacts and Present Policy Issues, May 28–29, New Orleans.

Dudek, D. J. 1986. *Stratrospheric Ozone Depletion: The Case for Policy Action.* Environmental Defense Fund, New York.

Dudek, D. J. 1987. The economic implications of climate change for agriculture in the southern United States. Paper presented at the Symposium on Climate Change in the Southern United States: Future Impacts and Present Policy Issues, May 28–29, New Orleans.

Dudek, D. J. 1988a. Climate change impacts upon agricultural resources: A case study of California. In *The Potential Effects of Global Climate Change on the United States,* J. B. Smith and D. A. Tirpak (eds.), pp. 4–33 to 4–37, EPA–230–05–89–0. US Environmental Protection Agency, Washington, DC.

Dudek, D. J. 1988b. Implications of global warming for natural resources. Statement before the House Subcommittee on Water and Power Resources, September 27.

Dudek, D. J. and G. L. Horner. 1982. An integrated physical-economic analysis of irrigated agriculture. *Nonpoint Nitrate Pollution of Municipal Water Supply Sources: Issues of Analysis and*

Control, K. H. Zwirnmann (ed.), pp. 247–299. International Institute of Applied Systems Analysis, Luxemburg, Austria.

Exner, M. E. and R. F. Spaulding. 1985. Groundwater contamination and well construction in southeast Nebraska. *Ground Water* 23:26–34.

Garcia, P., B. L. Dixon, J. W. Mjelde, and R. M. Adams. 1986. Measuring the benefits of environmental change using a duality approach: The case of ozone and Illinois cash grain farms. *J. Environ. Econ. Management* 13:69–80.

Gianessi, L., H. Peskin, and C. A. Puffer. 1986. *A National Data Base of Nonurban-Nonpoint-Source Discharges and Their Effect on the Nation's Water Quality.* Resources for the Future, Washington, DC.

Hallberg, F. R. 1986. Agricultural chemicals and water quality. In *Colloquium on Agrichemical Management to Protect Water Quality,* p. 46. National Academy of Sciences, Washington, DC.

Harrington, W. 1987. *The State of Wildlife Resources.* Resources for the Future, Washington, DC.

Harris, T. and J. Morris. 1985. Toxic chemical threatens west. *Sacramento Bee,* September 8, 1985.

Heck, W. W., R. Adams, W. Cure, A. Heagle, H. Heggestad, R. Kohut, L. Kress, J. Rawlings, and O. Taylor. 1983. A reassessment of crop loss from ozone. *Environ. Sci. Technol.* 17:573A–581A.

Horner, G. L., S. Putler, and S. E. Garifo. 1985. *The Role of Irrigated Agriculture in a Changing Export Market,* ERS Staff Report AGES850328. Economic Research Service, US Dept. Agriculture, Washington, DC.

Humenik, F. J., M. D. Smolen, and S. A. Dressing. 1987. Pollution from nonpoint sources. *Environ. Sci. Technol.* 21:737–742.

Jacobsen, T. and R. M. Adams. 1958. Salt and silt in ancient Mesopotamian agriculture. *Science* 128:1251–1258.

Judy, R. D., P. N. Seeley, T. Murray, S. C. Svirsky, M. R. Whitworth, and L. S. Ischinger. 1984. *1982 Fisheries Survey, Vol. I, Technical Report: Initial Findings,* Report No. FWS/OBS-84/06. US Fish and Wildlife Service, Dept. of the Interior, Washington, DC.

Klemes, V. 1983. Climatic change and the planning of water resource systems. In *Proceedings of Sixth Canadian Hydrotechnical Conference of the Hydrotechnical Division of the Canadian Society of Civil Engineering,* Ottawa, pp. 485–500.

Krutilla, J. V. and A. C. Fisher. 1975. *The Economics of Natural Environments: Studies in the Valuation of Commodity and Amenity Resources.* Johns Hopkins Press, Baltimore.

Manabe, S. and R. T. Wetherald. 1986. Reduction in summer soil wetness induced by an increase in carbon dioxide. *Science* 232:626–627.

Muller, R. A. and N. L. Tucker. 1982. Climatic opportunities for the long-range migration of moths. In *Long-Range Migration of Moths of Agronomic Importance to the United States and Canada: Specific Examples of Occurrence and Synoptic Weather Patterns Conducive to Migration,* A. N. Sparks (ed.), pp. 1–104. Proceedings of the Symposium of the Entomological Societies of America and Canada. Entomological Society of America, Lanham, MD.

National Academy of Sciences. 1982. *Impacts of Emerging Trends on Fish and Wildlife Habitat.* Washington, DC.

Parry, M. S. 1985. The impact of climate variations on agriculture margins. *Climate Impact Assessment: Studies of the Interaction of Climate and Society, Scope 27,* R. W. Kates, J. H. Ausubel and M. Berberian (eds.), pp. 351–367. John Wiley, New York.

Parry, M. S., T. R. Carter, and N. T. Konijn. 1988. *The Impact of Climatic Variations on Agriculture,*

Volume 1: Assessment in Cool Temperate and Cold Regions. Kluwer Academic Publishers, Norwall, MA.

Rader, D. N. 1988. Albemarle and Pamlico Sounds: Threats and protection strategies, from a working paper for the Albemarle Pamlico Estuarine Study.

Rosenzweig, C. 1986 (October). Potential effects of future climate changes on forests and vegetation, agriculture, water resources, and human health. In *An Assessment of the Risks of Stratospheric Ozone Depletion*, pp. 55–94. US Environmental Protection Agency, Washington, DC.

Smith, J. B. and D. A. Tirpak (eds.). 1988. *The Potential Effects of Global Climate Change on the United States*, Report No. EPA–230–05–89–0##. US Environmental Protection Agency, Washington, DC.

Smith, A., R. B. Alexander and M. Wolman. 1987. Water trends in the nation's rivers. *Science* 27:1607–1615.

Teramura, A. H. 1986. The potential consequences of ozone depletion upon global agriculture. In *Effects of Changes in Stratospheric Ozone and Global Climate, Vol. 2: Stratospheric Ozone*. J. G. Titus (ed.), pp. 255–262. US Environmental Protection Agency and United Nations Environmental Programme, Washington, DC.

US Bureau of Reclamation. 1986. *San Joaquin Valley Drainage Program*, Status Report 5, Sacramento, CA.

US Department of Agriculture. 1986. *1986 Agricultural Chartbook*, Agriculture Handbook No. 663. US Dept. of Agriculture, Washington, DC.

US General Accounting Office. 1978. *Water Quality Management Planning Is Not Comprehensive and May Not Be Effective for Many Years*, Comptroller General's Report to the Subcommittee on Investigations and Review. Committee on Public Works and Transportation, House of Representatives, December 11, Washington, DC.

US Dept. of the Interior. 1987. U.S. and Canada release preliminary findings of study on stabilized duck hunting regulations. *Fish and Wildlife Service News Release*, May 29. US Department of the Interior, Washington, DC.

Waggoner, P. E. 1983. Agriculture and a climate changed by more carbon dioxide. In *Changing Climate*, pp. 383–418. National Academy of Sciences, Washington, DC.

Warrick, R. A., R. M. Gifford, and M. L. Parry. 1986. CO_2, climatic change and agriculture: Assessing the response of food crops to the direct effects of increased CO_2 and climate change. In *The Greenhouse Effect, Climate Change, and Ecosystems, SCOPE 29*, B. Bolin, B. R. Doos, J. Jaeger, and R. A. Warrick (eds.), pp. 393–473. Wiley and Sons, New York.

Williams, J. R. and K. G. Renard. 1985. Assessments of soil erosion and crop productivity with process models (EPIC). In *Soil Erosion and Crop Productivity*, R. G. Follett and B. A. Steward (eds.), pp. 68–102. American Society of Agronomy, Madison, WI.

12

Global Climate Change: Potential Impacts on Public Health

Janice Longstreth

Introduction

The consequences of global climate change include impacts due to stratospheric ozone depletion and global warming. These two phenomena and their associated health effects are somewhat different, in that the effects of ozone depletion are reasonably direct and can therefore be evaluated semiquantitatively, whereas the potential effects of global warming are more indirect and can only be estimated qualitatively. I first deal with the two phenomena separately and then discuss how the two may intersect with regard to human health effects. A more detailed review of this information is presented in the health effects chapters which I prepared for two reports by the Environmental Protection Agency (1987, 1989, Longstreth 1989).

Stratospheric Ozone Depletion

The stratospheric ozone layer acts as a protective shield, preventing much of the sun's ultraviolet radiation (UVR) from hitting the earth. This protection is somewhat selective because the shorter wavelengths of UVR are absorbed preferentially. The shortest wavelength region of UVR is 200–290 nm and is termed UV-C; virtually all of it is absorbed by the ozone layer. UV-B, 290–320 nm, is only partially absorbed, and UV-A, 320–400 nm, is not absorbed at all. With depletion of the ozone layer, more UV-B will reach the earth, whereas the amount of UV-A will remain unchanged and UV-C is still expected to be completely absorbed. Of the UV-B and UV-A that reaches the earth, UV-B has the most biological activity per unit of energy. Irradiation with UV-B has been shown to cause cancer in animals and is also responsible for skin cancer and to some degree, cataracts in humans. In addition, UV-B has an adverse effect on the immune system, suppressing the responses to foreign substances that enter the body via the skin. Data from several animal models of infectious diseases suggest that one possible consequence of UV-B-induced immunosuppression is a decrease in the ability of animals to respond to infectious diseases (Environmental Protection Agency 1987).

As a part of an effort to assess the risks of stratospheric ozone depletion, the Environmental Protection Agency (1987) estimated the health risks associated with UV-B increases that would accompany decreases in the ozone layer. Quantitative estimates were developed for risks of skin cancer and cataracts, whereas effects on the immune system could only be addressed qualitatively.

Skin Cancer

Skin cancer is generally divided into two forms on the basis of the cell type affected. Cutaneous melanoma (CM) results from the transformation of melanocytes, the pigment-producing cell of the skin, and nonmelanoma cancer results from the transformation of keratinocytes, the major cell structure. Cutaneous melanoma is the most dangerous form of skin cancer; in the United States, it accounts for approximately 26,000 cases and approximately 7,800 deaths, annually. Over the past 35 years, there has been a 200% increase in incidence and a 150% increase in mortality (National Cancer Institute 1988). Nonmelanoma skin cancer (NMSC), which includes basal and squamous cell carcinoma (BCC and SCC, respectively), is more benign, so benign, in fact, that accurate records of incidence are not maintained. The last attempt to evaluate incidence in a systematic fashion in the United States was a survey performed in the period 1977–1978. This study found that between 400,000 and 500,000 individuals developed NMSC annually; compared to a similar survey performed in 1970–1971, this represented a 15–20% increase in incidence rate (Scotto et al. 1981).

The data linking sunlight and UV exposure to NMSC is reasonably solid and consists of the fact that (1) individuals at highest risk are those who have the greatest sun exposure and the lightest skin (i.e., have the least amount of protective pigment), (2) sites with the most exposure (e.g. face and hands) are at greatest risk, (3) there is a latitude gradient, such that individuals living closer to the equator (and therefore exposed to more UV) have a higher risk, and (4) UV induces NMSC in animals models.

On the basis of dose-response information drawn from the 1978–1979 survey information, the Environmental Protection Administration (1987) estimated that for every 1% increase in UV there would be between a 4 and 6% increase in NMSC depending on the type. A similar range of estimates for BCC and SCC has been calculated on the basis of data from an animal model of NMSC (Van der Leun et al. 1989).

The data linking CM to sunlight exposure has been considered less clear cut than that for NMSC. Although individuals with lighter skin are at greater risk, the sites that receive intermittent exposure show the greatest risk of CM. Individuals affected with the genetic disorder, xeroderma pigmentosa (XP), who have a defect in DNA repair such that they cannot repair UV-induced DNA damage show a 2,000-fold increase in risk of CM. However, those individuals who spend much of their time outdoors are at less risk than individuals who are exposed only on vacations and during occasional recreation exposure. Thus there was some concern as to a relationship between UV and CM. Recently the EPA completed a review of the available data and literature to assess the relationship of CM to UV-B exposure (Longstreth 1987). The salient conclusions were that (1) the older literature, taken in conjunction with some very recent case-control epidemiologic studies, clearly indicated a role for sunlight in the etiology of CM, (2) the active portion of the solar spectrum was most likely to be in the UV-B region based on animal studies implicating UV-B in nonmelanoma etiology and immunosuppression and on the sensitivity of XP patients, and (3) dose-response relationships for incidence and mortality could be estimated such that for every 1% decrease in ozone there would be up to a 2% increase in CM incidence and between 0.3 and 2% increase in CM mortality. Very recent evidence confirms the role of UV-B in CM etiology, in that UV-B has now induced CMs in two animal models, one in fish (Setlow et al. 1989) and one in marsupials (Ley et al. 1989).

Cataracts and Other Eye Diseases

Exposure to UVR has been associated with damage to the cornea, the lens, and the retina, as well as with intraocular melanoma. The best known example of UVR-associated damage to the cornea is "snowblindness," a form of photokeratitis often observed in skiers. Photokeratitis is somewhat like a sunburn of the eye in which the front of the eye, the eyelids, and the skin surrounding the eye become reddened. Unlike the skin which thickens or adds pigment following exposure, the cornea of the eye does not develop a tolerance to exposure. The major form of lenticular damage due to UVR is cataract, a disease in which opacities (cataracts) develop in the lens of the eye. These impair vision and gradually result in blindness as an individual ages unless surgically removed. In the United States and other developed countries, such operations generally prevent most cataracts from causing blindness. Nevertheless, in the United States, cataracts remain the third leading cause of legal blindness (Pitts et al. 1987). Worldwide, senile cataract is responsible for significant visual impairment in 30–45 million people, of which perhaps 12–15 million are blind. Current treatment rates are not keeping pace with incidence. In addition, as the population ages, incidence rates will increase, and thus the problem will continue to grow (Maitchouk 1985).

The exact mechanism of the formation of cataracts is still unknown. Epidemiological studies, laboratory animal studies, and biochemical analysis suggest that some cataracts are related to exposure to UV-B (Environmental Protection Agency 1987). Ultraviolet radiation A and other causes, for example, nutritional deficiency, may also contribute to cataract formation. Recent epidemiologic studies of occupationally exposed individuals have indicated that the incidence of cortical and posterior subcapsular cataracts are associated with cumulative exposure to UV-B (Taylor et al. 1988, Bochow et al. 1989), thus increases in the amount of ambient UV-B radiation due to ozone depletion are likely to increase the incidence of cataracts. Ultraviolet radiation B may also play a role in causing or exacerbating other eye disorders. The Environmental Protection Agency (1987) has estimated, on the basis of epidemiologic data, that for every 1% decrease in stratospheric ozone, there will be between a 0.3 and 0.6% increase in cataracts.

Immunologic Effects

Ultraviolet irradiation of the skin has been shown to induce local (in the skin) and systemic immunosuppression in humans and experimental animals (Kripke 1986). Inactivation of Langerhans cells, the principal antigen-presenting cell (APC) in the skin, is the first impact noted. Antigen-presenting cells are required in the development of cell- or antibody-mediated immune responses (ImRs) (Stingl et al. 1983). In humans, loss of Langerhans cells is accompanied by the migration into the skin of another type of APC, which apparently has a predilection for interacting with a subset of T lymphocytes, which suppress the immune response. These cells are termed suppressor T cells (Ts). With low doses of UVR, the Ts that arise in the skin are specific for antigens administered via that skin and prevent the development of ImRs to such antigens; this is termed local immunosuppression. At high doses of UVR, systemic immunosuppression has been induced experimentally in animals. In a tumor-bearing animal, this immunosuppression may result in the outgrowth of tumor cells, which in normal animals would have been destroyed by the immune system (Kripke and Fisher 1976). Although it is not certain that the damage to the Langerhans cells is entirely responsible for the immunosuppressive effect of UVR, it is clear that UV irradiation of skin reduces the ImR of that skin. Even more important, it is also clear that it is the UV-B portion of the UV spectrum that is responsible for the depression of the ImR.

The immunosuppressive effects of UVR may also have a deleterious effect on the ImR to those infectious diseases that enter through the skin, especially if the initial ImR to the agent takes place in the skin (Fig. 12.1). As yet, little research has been done in this area. Recently published reports indicate, however, that UV irradiation during a first cutaneous infection with two very different organisms, the parasite *Leishmania sp.* and *Herpes simplex* virus, may result in an impairment of the ImR of the host to subsequent infections (Giannini and DeFabo 1987; Perna et al. 1987). In the case of leishmaniasis, this could lead to the development of the more lethal form of the disease, visceral leishmaniasis. There is also some very preliminary evidence that other immune systems, for example, the ImR to malaria, may also be affected by UV-B irradiation (Taylor pers. comm.).

The effects of UV-B and solar radiation on the human immune system have not been studied in sufficient detail to allow estimation of dose-response relation-

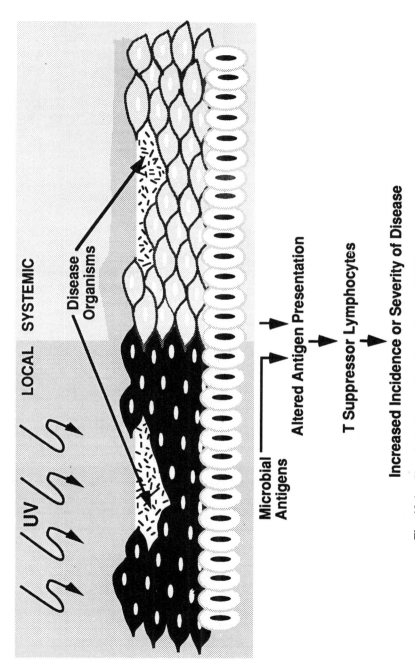

Fig. 12.1. Hypothetical mechanism for an impact of UVR on infectious diseases.

ships for these effects. Qualitatively, it is known from animal studies that the doses of UV-B needed to induce immunosuppression are much lower than those required for carcinogenesis. This may mean that exposure to low doses of UVR, even doses that do not cause a sunburn, may decrease the ability of the human immune system to provide an effective defense against neoplastic skin cells or skin infections. In addition, one theory of the mechanism of the immunosuppression suggests that the active photoreceptor lies above the melanin; if so then all races may be equally at risk for UV-B induced immunosuppression.

Estimates of Risk

The Environmental Protection Agency (1987) has assessed the risks of skin cancer due to ozone depletion with and without the controls of CFC production mandated by implementation of the Montreal Protocol. That analysis (summarized in Fig. 12.2) showed that under the assumptions used, implementation of the Montreal Protocol would have protected the population from the majority of additional skin cancers. However, recent data indicate that the assumptions used in the analysis may have underestimated the current ozone depletion and therefore that the conditions of the Montreal Protocol may not have been stringent enough.

Global Warming

That weather may affect certain diseases has been known since the time of Hippocrates (Kutschenreuter 1959). Seasonality of disease—flu epidemics in winter, measles in fall, and sunburn in summer—is something with which we all learn to live. With global warming one question of concern is whether we can expect to see changes in these disease-weather relationships. The Environmental Protection Agency (1989) asked to address this issue in a *Report to Congress on the Potential Impacts of Climate Change.*

In its request, Congress suggested that the evaluation combine analysis of old information, new studies, and expert advice. In the case of the health effects chapter, this approach was achieved through a review of what is known currently about weather–disease relationships integrated with modeling studies of the impact of potential weather patterns on certain types of diseases. Because it is unknown exactly how global warming will modify weather patterns, the modeling studies evaluated the probable impact of new weather conditions derived from a set of scenarios of future weather.

Health Effects Sensitive to Weather

As a first step in the process of evaluating the potential impacts of global warming on human health, those health effects that showed a relationship to

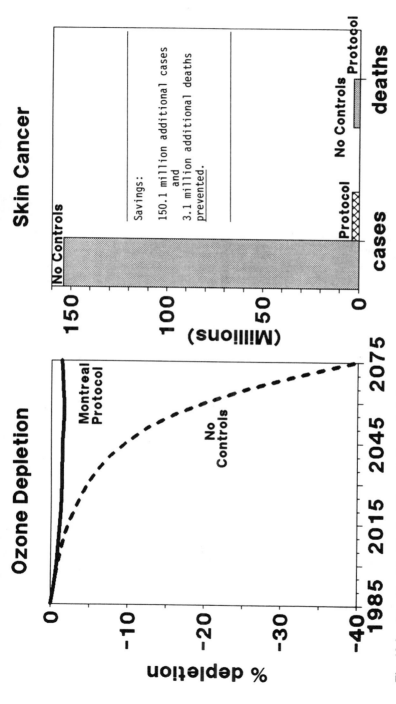

Fig. 12.2. Benefits of the Montreal Protocol. Ozone depletion computed with parameterized 1-D atmospheric model, with baseline growth in CFCs of approximately 2.7%/year. Assumes that 94% of developed and 65% of developing nations join the Protocol. Skin cancer estimates shown for populations born before 2075, based on dose-response models developed for risk assessment. Reprinted from Environmental Protection Agency (1987).

season, temperature, or other weather-related factor were identified, either via review of the literature or via conversations with experts in the field.

A variety of the relationships were identified (Fig. 12.3). They include heat stress, respiratory disease (both as a chronic disease, e.g. obstructive lung diseases, and an infectious disease, e.g. respiratory viruses), allergic disease, vector-borne disease, reproductive effects and to some extent secondary health effects due to compromised nutrition. Note that the *Report to Congress* was limited to effects that might occur within the United States and that the secondary effects due to compromised nutrition will probably not be an issue for United States populations. This is because it is likely that the impacts on agriculture that might occur in the United States, which could be devastating to the less developed countries, could be compensated for by our well-developed distribution system.

Heat stress as an impact of weather has received much attention. Hot weather (indeed temperature extremes in either direction) places additional stress on the circulatory system. This effect is magnified in individuals ill with various diseases. Heat waves thus are often accompanied by increased mortality in individuals with cardiovascular, cerebrovascular, or respiratory disease (Kalkstein, this volume; Rogot and Paget 1976; White and Hertz-Picciotto 1984). Respiratory disease has several links to weather. Not only do heat or cold waves put additional stress on individuals with respiratory disease, but individuals with asthma and chronic respiratory problems are very sensitive to air pollution, which is driven in large part by weather patterns (Grant 1988). In addition, asthmatics and individuals with hay fever respond to allergens, such as pollens and molds, the production of which is driven by humidity, sunshine, and temperature (Lopez and Salvaggio 1983).

Diseases spread to man from insects and arachnids, such as mosquitos and ticks, respectively, are called vector-borne diseases. All such diseases have favored weather patterns; generally the relationships are very complex and depend not only on the response of the disease agent and its vector to temperature, humidity, and light, but also on the response of the surrounding habitat and its animal inhabitants, which serve as intermediate hosts for the vector (Longstreth and Wiseman 1989).

The link between human reproductive effects and weather is far less solid than that between the other effects discussed above. However, in two recent studies of perinatal mortality and preterm birth (Keller and Nugent 1984, Cooperstock and Wolfe 1986), a summertime increase in these adverse effects was seen in two northern locations. One possible explanation is that perinatal infections are also increased during this time period. Further study will be required to determine if the observed seasonality is temperature related. If this were a temperature-related phenomenon, one might expect to see a latitude gradient in this effect in the United States with the warmer southern states showing a higher incidence of these outcomes. The South does have a greater problem with infant mortality, which heretofore has been ascribed to differences in socioeconomic status. Further

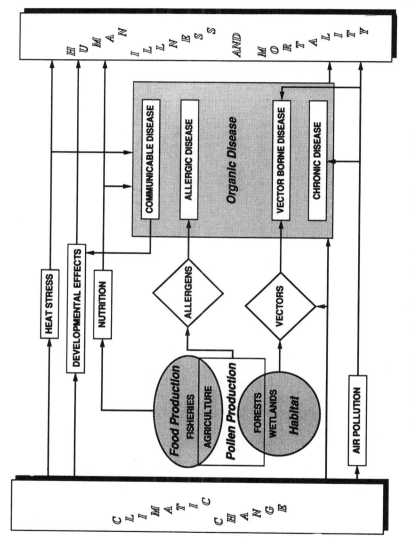

Fig. 12.3. Schematic of how climate may affect human health.

209

study of this issue will be required to determine whether temperature contributes to perinatal mortality or preterm birth.

There is a high probability that climate change will cause disruptions in food production and water supplies. In the United States, most of the potential disruptions envisioned will require some response but will not lead to an impact on nutrition because local shortages can be compensated for by goods from elsewhere around the country. In other countries, however, disruptions of food and water supplies are likely to affect human nutrition, leading to decreased resistance to disease and possibly an increase in epidemics. In addition, water-borne infections may become more of a problem. This impact on other populations may have an indirect effect on the United States via an increased requirement for foreign aid.

Modeling to Evaluate the Impact of Global Warming

The most likely health effects of global warming are increased mortality due to increased temperatures and an increase in mosquito- or tick-borne diseases (should warming provide more favorable conditions for these vectors) (Environmental Protection Agency 1989). To investigate these health effects of global warming, the Environmental Protection Agency commissioned two modeling studies, one on mortality (Kalkstein 1989) and one on vector-borne diseases (Haile 1989). Because there is a large degree of uncertainty with regard to exactly how global warming will affect the climate, scenarios of future change were derived from global scale weather models (general circulation models). The study on mortality evaluated the impact of temperature on mortality for 15 cities, examining how mortality occurring above or below certain critical temperatures (termed threshold temperatures) would change with global warming (Kalkstein 1989, Kalkstein, this volume). Mortality was evaluated either with or without the assumption that populations would acclimatize, and it was concluded that, on a national basis, if the population fails to acclimatize, there would be an increase in summertime mortality and, to a lesser extent, a decrease in winter mortality, or a net increase in mortality. If full acclimatization were to occur, the predicted increases in mortality would be much smaller.

The modeling study of vector-borne disease evaluated the potential impact of future weather on mosquito-borne malaria and tick-borne Rocky Mountain spotted fever (RMSF). The goal of these studies was to determine if there might be parts of the United States that would be more favorable to malaria or RMSF development under scenarios of future weather conditions. Estimates under these conditions were derived for a number of cities. In general, the climate change scenarios used did not result in any great increased potential for malaria or RMSF development. For malaria, the study evaluated the impact of weather not only on the vector but also on the parasite. In the case of Rocky Mountain spotted fever (RMSF), the approach taken was to evaluate whether future weather conditions would be more favorable for the development of the American dog tick, the vector for RMSF. (Previous information indicated that there is a fairly good correlation between the size of the dog tick population and the incidence of RMSF). The models used in both these studies are based on existing information about the importance of weather parameters (e.g., rainfall and temperature) on the development and life cycle of the vectors and, in the case of the malaria model, the parasite. One limitation of this study was that it held constant both the density of the intermediate host populations (field mice, birds, and/or deer) and the distribution of habitat between meadow and forest for both current as well as future weather conditions. Changes in weather could significantly affect both of these parameters. In an analysis of how changes in these two factors might affect the predictions, changes in the sizes of the host populations could cause the estimates to vary as much as 16 times.

Implications

There are many interrelationships between weather and human health effects. As indicated in Fig. 12.3, most of these are indirect. Thus weather patterns do not directly induce mortality (except perhaps in the case of lives lost during a hurricane); rather unusual weather sets up a situation in which mortality is more likely (for example, hot weather increases the chance of heart attack). Some of the relationships are even more tenuous. For instance, poor weather may result in crop failure leading to famine and death due to starvation or decreased resistance to disease. In developed nations such as the United States, this category of weather-related deaths does not seem that likely, but in the lesser developed countries, where populations exist on the borderline of starvation, such disruptions in agriculture are known to have terrible consequences in terms of human suffering.

In the United States, the modeling analyses performed for the report to Congress suggest that global warming will have a net adverse impact on human mortality. More research needs to be done in this area, however. With regard to infectious diseases, the modeling studies do not suggest that global warming will lead to significant problems *per se*. This conclusion also should be accepted cautiously, because the analysis did not include an estimation of the impact of global warming on the intermediate host. If global warming favors an increase in the population size/density of the mice, deer, or birds that act as intermediate hosts for any of these vectors, then the estimates may be totally erroneous. One further area that needs research is that of infant mortality and temperature. Not only would this be an important observation, but such a relationship would have consequences for assessing the impact of climate change.

Interactions of Environmental Insults

There are many forces acting concurrently to change our environment. These include not only the greenhouse effect and stratospheric ozone depletion, but also acid rain, deforestation, and desertification. Although historically these impacts have all been evaluated separately, it is becoming increasingly clear that such separate treatment does not represent the real situation. These insults compound each other and we need to be aware and to plan for these combined insults.

With regard to human health effects, the largest area of overlap appears at this time to be between stratospheric ozone depletion and global warming. To date there are at least two end points that are predicted to show an interaction: respiratory diseases and infectious diseases. A combined impact on respiratory diseases seems likely because both global warming and stratospheric ozone depletion will both increase tropospheric ozone concentrations and global warming will contribute to higher reaction rates contributing to increased levels of other air pollutants as well. Increased air pollution will result in a higher incidence and/or severity of respiratory diseases. The second end point, infectious disease, is likely to be doubly affected by virtue of a potential increase in the prevalence and distribution of vectors due to global warming, increases in communicable and water-borne diseases due to sea level rise and the resulting population disruptions and stress, and a potential impact on the immune system from increases in ultraviolet radiation.

The above mentioned interactions are fairly easy to identify. In the coming decades, it seems likely that many other interactions will be revealed. One possible example is that global warming could increase cancer incidence by increasing the amount of aflatoxin present in food supplies. In populations already stressed due to malnutrition or crowding, an increased level of such toxins could have serious repercussions.

Policy Implications

Many of the policies required to prepare for global climate changes are those that are necessary to address already pressing problems both in the United States and elsewhere. The United States is already struggling to cope with unhealthy levels of ozone and other air pollutants; however, it seem likely that, with the passage of a new Clean Air Act, we will be far ahead of many other nations in the development of strategies to address these issues. Many of the less developed nations, where populations are crowded into megacities, have yet to develop any such plans, and it seems likely that some such cities, for example, Mexico City, Calcutta and Nairobi, will need help to respond adequately to the health impacts of increasing air pollution.

It seems likely that any plan to provide aid to the lesser developed nations needs to take into account potential changes in climate due to warming. The plans to build water systems so that populations will have an adequate water supply may need to be designed with larger capacities, hydroelectric projects may need to take into account lower water levels and less rainfall, and vaccination programs may be needed for diseases in areas where they have not been seen before.

Beyond all else, developers and planners need to be aware of the potential consequences of global climate change and wherever possible need to build flexibility into their designs. We do not know what the rate of change will be, so that any project involving land and/or natural resources currently in the design phase must consider the consequences of a very different environment.

Summary

The potential impacts on public health of global climate change pale by comparison to the ecological effects that are likely to occur. However, this is not to say that the public health consequences will be negligible, particularly in nations at an early stage of development. In the United States and probably most other developed nations, it seems likely that the greatest public health impacts will be on respiratory diseases. Health effects related to heat stress are also possible, but the degree to which such effects occur will be dependent to a large extent on the ability of populations to adapt. This, in turn, will depend to some extent on the rate of climate change. If it occurs slowly, populations may have time to adapt. Poorer populations in the developed nations are also likely to be at greater risk than those with sufficient resources to afford mitigative measures, such as air conditioning. If perinatal mortality and/or preterm birth are exacerbated by summertime conditions, then it is not unlikely that global warming will make these problems worse in the United States, which already has an abysmal record among the developed nations in premature birth and infant mortality.

In the developing nations, it seems likely that the potential public health consequences of global warming will be many. Impacts on agricultural productivity could prove devastating to countries that currently are only marginally able to provide adequate nutrition for their populations. If droughts occur, famine will follow and with famine, malnutrition. Malnutrition in turn results in lowered resistance to infection, so epidemics will be more likely. If vectors change venues, then we may also see significant shifts in disease, and it is also conceivable that UVR will lower resistance, potentially also contributing to an increase in infectious diseases. These are not insurmountable problems; however, even without global climate change, starvation and disease are major problems throughout much of the world today.

Research is needed to determine what crops/cultivars are likely to be resistant to the impacts of global climate change and to develop substitutes for any important crops for which no resistant cultivars can be found. It seems likely that any research to develop drought-resistant strains that are also heat tolerant will be very worthwhile. Much more research is needed into the immunologic effects of UVR and infectious diseases on humans. Furthermore, it is critical to determine if vaccination programs might be compromised by UVR. Finally, the role of temperature and/or humidity in reproductive effects such as perinatal mortality and preterm birth needs further exploration.

References

Bochow, T. W., S. K. West, A. Azar, B. Munoz, A. Sommes, and H. R. Taylor. 1989. Ultraviolet light exposure and the risk of posterior subcapsular cataract. *Arch. Opthalmol.* 107:369–372.

Cooperstock, M. and R. A. Wolfe. 1986. Seasonality of preterm birth in the collaborative perinatal project: demographic factors. *Am. J. Epidemiol.* 124:234–241.

Environmental Protection Agency (EPA). 1987. *Assessing the Risks of Trace Gases that can Modify the Stratosphere*, EPA 400/1–87/001A-H. Government Printing Office, Washington, DC.

Environmental Protection Agency (EPA). 1989. *Report to Congress: Potential Effects of Global Climate Change on the United States*. Office of Policy, Planning, and Evaluation and Office of Research and Development, Washington, DC.

Giannini, S. H. and E. C. De Fabo. 1987. Abrogation of skin lesions in cutaneous leishmaniasis by ultraviolet B irradiation. In *Leishmaniasis: The First Centenary (1885–1985), New Strategies for Control*, D. T. Hart (ed.), Plenum, London.

Grant, L. D. 1988. Health effects issues associated with regional and global air pollution problems. Draft document prepared for World Conference on the Changing Atmosphere, Toronto.

Haile, D. G. 1989. Computer simulation of the effects of changes in weather patterns on vector-borne disease transmission. In *The Potential Effects of Global Climate Change on the United States*, J. B. Smith and D. A. Tirpak (eds.), EPA 230–05–89–057, Pages 2–1 to 2–11. Government Printing Office, Washington, DC.

Kalkstein, L. S. 1989. The impact of CO_2 and trace gas-induced climate change upon human mortality. In *The Potential Effects of Global Climate Change on the United States*, J. B. Smith and D. A. Tirpak (eds.), EPA 230–05–89–057, pp. 1–1 to 1–35. Government Printing Office, Washington, DC.

Keller, C. A. and R. P. Nugent. 1983. Seasonal patterns in perinatal mortality and preterm delivery. *Am. J. Epidemiol.* 118:689–698.

Kripke, M. L. 1986. Photoimmunology: The first decade. *Curr. Prob. Dermatol.* 15:164–175.

Kripke, M. L. and M. S. Fisher. 1976. Immunologic parameters of ultraviolet carcinogenesis. *J. Nat. Cancer Inst.* 57:211–215.

Kutschenreuter, P. H. 1959. A study of the effect of weather on mortality. *NY Acad. Sci.* 22:126–138.

Ley, R. D., L. A. Applegate, R. S. Padilla and T. D. Stuart. 1989. Ultraviolet induced malignant melanoma in *Monodelphis domestica*. *Photochem. Photobiol.* 50:1–5.

Longstreth, J. D. (ed.). 1987. *Ultraviolet Radiation and Melanoma with a Special Focus on Assessing the Risks of Stratospheric Ozone Depletion*. EPA 400/1–87/001D. Government Printing Office, Washington, DC.

Longstreth, J. D. 1989. Human health. In *The Potential Effects of Global Climate Change on the United States*, J. B. Smith and D. A. Tirpak (eds.), EPA 230–05–89–050, pp. 219–235. Government Printing Office, Washington, DC.

Longstreth, J. D. and J. Wiseman. 1989. The potential impact of climate change on patterns of infectious disease in the United States—background paper and summary of a workshop. In *The Potential Effects of Global Climate Change on the United States*, J. B. Smith and D. A. Tirpak (eds.), EPA 230–05–89–057, pp. 3–1 to 3–48. Government Printing Office, Washington, DC.

Lopez, M. and J. E. Salvaggio. 1983. Climate-weather-air pollution. In *Allergy*, E. Middleton and C. E. Reed (eds.), Ch. 24. C. V. Mosby, St. Louis.

Maitchouk, I. F. 1985. Trachoma and cataract: Two WHO targets. *Int. Nursing Rev.* 32:23–25.

National Cancer Institute (NCI). 1988. *1987 Annual Cancer Statistics Review, Including Cancer Trends: 1950–85*. Division of Cancer Prevention and Control, Washington, DC.

Perna, J. J., M. L. Mannix, and J. E. Rooney. 1987. Reactivation of latent herpes simplex virus infection by ultraviolet light: A human model. *J. Am. Acad. Dermatol.* 17:473–478.

Pitts, D. G. 1987. Optical radiation and cataracts. In *Visual Health and Optical Radiation*, M. Waxler and V. Hitchens (eds.), CRC Press, Boca Raton, FL.

Rogot, E. and S. J. Paget. 1976. Association of coronary and stroke mortality with temperature and snowfall in selected areas of the United States 1962–1966. *Am. J. Epidemiol.* 103:565–575.

Scotto, J., T. R. Fears, and J. F. Fraumeni, Jr. 1981. *Incidence of Non-melanoma Skin Cancer in the United States*, (NIH) 8202433. National Cancer Institute, US Department of Health and Human Services, Washington, DC.

Setlow, R. B., A. D. Woodhead, and E. Grist. 1989. Animal model for ultraviolet radiation-induced melanoma: Platyfish-swordtail hybrid. *Proc. Nat. Acad. Sci.* 86: 8922–8926.

Stingl, L. A., D. N. Sauder, M. Iijima, K. Wolff, H. Pehamberger, and G. Stingl. 1983. Mechanism of UV-B induced impairment of the antigen presenting capacity of murine epidermal cells. *J. Immunol.* 130: 1586–1591.

Taylor, H. R., S. K. West, F. S. Rosenthal, M. Beatriz, H. S. Newland, H. Abbey, and E. A. Emmett. 1988. The effect of ultraviolet radiation on cataract formation. N. Engl. J. Med. 319:1411–1415.

Van der Leun, J. C., Y. Takizawa, and J. D. Longstreth. 1989. Chapter 2—Human Health. In *Environmental Effects Panel Report*. United Nations Environment Programme. United Nations, NY pp. 11–24.

White, M. R. and I. Hertz-Picciotto. 1984. Human health: analysis of climate related to health. In *Characterization of Information Requirements for Studies of CO$_2$ Effects: Water Resources Agriculture, Fisheries, Forests, and Human Health*, M. R. White (ed.), DOE/ER/0236. Dept. of Energy, Washington, DC.

13

Potential Impact of Global Warming: Climate Change and Human Mortality

Laurence S. Kalkstein

Introduction

The impact of potential climate change upon society has been the subject of intensive study, but very little has been done to estimate how predicted changes in climate might affect the health of the general population. The objective of this study is to evaluate changes in human mortality attributed to predicted changes in climate due to increased concentrations of CO_2 and other trace gases in the atmosphere. Estimates of the number of deaths attributed to the increased incidence of extreme weather episodes predicted by various climate change models are presented.

In addition, the historical relationships between weather and mortality are evaluated, and those weather variables most influential upon summer and winter mortality are identified. Finally, results from a preliminary study to determine the differential impact of weather and pollution on mortality in a sample city, St. Louis, are briefly discussed.

The evaluation covers 48 cities around the country, and daily mortality data for 11 summer and winter seasons are extracted and standardized in a manner that facilitates intercity comparisons (refer to Lilienfeld and Lilienfeld 1980 for an explanation of standardization procedures). The mortality totals are divided into various age and race categories, and separate evaluations are developed for all causes of death and those causes considered to be "weather related."

Methods

The initial step involves the determination of historical weather/mortality relationships. The National Center for Health Statistics (1978) provided a very detailed mortality database, which contains records for every person who died in the United States from 1964 to 1978. The data contain cause of death, place of death, date of death, age, and race, extracted for the Standard Metropolitan Statistical Areas (SMSAs) of the 48 cities for 11 years: 1964–1966, 1972–1978, and 1980.

Threshold temperatures, that is, the temperature beyond which mortality increases, are developed for total deaths and weather-related causes within each city using an objective procedure (for a detailed discussion of all procedures used here, refer to Kalkstein et al. 1987 and Kalkstein and Davis 1989). Once established, 12 weather elements that, based on previous research, might have some influence on human health are correlated with the mortality data for days beyond the threshold temperature. The weather elements include:

maximum daily temperature	3 AM visibility
minimum daily temperature	3 PM visibility
maximum daily dew point	3 AM windspeed
minimum daily dew point	3 PM windspeed
cooling degree hours	mean 10 AM to 4 PM cloud cover
heating degree hours	Time

Cooling degree hours (CDH calculated for summer only) measures the daily accumulation of degree hours above the temperature that exceeds the mean daily maximum by one standard deviation. Heating degree hours (HDH calculated for winter only) measures the daily accumulation of degree hours below the temperature that is one standard deviation below the mean daily minimum. Time evaluates the intraseasonal timing of the weather event. Time assigns each day a number (i.e., June 1 is 1, June 2 is 2, July 1 is 31, etc.) representing its position in the summer (defined as June 1 to August 31) or winter (defined as December 1 to February 28).

An all-regression procedure is used to determine which combination of weather elements produces weather/mortality models with the highest coefficient of determination (R^2) for days beyond the threshold temperature. In all-regression R^2 is computed for all possible combinations of weather elements and the best twelve variable models (in terms of R^2) are determined (Draper and Smith 1981). The next step involves choosing which of the twelve all-regression models best represents the historical relationships for that SMSA. Complete multiple linear regressions were run for each model, which included regression diagnostics, such as residuals plots and variance inflation factors (VIFs) (Draper and Smith 1981 SAS Institute 1985). A high VIF indicates that two or more colinear independent variables are included in the model. When this occurs one of the colinear variables is omitted from the model; the remaining variable then explains a greater amount of the variance in mortality than the omitted variable.

The next step attempts to estimate changes in mortality that might occur with predicted climatic warming for 15 of the 48 cities. This study uses three general circulation models (GCM) transient runs provided by the National Center for Atmospheric Research (NCAR) and the United States Environment Protection Agency (Jenne 1987), with predictions of future climate developed for the cities in this study. The three runs are GISS (Goddard Institute for Space Studies) transient A_1 (covering a 17-year period 30 years after the base period of 1951–1980), GISS transient A_2 (covering a 17-year period 60 years after the base period), and GISS $2 \times CO_2$ (the double-CO_2 model). The GISS transient A_1 scenario estimates mortality for the period 1994–2010. The GISS transient A_2 scenario estimates mortality for the period 2024–2040. The GISS $2 \times CO_2$ scenario assumes double-CO_2 atmospheric concentrations (over 1950 levels) during the base period 1964–1980. The historical algorithms for these cities produced from the all regression procedures provided "unacclimatized" estimates of mortality for each city using climate data from the transient runs. "Analog cities," whose present weather duplicates a city's future weather predicted from the transient runs, were determined from a large pool of cities, and their historical mortality algorithms were used to predict "acclimatized" estimates of mortality for each of the 15 cities. "Partially acclimatized" estimates were produced as well, and were calculated by determining the mortality value midway between the acclimatized and unacclimatized estimates.

Results and Discussion

Threshold temperatures calculated for summer and winter suggest that the impact of weather upon mortality is relative rather than absolute. The highest summer threshold temperatures were found in the South and Southwest (e.g., Dallas 39°C, Phoenix 44°C), whereas the lowest were found in the Pacific and Northeast regions of the country (e.g., Boston 29°C, San Francisco 29°C). Thus, weather-induced increases in summer mortality were noted in cooler climates at much lower temperatures. During the winter, the lowest threshold temperatures were found in the coldest regions (e.g., Fargo −22°C, Milwaukee −13°C), whereas relatively high thresholds were uncovered for mild cities (e.g., Jacksonville, 10°C, San Francisco 9°C). These results suggest that people respond to weather in relative fashion; what is considered "extreme" weather in one locale (based on a negative human response) is quite common in another and elicits little human response. This suggests that regional acclimatization appears to be very important in the weather/mortality relationship.

During summer, the lag time between the weather mechanism and the associated mortality was short for all cities, never exceeding a day. In most cases, the mortality response occurred on the same day as the responsible weather mechanism. However, in winter, the lag time was much greater, and, in a number of cases, the mortality response occurred 3 days after the responsible weather mechanism.

In both seasons, the age/race categories that appeared most sensitive to weather were total deaths (rather than "weather-related") and elderly deaths (greater than 65 years old). Thus it appears that mortality from a wide variety of causes increases during extreme weather, and the notion that a few specific weather-related causes are very important (i.e., heat stroke, heat exhaustion, etc.) is specious. There seemed to be little difference in racial response to extreme weather in summer, but, in winter, nonwhites seemed more vulnerable in southern cities, possibly due to inadequate housing and increased exposure to hostile weather elements. During both seasons, the smallest number of statistically significant weather/mortality models were found within the youngest age classes (ranging from 0–44 years old).

The weather variables that seemed to have the greatest impact on mortality varied by season. For the total deaths in summer (all causes and all age groups), the most important independent variables influencing mortality were CDH and Time. The strength of CDH (and relative unimportance of maximum temperature) suggests that the *intensity* of the heat event may be of lesser importance than the *duration* of the event. Thus a day where the temperature is hovering near 35°C for many hours (accumulating a large value for CDH) appears to have a greater influence on mortality than a day when the maximum temperature approaches 38°C but rapidly falls to more tolerable levels. The Time variable was almost always inversely proportional to mortality, indicating that heat waves earlier in the season are more important than those late in the season. The importance of Time implies that some degree of acclimatization might take place within a season.

Other weather variables appearing commonly in summer total death models were minimum dew point, afternoon visibility, and minimum temperature. In most cases it appeared that humid, uncomfortable conditions with warm nighttime temperatures contribute to heightened mortality, although in a minority of cities hot, dry conditions were most responsible.

Even stronger models were uncovered for the 65 and older age group, and the responsible weather variables were somewhat different. For example, maximum temperature was much more important here than in the total death models and CDH was less important. This suggests that the intensity of the heat wave is more important than duration for this age group. The impact of hot, dry weather was more noteworthy in the elderly models.

A regional comparison of summer models indicated a differential sensitivity to weather. The two most weather-sensitive areas were the Pacific and upper Midwest regions of the nation, areas noted for a reduced frequency of extremely high temperatures. The least weather-sensitive regions were in the South and desert Southwest, where extreme heat is commonplace and human response is less dramatic. These findings again suggest that human acclimatization to heat is substantial.

During winter it appeared that overcast, damp days contributed to heightened mortality in many areas, regardless of temperature (but assuming that the temperature was below the threshold). Dew point, windspeed, and cloud cover seemed more influential in winter than summer, and surprisingly, windspeed was generally inversely related to mortality. This may imply that "wind chill" has less of an impact on winter mortality than expected. Unlike the summer results, Time

Table 13.1. Estimates of future total mortality in summer assuming no acclimatization

City	Present	GISS Trans A_1	GISS Trans A_2	GISS $2 \times CO_2$	Absolute Change, Present to $2 \times CO_2$
Atlanta	38	112	293	379	341
Chicago	95	168	289	236	141
Cincinnati	94	258	542	629	535
Dallas	0	92	298	469	469
Detroit	103	177	449	519	416
Kansas City	98	105	199	200	102
Los Angeles	46	82	168	783	737
Memphis	94	130	349	792	698
Minneapolis	86	194	353	286	200
New Orleans	0	0	0	0	0
New York	139	303	537	651	542
Oklahoma City	0	0	0	0	0
Philadelphia	118	239	654	768	650
St. Louis	183	527	1,214	1,207	1,024
San Francisco	29	53	87	294	265
Total	1,123	2,440	5,432	7,243	6,120

was poorly represented in the winter models, indicating that the seasonal timing of offending weather is relatively unimportant. In addition, unlike the summer, differential regional responses were difficult to uncover in winter, and weather variables that exerted the greatest influence upon mortality also demonstrated a lesser interregional variation than in summer. Thus regional and seasonal acclimatization, which was so apparent in the summer months, is not evident during winter.

Predictions of weather-induced mortality occurring during summer were attempted for 15 large cities, and it is estimated that over 1,100 deaths (standardized to allow for intercity comparison) occur during an average summer season in the SMSAs of the 15 cities (Table 13.1). St. Louis, New York City, and Philadelphia ranked first, second, and third, respectively, and each city averaged over 100 standard city deaths per summer. The seven highest ranking cities were all found in the Midwest or Northeast. Four of the five lowest ranking cities were found in the South, with New Orleans and Oklahoma City experiencing virtually no deaths attributed to weather in the summer.

Predicted future unacclimatized mortality in summer rose rapidly as the scenarios become warmer (Table 13.1). The $2 \times CO_2$ transient run yielded an estimated weather-induced mortality exceeding 7,200 standardized deaths per year in the SMSAs of the 15 cities. Predicted future acclimatized mortality (using analog cities, Table 13.2) indicated that warming might have little impact on weather-induced mortality if acclimatization is complete. Estimates of future mortality

Table 13.2.   Summer analogs for the fifteen cities using the three warming scenarios

Target City	Analog Cities		
	GISS Trans A_1	GISS Trans A_2	GISS $2 \times CO_2$
Atlanta	Kansas City	Wichita	New Orleans
Chicago	Des Moines	St. Louis	St. Louis
Cincinnati	Philadelphia	Nashville	Birmingham
Dallas	Dallas	Phoenix	Phoenix
Detroit	Minneapolis	Omaha	Omaha
Kansas City	Omaha	Memphis	Memphis
Los Angeles	San Diego	Pittsburgh	Norfolk
Memphis	Nashville	New Orleans	San Antonio
Minneapolis	Des Moines	Nashville	St. Louis
New Orleans	New Orleans	San Antonio	San Antonio
New York	Norfolk	Kansas City	Kansas City
Oklahoma City	Dallas	Dallas	Dallas
Philadelphia	Norfolk	Kansas City	Birmingham
St. Louis	Wichita	Memphis	Jacksonville
San Francisco	Seattle	Seattle	Pittsburgh

assuming partial acclimatization (Table 13.3) indicated that sizable increases in mortality will occur as the weather becomes warmer. Over 4,900 added deaths will occur during an average summer in these 15 cities due to weather alone under $2 \times CO_2$ conditions if people partially acclimatize to the warmth. This represents a fourfold increase over present weather-induced deaths. The partial acclimatization scenario is probably the most realistic, since it is expected that humans might acclimatize rather quickly, but the physical structure of the city (especially the construction of dwellings and work places to conform to the prevailing climate) will take much longer to change (Kalkstein 1988).

Present-day estimates of winter mortality indicated that weather-induced deaths were much less important in winter than in summer. The results differed from those uncovered in summer regarding the relative impact of weather. Most of the estimated winter deaths occurred in regions with relatively severe winter climates, whereas the smallest number of deaths were found in mild weather cities. It appeared that the impact of weather in winter is more absolute, whereas the impact of weather in summer tends to be relative.

Winter unacclimatized, partially acclimatized, and acclimatized predictions indicated that sharp drops in mortality are expected if the weather becomes warmer. The unacclimatized results differed from those uncovered in summer, when dramatic rises in mortality were predicted. The unacclimatized drop in winter may be related to fewer numbers of days below the threshold. Acclimatized mortality predictions approached zero under $2 \times CO_2$ conditions.

A major difficulty in this research is separating weather-induced mortality from pollution-induced mortality, as it is widely believed that weather situations that

Table 13.3. Estimates of future total mortality in summer assuming partial acclimatization

City	Present	GISS Trans A_1	GISS Trans A_2	GISS $2 \times CO_2$	Absolute Change, Present to $2 \times CO_2$
Atlanta	38	56	146	190	152
Chicago	95	84	294	274	179
Cincinnati	94	262	271	476	382
Dallas	0	88	200	370	370
Detroit	103	140	224	260	157
Kansas City	98	52	205	308	210
Los Angeles	46	41	116	392	346
Memphis	94	65	174	396	302
Minneapolis	86	97	176	370	284
New Orleans	0	0	0	0	0
New York	139	152	270	345	206
Oklahoma City	0	31	73	122	122
Philadelphia	118	120	327	570	452
St. Louis	183	264	653	604	421
San Francisco	29	28	44	245	216
Total	1,123	1,480	3,374	4,922	3,799

seem to be associated with high mortality are also associated with high pollution levels. However, there is new evidence to suggest that weather has a much larger impact on day-to-day mortality than does pollution concentration (Kalkstein 1990). Using a synoptic climatologic approach, air mass categories were developed for St. Louis, and each day in the study period was categorized (refer to Kalkstein et al. 1987 for a discussion of synoptic methodology). Mean daily mortality was computed for each air mass category, and it is apparent that one air mass type (which possesses particularly sultry weather conditions) has a 30% higher mean mortality than the others. In addition, 8 of the 10 highest mortality days in St. Louis fell within this synoptic category, even though this category occurred only 7% of the time during the period of study. Interestingly, this particular synoptic situation possesses average or below average readings of total suspended particulates, oxidants, ozone, nitrous oxides, and sulfur dioxide, even during the very highest mortality days. Thus, our initial results for St. Louis suggest that weather, rather than pollution concentration, has a more important impact on the day-to-day variation in mortality. This topic obviously requires further investigation, and this study is being expanded to nine additional cities.

Summary

This study has suggested that weather has a profound effect on human mortality and that the impact is different depending on a seasonal and regional variations.

In addition, it appears that human mortality may increase substantially if a global warming occurs similar to what is predicted by the GCMs. If the population does not acclimatize, over 7,000 additional annual deaths attributable to the increasingly harsh weather can be expected in the SMSAs of the 15-city sample. This figure is more startling when it is considered that these numbers correspond to *average summer* conditions. An analog of the very hot summer of 1988 occurring in the 21st century will no doubt increase weather-induced mortality to a much higher number. Although estimates for partial acclimatization are more modest, general increases are still expected and deaths attributable to weather are predicted to increase by four to five times the present levels.

The global implications of these findings are possibly more alarming. Similar climate changes are predicted for Third World and other lesser developed countries, and there is no reason to expect that the mortality response to more stressful weather will be any less in these regions. In fact, the migration of insect vectors, which transmit a variety of infectious diseases, may exacerbate the problem even further in underdeveloped countries where health care facilities are inadequate (Watts et al. 1987). Thus it appears that specific policy decisions are necessary to prepare for a significant rise in human mortality if the warming scenarios accurately reflect climate conditions into the 21st century.

References

Draper, N. and H. Smith. 1981. *Applied Regression Analysis*. John Wiley, New York.

Jenne, R. 1987. *GISS Transient Runs*, NCAR/EPA Document 4. US Environmental Protection Agency, Washington, DC.

Kalkstein, L. S. 1988. The impacts of predicted climate change on human mortality. *Publ. Climatol. 41:132*.

Kalkstein, L. S. 1990. A new approach to evaluate the impact of climate upon human mortality. *Environ. Health Persp.* in press.

Kalkstein, L. S. and R. E. Davis. 1989. Weather and human mortality: An evaluation of demographic and interregional responses in the United States. *Ann. Assoc. Am. Geogr.* 79:44–64.

Kalkstein, L. S., G. Tan, and J. Skindlov. 1987. An evaluation of three clustering procedures for use in synoptic climatological classification. *J. Climate Appl. Meteorol.* 26:717–730.

Lilienfield, A. M., and D. E. Lilienfield. 1980. *Foundations in Epidemiology*. Oxford Press, London.

National Center for Health Statistics. 1978. Standardized microdata tape transcripts. US Department of Health, Education, and Welfare, Washington, D.C.

SAS Institute, Inc. 1985. *SAS User's Guide: Statistics*, Version 5 Ed. SAS Institute, Cary, NC.

Watts, D. M., D. S. Burke, B. A. Harrison, R. E. Whitmire, and A. Nisalak. 1987. Effect of temperature on the vector efficiency of *Aedes aegypti* for Dengue 2 virus. *Am. J. Trop. Med. Hyg.* 36:143–152.

14

Energy Policy and Global Warming

Jan Beyea

Introduction

Because of the scale at which humans use energy, particularly fossil fuels, we are now a major player in setting the composition of the Earth's atmosphere. As a result, we affect the global temperature balance. Climate disruption is the biggest environmental problem we have ever faced. A good way to remember the rate of projected climate change is in terms of temperature migration. Think of temperature regimes moving northward at a rate of 16 km per year. That means 160 km per decade, 1600 km per century (See Andresko and Wells 1988). Although we cannot be sure that these projections are correct, we must act as if they are correct. We cannot take the risk that the global climate models (GCMs) are wrong. Thus, I will assume for the rest of the discussion that they are correct.

In 50 years, a northern state like New York will have the temperature climate of the deep South. Actually, New York will be relatively well off compared to other states, but not for long. As climate change proceeds 10 times more rapidly than experienced in the past, conflicts between humans and wildlife will heighten. Many of our hard-won environmental victories will be overwhelmed (Peters, this volume).

Climate change is likely to take place in an overpopulated and deforested world, with air pollution threatening the survivability of the forests that are not being cut down and that are not being driven to extinction by climate change. A new technology, biotechnology, will be invading the remaining natural lands (Beyea and Keeler 1990). Initially the invasion will be for economic purposes: better crops, better livestock, better suburban lawns, better trees. These new genetically engineered products will turn uneconomic lands into biological factories, ruining them for the wildlife that now depend on them. Unintended migrations will introduce genetically engineered exotics into our National Parks, Forests, and protected Wilderness lands.

After this initial biotechnologic revolution, a second wave of life designers will replace dying trees and wildlife with genetically engineered creatures that can tolerate a deteriorating planet. The prospects are very bleak for the natural world and wildlife as we know it today. These four factors (population increase, climate change, deforestation, and biotechnology) are the four horsemen of the modern apocalypse.

Climate change is discussed in terms of a 50-year horizon, but the effects do not stop after 50 years. Consider this. We have a 400-year supply of coal in the United States. The other countries with major resources are China and the Soviet Union (International Institute for Applied Systems Analysis 1981). If we burn all of ours and tap into our shale and tar oils, if the Soviets and Chinese burn theirs, and, if at the same time, we fail to clamp down on greenhouse gases and deforestation, then the tropics will end up at the poles according to my projections, possibly with an interlude of an ice age up north. In light of possible climate interludes and fluctuations, it is more accurate to refer to "climate disruption" when speaking of the future, rather than global warming. Ultimately, however, any regional cooling trend will be overtaken by increased warmth as more and more carbon dioxide enters the atmosphere.

We cannot expect that tropical wildlife will migrate and that trees will survive. Not even tropical wildlife will be able to stand the summers, which will soar to killing extremes. Trees as we know them will be largely gone. None of the wildlife that many of us love will be able to survive. Wilderness will be a memory. Wildlife remnants will be relegated to air-conditioned zoos, possibly underground, with the remnants of humanity, breathing artificially maintained air. According to these extrapolations, we literally face the end of the natural world as we know it.

But then who cares about what happens in 400 years? Actually, we probably care more than we realize. Four hundred years is not that long in historical terms. Most of us, when we studied history, identified with those who lived 1,000 and 2,000 years ago. Can we accept no future for the natural world in 400 years? Suppose people in the Middle Ages had knowingly used up the land so that nothing natural remained for us? Would we not curse them as monsters?

Climate protection requires a fundamental change in how we, as a society, cope with problems. It requires us to act now to stop destruction long into the future. We must act before the evidence of the destruction is actually visible. We must act on the wisdom of scientific predictions. Those of us alive today have a special responsibility the future. If we do not reverse our course over the next decades, there will be little hope of later generations doing anything but surrendering to the effects of climate disruptions.

There is a key point that must be repeated about global warming, over and over again, until it is widely appreciated. The gases we spew out today will take a long time before they are absorbed into vegetation and oceans. Approximately 50–70% of our CO_2 emissions are recycled into the ocean surface waters rather rapidly (Oeschger et al. 1975). However, the residence time in the atmosphere for the remainder is hundreds of years (Maier-Reimer and Hasselman 1987,

Solomon et al. 1985). The fraction that stays up for the long haul will determine the climate of our descendants. Every time we drive our car, heat our homes with fossil fuels, or use electricity generated by fossil fuels, we ever so slightly narrow the options of future societies. The analogy with nuclear wastes is very strong. Environmentalists have held it immoral to benefit from nuclear power while passing on the risks to future generations. Our descendants will be the ones who will have to deal with nuclear wastes escaping from repositories, not us. Similarly, they are the ones who will have to cope with fossil wastes, the wastes in the atmosphere after we have reaped the energy benefits for ourselves. Focusing on the moral issue is going to be important for developing an adequate political response to the threat of climate disruption.

Because of the long residence time of CO_2, we cannot treat CO_2 like other pollutants, such as SO_2 and NO, with which we are familiar because of the debate over clean air and acid rain. To prevent climate disaster for future generations, we must reduce emissions essentially to zero within the next 100 years, not simply cut emissions in half. Lightheartedly I advise my daughters and their friends that it is important that they be left at least one challenging problem to solve. No problem of this magnitude can be solved by forgetting one's sense of humor. We cannot afford to let the sheer magnitude of the greenhouse problem constipate us into inaction.

The United States contributes approximately 20% of world CO_2 (Krause et al. 1989). Thus, the United States cannot solve the greenhouse problem on its own. Yet, because we are the worst CO_2 polluters on a per capita basis, we must put our own house in order first. Only then can we expect other nations to put much effort into controlling emissions. Furthermore, it is up to us and other highly industrialized countries to develop the technology to ease the pain that may be involved in stabilizing the world's climate. In assessing energy policy, it should be understood that no energy solution can make sense without a simultaneous commitment to the stabilization of the human population, a reversal of deforestation, and control of trace gases, like CFCs and methane.

As a result of potential climate disruption, United States and world energy policy must change radically. We need to make every rational effort to conserve energy, to become more efficient, and to steadily shift our economies away from burning hydrocarbon-based fuels. Every time that we advocate one form of energy policy or another, we should make sure that climate protection is part of the equation. We have not always done so. For instance, the environmental community for the last 15 years, out of concern for the dangers of nuclear power, has either explicitly or implicitly supported conventional use of coal.

Before expanding on an overall energy policy, it is appropriate to look at the various options we have. There are many. The world is not going to run out of energy. The real question is how much will we pay for energy and what will happen to economic growth and the environment as a result.

Energy Options

Fossil Fuels

Natural gas emits the least CO_2 per unit of energy (approximately half that of coal) (JASON 1979). Oil is next in this regard, followed by coal. The worst CO_2 emitters are synthetic fuels from coal. A movement toward natural gas will reduce total CO_2 emissions, so it has promise as a short term strategy, provided emissions of unburned natural gas, a greenhouse gas itself, are reduced during production and transmission. Oil and gas will be the most difficult to forego, because of their usefulness in transportation. The nontraditional fossil fuels, shale and tar oils, represent another enormous potential supply of energy, comparable to the world coal resources (Jason 1979). If we should ever tap significant amounts of these dirty fuels, any hope of controlling climate disruption will be lost (Sundquist and Miller 1980).

Novel Ways of Using Fossil Fuels

Fossil fuels, however, should not be written off completely (Fig. 14.1). There may well be ways to improve the consumption of fossil fuels from the climate perspective. CO_2 removal is one example. It is possible to remove CO_2 from the exhaust gases of fossil fuels at power plants, such as those at utilities and large industries. One estimate is that a 90% removal of CO_2 will approximately double the cost of electricity (Cheng and Steinberg 1985). However, in the absence of hard engineering data on costs, it would be wise to expect higher figures.

A possible way to reduce those costs is to burn the coal from the start with pure oxygen. Ordinary air contains lots of elements other than oxygen that are carried along during the burning process and end up as part of the effluent stream. Disposal of the CO_2, then, requires either separating out the CO_2 prior to disposal or disposing of the whole volume. Either alternative is expensive. In contrast, this new way of burning coal with pure oxygen produces an output that is practically pure CO_2. Of course, the oxygen must be separated from air in the first place, but one research group claims the new process is cheaper overall (Golomb et al. 1989).

In any case, disposal of the removed CO_2 accounts for a significant fraction of the cost. The most likely way to dispose of large quantities of CO_2, beyond that which can be used in industrial processes, is to pipe it down into deep ocean waters, the place it would end up anyway in thousands of years if we allowed it to escape today into the atmosphere. If we put it deep enough, CO_2 will sink to the bottom (Cheng and Steinberg 1987). But critics of this approach argue that transporting the scrubbed CO_2 across the country to the oceans is too clumsy and impractical. However, this objection seems to be relevant to inland use. Because

TECHNOLOGY	SOME ASSOCIATED ENVIRONMENTAL PROBLEMS	MITIGATABLE?
Ocean Disposal of CO-2 Removed From Fossil Fuel Effluents.	Unknown Impacts on Ocean Cycles.	?
Hydrogen Stripping From Coal.	Possible Oxidation of Residual Carbon Leading to Delayed CO-2 Emissions.	?

Fig. 14.1. Some novel ways of using fossil fuels, associated environmental problems, and comments on whether the environmental problems can be mitigated.

most of the population lives close to the coasts, restricting coal to coastal locations would still allow significant quantities of coal to be consumed. Thus, it is likely that economics will be the key to scrubbing CO_2, not infrastructure requirements.

The real problem with ocean disposal of CO_2 is environmental. We do not know how the ocean systems will be affected. Environmental research is needed before the method can be considered an acceptable alternative. In any case, like all the other supply alternatives being discussed, costs are likely to be higher than the cost of electricity from coal today (Fig. 14.1).

Other options are also of interest. Recent work at Brookhaven Laboratory (Steinberg 1988) involving the "stripping" of hydrogen from coal is so original that it overturns the conventional wisdom that coal consumption is synonymous with CO_2 production. By settling for less than maximally extractable energy, the Brookhaven group avoids CO_2 as an end product.

Coal is made up of carbon, hydrogen, and oxygen. When coal is burned in conventional fashion, the energy locked up in both carbon and hydrogen is released when combined with atmospheric oxygen. Steinberg's method separates carbon into pure form and makes only the hydrogen available for combination with oxygen. If the carbon is sequestered and not burned, no CO_2 is formed. The hydrogen is actually an intermediate product, which can serve as a mobile energy carrier, providing energy when it is eventually burned.

On the negative side, only 25% or so of the potential energy in the coal is obtained. The rest must stay locked up in the pure carbon to prevent CO_2 from being produced. However, to make hydrogen from coal through normal means would require producing electricity first, itself a wasteful process, and then separating hydrogen from water. In fact, electricity from coal requires two-thirds of the initial energy as well, so that the Brookhaven method for making hydrogen is not much more wasteful than electrical methods. Thus, to the extent that hydrogen is a desired product, the Brookhaven process looks very interesting. Should hydrogen become the future fuel of choice for transportation, a real possibility according to many analysts, fossil fuels may gain a new lease on life through this process.

Research into this technology makes sense. Its novelty makes one wonder what other original ideas about use of fossil fuels are out there waiting to be discovered? Research dollars now going into conventional fossil fuel technology need to be redirected into these innovative areas.

Energy Efficiency

Using energy more efficiently is the cheapest and fastest way to reduce CO_2 emissions while maintaining economic growth. Also it can be the most environmentally benign. I refer here particularly to eliminating energy waste by modernizing equipment in the home, office, factory, and transportation sectors (Morrison 1990, Carlsmith et al. 1989).

The technologic potential is awesome; the political will weak. Hopefully, concern over climate change will motivate societies to curb bad energy habits and shift dollars away from investment in energy supply to efficient utilization of energy. A reasonable target for conservation is to keep energy consumption constant while the economy grows. Such a target can be achieved with a net economic saving to the consumer, a saving that can be used to offset the cost of supply options that reduce CO_2.

Because in the minds of the general public energy efficiency is still a rather esoteric concept, often is confused with "freezing in the dark," there is a need for a dramatic demonstration of the power of the concept. Why not a national effort, comparable to putting up a space station, to develop a 100 km/l car. Such an effort will require years of work from our best engineers, but it will make efficiency chic as well as make possible huge reductions in CO_2 emissions.

In addition to the saving of energy with improved vehicles, there is a great potential associated with changing the transportation infrastructure itself. Optimal integration of mass and personal transportation systems is needed. We need special lanes everywhere for vehicles with multiple passengers. We need the promotion of lanes for bike and motor-bike travel, which has barely started in this country. Admittedly, changing the transportation infrastructure is a slow process, but the time frame is matched to the time frame over which we must reduce our CO_2 emissions.

All energy options have drawbacks. The biggest one associated with efficiency is potential increases in indoor air pollution associated with tighter buildings. However, buildings with reduced air-quality need not be a part of our efficiency

TECHNOLOGY	SOME ASSOCIATED ENVIRONMENTAL PROBLEMS	MITIGATABLE?
Photovoltaics, Solar Thermal.	Landuse Competition. Pollution During Production of Materials.	No, but tolerable amounts involved. To some extent.
Biomass (Solar energy Collected in the Form of Biological Material).	Destruction of Habitat and Loss of Biological Diversity.	To some extent.
Wind	Aesthetic. Noise.	No. Yes.
Hydro (Big and Small)	Loss of Key Wildlife Habitat and Recreation Opportunities.	Only by scaling number of projects way down.
Geothermal	Water Pollution.	Yes.
Ocean Thermal	Interference with Ocean Cycles.	?

Fig. 14.2. List of solar-related and geothermal technologies, associated environmental problems, and whether the environmental problems can be mitigated.

strategy. Such conservation measures only contribute a small part to the overall efficiency potential.

Recycling

Recycling can reduce emissions of greenhouse gases directly and indirectly. After the United States establishes a recycling infrastructure, material recycling would lead to a major, cost-effective reduction in direct CO_2 emissions now associated with the combustion of used materials. Unfortunately the development of appropriate infrastructure is proceeding slowly. Many communities have established mandatory recycling only to find that they must deposit the presorted and cleaned materials into landfills because the markets are saturated. Indirectly recycling reduces emissions because less energy is needed, and hence less fuel is burnt and fewer emissions produced, to process recycled materials than is required to mine, transport, and manufacture products from raw natural resources.

Solar Technologies

A number of reports discuss the promising status of solar energy (Andrejko 1989, Chiles 1990). Solar-related technologies (Fig. 14.2) derive their potential power at some point from the sun. Wind, for instance, arises from unequal heating of the earth by solar energy. The success of technologies like wind turbines has shown that such alternatives can make a real contribution to the United States energy supply under the right regulatory climate (Chiles, 1990). California has led the way and shown that they can be practical. However, there is no free lunch when it comes to energy sources, so care must be exercised even with solar technologies (Medsker 1982).

Direct solar. On the supply side, one of the most promising options is solar electricity. It can be derived from steam produced by high-temperature solar heat, assisted by the burning of natural gas. The cost of producing electricity, at least in the daytime, by this method is not too much greater than the cost of electricity from the latest nuclear power plants (Chiles 1990).

The "hottest" form of solar electricity today is that which is produced directly when sunlight hits photovoltaic cells. The costs of these cells have been dropping dramatically, with the potential for producing electricity at costs well below that of nuclear power (Carlson 1989, Hubbard 1989, Ogden and Williams 1989). Expanding research into photovoltaics would seem to be the most important energy research step that can be taken for the long term. In the United States, replacing fossil fuel units would be a massive job, requiring the laying down of collectors on an area of perhaps the size of the interstate highway system or 5% of the farmland, an equivalent area. These engineering projects are so vast that engineers would clamor to be a part of them. Although a complex undertaking, it would certainly be possible to accomplish the task over a 50-year period.

Although land use of this magnitude would raise eyebrows, the other advantages of solar energy would ensure its widespread public acceptance. In fact, development of photovoltaic cells may represent the most politically viable way of forestalling massive climate change in the next century. However, solar energy is difficult to store. The cost of nighttime power may prove very expensive. In fact, the cost of electric storage will dominate the cost of solar electricity.

Here is a vision of how this system might work in the future: Central station generation during the day time will consist of large fields of photovoltaics. Utility arrays of photovoltaics will consist of 13,000-v panels that can be connected, after conversion to AC, directly into the electric distribution system. Centralized arrays will dominate over decentralized installations because of economies of scale. Land-use regulations will be needed to prevent use of high-quality farm and forest land for photovoltaics and to shift uses to lands that are not biologically productive.

Electricity from photovoltaics installed on top of commercial establishments and, to a lesser extent, on (or near) residential buildings will feed power into the grid during daytime, where it will be stored by utilities for nighttime use. At night, electricity will flow from the utility as it does today. Under this scenario, electric utilities will play the major role in providing electricity storage. Compressed gas, pumped hydro, and hydrogen production will be the major utility storage technologies. Electricity will cost twice as much to produce at night and will be priced accordingly, leading to the development of home technologies for storing heat and the maintenance of cool temperatures. Computer control of homes will allow for painless scheduling of energy-intensive tasks for hours when electricity costs are cheapest, that is during sunlight hours. Cleaning of the arrays may lead to water pollution. Photovoltaics will be used to make some of the hydrogen that will be used as a transportation fuel (Ogden and Williams 1989). Electricity will be transported across the country along the transmission network to follow the sun. In the early hours of the day on the East Coast, electricity will move westward, whereas late in the day on the West coast, electricity will move eastward.

Based on costs today and costs of storage, in constant dollars, electricity will cost less than 30 cents/kWh during the day, less than 45/kWh during the 2-h-period prior to sunrise and after sunset. It will cost less than 60 cents/kWh at night. Environmental problems from photovoltaic technology will be significant, but nothing compared to the problems that would arise from use of fossil fuels. Pollution from the production of the solar cells will be a problem, as will use of herbicides to keep solar arrays free of vegetation. Are these predictions of the development of photovoltaics valid? We will know in 20 years.

Hydropower. Hydropower in moderation is fine, but too much would be a disaster. We have all too few crucial sites left for wildlife and river recreation. The natural flow of rivers is essential to ecosystems. For instance, in the spring when ice melts, the resulting rush carries much-needed nutrients for wildlife far and wide. Dams change the natural rhythms by regulating the flow (Beyea and Rosenthal 1989). By the way, even small hydropower can be a problem, because it requires many dams to make the electrical equivalent of a large dam.

There is a hydropower option that needs consideration, the so-called "run of the river" turbines, which operate during peak flows only. It is not the turbines themselves that cause the major environmental problems, but the flooding of land from dams and the smoothing out of the natural flows. Therefore, by generating electricity in phase with the natural flows (which does not require the construction of a large dam), we can eliminate the greatest problems with hydropower. Although run-of-the-river systems are more expensive, they do offer hope that hydropower can help offset global warming, without causing major damage to natural ecosystems and the creatures that depend on them.

Wind. Germany is planning to get 20% of its energy from electricity generated by wind. Wind is a real option from a technical point of view. The tendency is to place wind-turbines on mountain path sites where there are high winds. These sites may be environmentally sensitive. Turbines could be spread out in the Great Plains, where there is less environmental risk but lower average power. Because of inherent aesthetic problems, photovoltaics may be preferred.

Ocean thermal. The ocean thermal (OTEC) option takes advantages of vertical temperature differences in the ocean to extract useful energy. However, the environmental impacts of large-scale use of OTEC are largely unknown. For this reason, this technology may not be a viable alternative to fossil fuels.

Geothermal. Geothermal energy is obtained from hot waters deep underground. The waters are heated as a result of radioactive decay deep in the earth. The practical potential for long-term replacement of fossil fuels by this technology is not well known. However, the world's geothermal energy base is very large, comparable to the world's coal resource base (Tester et al. 1988). Most current United States geothermal energy facilities are in California (Rhoads 1987). Its use elsewhere in the United States will depend on the price of competing fuels. To avoid environmental contamination, geothermal water should be reinjected, after the heat has been extracted, into the underground layers from which it was originally pumped. Otherwise, the chemicals in such waters will contaminate surface-water systems.

Biomass. Biomass refers to biological matter that contains stored energy. Consider trees and plants, which collect sunshine and use it, along with CO_2 extracted from the atmosphere, to build up biological molecules, storing energy in the process. The stored energy can be extracted from these molecules for human use. (Note that biomass also includes living matter that eats plants or other living things. With very rare exceptions, all of the energy in biological systems can be traced back along the food chain to solar energy.)

Considerable biomass in the form of wood is already consumed in this country (Energy Information Administration 1989). The real potential for biomass, however, lies in its ability to be converted to a transportation fuel, for example alcohol. It is quite conceivable that the costs of producing alcohol from biomass will be dramatically reduced due to bioengineering, making ethanol the cheapest alternative to gasoline (Bath 1989, Beyea and Keeler 1990).

Although biomass produces CO_2 when consumed for energy purposes, the next crop absorbs CO_2 back from the air. Equilibrium results when the next crop stores as much biomass as did the original. In contrast, should a forest be cut down and replaced with corn or short crops, the difference in biomass appears in the atmosphere as CO_2 (Houghton, this volume). Once equilibrium is reached with biomass, it is an energy source that does not contribute to global climate disruption. The problem is that too great reliance on this energy source could have disastrous environmental impacts on land and habitat, unless agricultural and silvicultural practices are radically changed. Suppose, for example, the current United States transportation fleet were powered by alcohol. It could take 400 million acres of land to grow the necessary crops and wood (Beyea and Keeler 1990). This is an area equivalent to our current crop base and would practically saturate our entire agricultural and silvicultural resource. The pressure to build so-called "biomass farms" would be enormous. If not properly designed, biomass farms could eliminate much of the wildlife habitat in the United States and put

TECHNOLOGY	SOME ASSOCIATED ENVIRONMENTAL PROBLEMS	MITIGATABLE?
Hot Fusion (Using Conventional Fuel Cycles).	Radioactive Wastes from Neutron Activation. Proliferation of Weapons-grade Material.	Yes, but expensive. ?
Cold Fusion	If works, and if power too cheap, will lead to massive interference in environment by humans.	No.

Fig. 14.3. Fusion technologies, their associated environmental problems, and whether the environmental problems can be mitigated.

equivalent stress on the environment in other countries. Environmentally sound biomass plantations should be designed to provide habitat diversity that will allow wildlife to survive.

Fusion

Fusion energy (Fig. 14.3), which powers the sun, would not produce CO_2. Hot fusion technology attempts to produce temperatures as hot as the sun and hence tap fusion power. So far, success has been elusive. Current fusion cycles under study in the United States with government support are inherently radioactive, because they produce neutrons. When neutrons stop in the matter surrounding the reactor, they generate long-lived radioactivity, unless very pure (and expensive) materials are used. Another problem with neutronic fusion is that neutrons can easily be made to produce fissionable materials that can be used in conventional nuclear power reactors and for making nuclear weapons. In fact, the most practical uses of neutronic fusion power will be as a fission breeder. As a result, I doubt that conventional fusion can compete with gentler technologies such as photovoltaics.

There do exist nonneutronic fusion cycles, but research into these cycles is not supported by the United States government because they are technologically less promising. True enough, but man does not live by technology alone. The alternate cycles would at least have a chance of proving politically acceptable (Beyea 1990).

During 1989, there was a flurry of media reports about the possibility of cold fusion, or fusion taking place at low temperatures inside a metal matrix. Most exciting was the apparent absence of neutrons and the possibility of cheap power. Cold fusion could solve the coming energy crisis. However, if true, the environmental implications could be disastrous. Why? If man can move mountains cheaply, the natural world will be transformed. As the saying goes, "power corrupts and cheap power corrupts absolutely."

Nuclear

Conventional. Nuclear power emits very little carbon dioxide and little is emitted indirectly during the mining and transportation of the fuel, but the current technology has lost so much credibility that it is unlikely to be a viable alternative. The majority view is that conventional nuclear power has proved too vulnerable to human error, too expensive, and the waste problem is not close to a solution. Although nuclear advocates vigorously dispute all these criticisms, their arguments have proven unconvincing. A Harris poll taken in January 1989 shows that two-thirds of the public does not want any more new nuclear plants. To replace coal electricity with nuclear power would require the siting of 500 facilities over the next 50 years. It is doubtful that there are even a fraction of 500 communities that would tolerate the siting of a new nuclear reactor. Any attempts to build new ones would generate strong community resistance, comparable to the current fights over Seabrook and Shoreham. It does not make sense to try to plan for our electricity future with a technology that polarizes our society.

Second generation. There is the possibility of developing new designs of nuclear power that are meltdown free (Weinberg 1990). Research into them should be started, but we must recognize that they do not address other problems and other public concerns. They do not address the transportation of radioactive materials, their disposal, and the proliferation of weapons-grade material. Furthermore, it is questionable that the new designs can compete economically with other methods for avoiding CO_2 emissions, especially if they are really built to reassure the public on safety and quality assurance.

More important than designing a reactor to meet tough goals will be demonstrating safety. It will be necessary to convince independent engineers and scientists, as well as the public, that the designs will work. That is certainly not going to happen based on engineering promises. Full-scale tests aimed at destroying a reactor will be required to build the necessary confidence. It is important to mention that successful demonstration of idiot-proof reactors is decades off, if it should prove possible at all. Even then, acceptance is problematic. The battleground of the nuclear debate will shift. Local communities will be skeptical that an actual plant will be built to the same standards as the demonstration plants. They will be afraid that small releases will still be possible. They will be unhappy that radioactive waste will have to be stored at the reactor, and transported through

TECHNOLOGY	SOME ASSOCIATED ENVIRONMENTAL PROBLEMS	MITIGATABLE?
New Nuclear Designs.	Radioactive Wastes.	?
	Proliferation of Weapons-grade Materials.	?

Fig. 14.4. Summary of potential new nuclear technologies and their associated environmental problems.

the community to waste repositories in which few people will have any confidence (Fig. 14.4).

For these reasons, the siting of even second-generation reactors is likely to meet strong public resistance. Only if all other alternatives to climate disruption have failed, do I see public acceptance of a second nuclear era. These reactors must be viewed as an insurance policy, not a component of our main line of defense.

An Energy Policy for a Greenhouse World

Vision

Based on this review of energy options, the most practical program for solving the greenhouse problem in the next century involves equal attention today to both the supply side and the demand side of the energy equation:

Demand side. Improved energy efficiency, material recycling, lifestyle changes.

Supply side. Direct solar technologies, such as photovoltaics.

The obstacle to this solution is not a shortage of technologies or resources, but concern about its economics. We can gradually eliminate CO_2, if we are willing to gradually pay more for energy. Whatever the costs turn out to be initially, research should be able to cut them.

Increasing costs will have an impact on economic growth, because the costs of living in a deteriorated world begin to dominate other costs. A hypothetical energy price scenario that might result from forcing a steady decline in CO_2 emissions by 2% per year shows that prices eventually triple over 1989 values. This an upper limit scenario, because it is based on current technology (Fig. 14.5). Although the overall growth rate is projected to slow, economic wealth would remain high and would eventually surpass the wealth in the baseline scenario (Fig. 14.6).

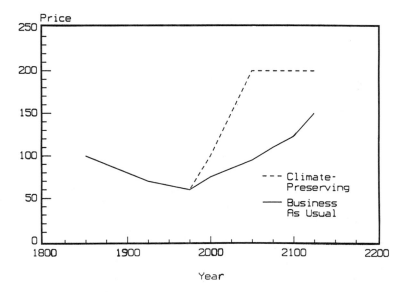

Fig. 14.5. Hypothetical future energy prices under a climate-preserving (worst case) scenario.

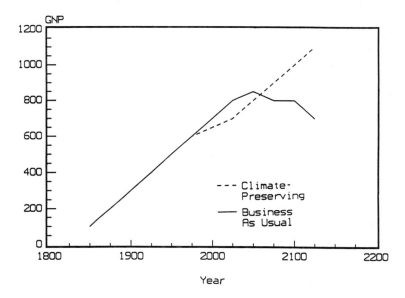

Fig. 14.6. Hypothetical future GNP under a climate-preserving (worse case) scenario.

When looking at the reduced economic growth in the early years, it is important to remember that conventional definitions of wealth, such as GNP, are necessarily limited. There are costs we pay other than those represented by dollars. These indirect costs—damage to the environment, to health, and to the quality of life—can be reduced as a by-product of following the CO_2 strategy I have outlined.

Practical Scenario

How can this future come about? How can we insure in a practical way that emission of CO_2 declines steadily, say at 2% per year over the next 50 years? (Note that a 2% per year reduction translates into approximately a 20% reduction by the year 2000.) The only realistic way to achieve this goal is by legislation, for instance, by placing a CO_2 limit per unit of energy on both new and existing plants, a limit that would tighten each year. To gain political acceptance, it will be important that any such law not specify a specific technology. We should give all non-CO_2 technologies a fair chance to compete.

On the supply side, efficiency (conservation) can reduce CO_2 emissions and we can therefore reduce the CO_2 limits accordingly. Practically, we can use efficiency to keep energy growth from rising, and possibly cause it to decline slightly, while still increasing GNP. As stated earlier, this strategy can actually save money, helping to offset the costs of solar power. To ensure that we get the full benefit from conservation, we must enact standards on buildings, automobiles, appliances, and so on. These standards should be imposed whenever engineering calculations predict that the standards will both save consumers money and reduce CO_2 emissions. Technically, this is interference in the marketplace. It is possible that engineers are wrong. But we have no choice. If we are serious about protecting our world, we will have to take some risks. It seems wiser to take the risk that investments elsewhere may earn more money than to take the risk that the climate will run out of control.

When it comes to setting energy standards, there are times when we need to interfere with the free market. For instance, it is an environmental crime to put up the inefficient buildings we build today. Why? They require more energy to operate than would be most cost-effective for the occupants; they are energy wasters. They will last for 75 years on average. They will be the energy guzzlers of the next century. Yet many still say the market must not be interfered with. Standards will be very important to ease the pain of other steps on the economy, for example, moving faster into solar than pure economics would warrant.

Suppose efficiency keeps energy consumption constant or slightly declining, while the economy is growing. Carbon dioxide emissions still need to be cut. Keeping them constant is not enough. The reduction of 2% per year will have to be met by changes in the supply mix. At the beginning, the easiest way for an industry to meet the fuel limit would be to add natural gas to coal. As time passed and the limit became more stringent, it would be necessary to phase out many fossil units, although flexibility could be introduced by allowing the purchase of emission offsets from facilities (like solar units) that do not surpass the CO_2 limit.

The use of emission offsets is a general strategy to improve economic efficiency. In this case, owners of energy sources with a margin to spare below the limit would be allowed to sell the margin to the highest bidder. Purchase of an offset would be made legally equivalent to a comparable CO_2 reduction. A facility above the limit would have the choice of either installing its own solar equipment or buying a solar (or other) offset from someone who could reduce CO_2 at lower cost. Economic allocation of CO_2 controls would thereby be promoted. An interesting offset concept involves reforestation, which one utility in Connecticut has already undertaken voluntarily (Trexler et al. 1989). At a trivial cost per kilowatt hour, they found they could pay for the planting of sufficient number of trees (which remove CO_2 from the atmosphere) to completely offset the CO_2 that will be emitted over the lifetime of the generating plant.

To obtain a 2% reduction in CO_2 in the transportation sector, fuel economy standards would have to tighten each year. Mixing grain or wood alcohol with gasoline should also count as a credit toward CO_2 reduction, because biomass energy offsets its own CO_2 in the growing process. Although it is difficult to estimate the cost of a 2% reduction in CO_2 transportation emissions, my preliminary calculations suggest average energy costs will increase a few percent a year. Although tolerable domestically, it would not take too many years before the United States would begin to be hurt competitively in international markets, unless other countries joined in. Consequently, international cooperation will be essential to make it politically feasible for the United States to continue CO_2 skimping. However, we cannot wait for international cooperation to start the process. We must take the first step.

There is an important geopolitical fact in favor of international cooperation: three countries (the United States, the Soviet Union, and China) control most of world's coal. Agreement need only be reached among them to gain the leverage to restrict coal use to globally responsible technologies.

Political Considerations

Although the scenario discussed here is technically possible, the likely result is that such efforts will fail, unless old patterns are broken. Environmentalists tend to be purists, taking on the automobile industry, the coal industry, the oil industry, and the nuclear power industry—industries that earn more than $400 billion per year. These industries will dig in their heels, fighting both environmentalists and each other. Deadlock. We have seen it happen with acid rain legislation over the last 10 years, with "only" a few billion dollars per year at stake. The potential for deadlock is much greater with global climate issues.

Because the political situation is so grim, environmentalists must propose a realistic CO_2 strategy that can pass Congress and other governing bodies around the world. We must minimize any compromises, but we must be sure that the CO_2 reduction goal is met. If no compromises are made, no legislation will be passed. On the other hand, if too much compromise is made, victory will not be worth much. Finding the right path will not be easy. Whatever strategy is followed domestically, it is essential to look outward. We must never forget that the problem is inherently international and that the role of the United States is to set an example. The United States must take the lead in developing technological and social solutions. No one is going to cut CO_2 emissions, if the rich United States is not out there ahead of them.

A key part of the solution is citizen activism. Millions of people are going to have to dedicate their lives to saving the planet from climate disruption. Become part of National Audubon's climate activist network. Write for a copy of the "Carbon Dioxide Diet" (Beyea et al. 1990). Moreover, elected representatives need to know that this issue is a priority and that your vote depends upon their support for a responsible public policy on climate protection. Let them know that climate protection is an international issue, a national security issue, and that you want our best scientists, best diplomats, and best planners tackling this one with all their energy. Write your senators and representative to tell them to support efforts to invest in climate protection. It is not necessary to support every item in each bill. Climate bills are at an early stage. However, do demand that we develop a concrete plan for reducing CO_2 emissions, no less than 2% per year. Urge that we draw other nations into this debate and commit to a 50% reduction in greenhouse gases by 2015.

I have outlined the necessary steps that must be taken to come to grips with global climate change. Many of them are difficult. Yet, there is hope. The Montreal convention restricting growth of CFCs to protect the ozone layer is an indication that it is possible to cooperate on global climate issues. The very magnitude of the climate issue raises hopes that the world will finally cooperate. Solving the greenhouse problem has benefits that will spill over into other areas of international concern.

We must not forget the need to develop a plan that can pass the Congress and equivalent governing bodies around the world. If we lose this fight it could be a disaster. We are out to save the world!

Summary

We have a moral responsibility to prevent climate disaster. We can do so without disruption by steadily cutting CO_2 emissions 2% a year over the next 50 years. The United States must set an example in developing an environmentally responsible energy policy, one that always takes climate protection into consideration. For their part, environmentalists must realize that conventional use of coal can no longer be considered an acceptable substitute for nuclear power.

We have many options and must consider the environmental pluses and minuses of each. As the first part of the solution, the public must be educated about energy efficiency, including the need to change transportation and recycling infrastructures. Keeping energy consumption constant or slightly declining while the economy is growing is a worthy goal. To accomplish it efficiency standards must be imposed, even at the risk of interfering with the free market.

The other half of the solution is solar technologies. They can make a big difference, for they cause much fewer environmental problems than fossil fuels. Expanding research into photovoltaics could be the most important energy research step that can be taken for the future. Photovoltaics alone could power the entire economy in an environmentally responsible manner. Other possibilities, such as hydropower, wind, ocean-thermal, geothermal, biomass, and fusion have less potential. Nuclear power does protect the climate but has other problems and is in public disfavor. For it to replace coal electricity would require the siting of 500 facilities over the next 50 years, which would certainly meet resistance. However, second-generation nuclear designs are worth researching as an insurance policy, to guard against failure of the solar option.

Over the long term, we will have to pay more for energy to cut down CO_2 emissions sufficiently, but the cost of living in a deteriorated world for our descendants would be much greater.

Acknowledgments

Discussions with Pete Myers and John DeCicco are gratefully acknowledged, as is the assistance of Valerie Harms in expanding and editing my original presentation.

References

Andresko, K. and J. B. Wells. 1988. North American forests during rapid climate change: Overview of effects and policy response options. In *Proceedings for the Second North American Conference on Preparing for Climate Change*, pp 282–291. Climate Institute, Washington, DC.

Andrejko, D. A. (ed.). 1989. *Assessment of Solar Energy Technologies*. American Solar Energy Society, Boulder, CO.

Bath, T. D. 1989. Testimony before the U.S. Senate Committee on Energy and Natural Resources, given March 4, 1989. Solar Energy Research Institute, Boulder, CO.

Beyea, J. 1990. The impact of environmental issues on public support for fusion research. *Phys. Soc.* 19:6–7.

Beyea, J., D. Bolze, J. Cook, and J. DeCicco. 1990. The Audubon Activist carbon dioxide diet. *Audubon Activist* Jan.–Feb.: 8–9.

Beyea, J. and K. Keeler. 1990. *Environmental Implications of Genetic Engineering Applied to Biomass Energy and Chemical Production*. National Audubon Society, New York, in press.

Beyea, J. and J. Rosenthal. 1989. *Long-Term Threats to Canada's James Bay from Human Development*, EPAD Report #29. National Audubon Society, New York.

Carlsmith, R. S., W. Chandler, J. McMahon, and D. Santini. 1989. *Energy Efficiency: How Far Can We Go?* US Department of Energy, Washington, DC.

Carlson, D. 1989. Low-cost power from thin-film photovoltaics. In *Electricity: Efficient End-Use and New Generation Technologies and their Planning Implications*. Lund University Press, Sweden.

Cheng, H. C. and M. Steinberg. 1985. *A Systems Study for the Removal, Recovery, and Disposal of Carbon Dioxide from Fossil Fuel Power Plants in the U.S.*, BNL–35666. Brookhaven National Laboratory, Upton, New York.

Cheng, H. C. and M. Steinberg. 1987. *Advanced Technologies for Reduced CO_2 Emissions*, BNL–40730. Brookhaven National Laboratory, Upton, New York.

Chiles, J. R. 1990. Tomorrow's energy today. *Audubon Mag.* 9:58–72.

Energy Information Administration (EIA). 1989. *Estimate of Biofuels Consumption in the U.S. during 1987*. US Department of Energy, Washington, DC.

Golomb, D., J. Herzog, J. Tester, D. White, and S. Zemba. 1989. *Feasibility, Modelling, and Economics for Sequestering Power Plants CO_2 Emissions in Deep Ocean*. Massachusetts Institute of Technology, Cambridge, MA.

Hubbard, J. M. 1989. Photovoltaics today and tomorrow. *Science* 244:297–304.

International Institute for Applied Systems Analysis. 1981. *Energy in a Finite World*. Ballinger, Cambridge, MA.

JASON, 1979. *The Long Term Impact of Atmospheric Carbon Dioxide on Climate*, Table 1–10. SRI International, Arlington, VA.

Krause, F. 1989. *Energy Policy in the Greenhouse*. International Project for Sustainable Energy Paths, El Cerrito, CA.

Maier-Reimer, E. and K. Hasselman. 1987. Transport and storage of CO_2 in the ocean—an inorganic ocean-circulation carbon cycle mode. *Climate Dynam.* 2:63–90.

Medsker, L. 1982. *Side Effects of Renewable Energy Sources*, EPAD Report #15. National Audubon Society, Washington, DC.

Morrison, D. L. 1990. *Alternative Energy Research and Development Strategies in the Context of Global Climate Change*. National Academy Press, New York, in press.

Oeschger, H., U. Siegenthaler, U. Schotterer, and A. Gugelmann. 1975. A box diffusion model to study the carbon dioxide exchange in nature. *Tellus* 27:178.

Ogden, J. M. and R. H. Williams. 1989. *Solar Hydrogen: Moving Beyond Fossil Fuels*. World Resources Institute, Washington, DC.

Rhoads, S. 1987. *California Energy Outlook*. California Energy Commission, Sacramento, CA.

Solomon, A. M., J. R. Trabalka, D. E. Reichle, and L. D. Voorhees. 1985. The Global Cycle of Carbon. In *Atmospheric Carbon Dioxide and the Global Carbon Cycle*, DOE/ER–0239. US Department of Energy, Washington, DC.

Steinberg, M. 1988. *An Option for the Coal Industry in Dealing with the Carbon Dioxide Global Greenhouse Effect Including Estimates for Reduced CO_2 Emissions Technologies*, BNL–42228. Brookhaven National Laboratory, Upton, New York.

Sundquist, E. T. and G. A. Miller. 1980. Oil shales and carbon dioxide. *Science* 208:740–741.

Tester, J. W., D. W. Brown, and R. M. Potter. 1988. The potential for geothermal energy. In *Proceedings of the Second North American Conference on Preparing for Climate Change*, p. 614. Climate Institute, Washington, DC.

Trexler, M. C., P. E. Faeth, and J. M. Kramer. 1989. *Forestry as a Response to Global Warming: An Analysis of the Guatemala Agriforestry and Carbon Sequestration Project*. World Resources Institute, Washington, DC.

Weinberg, A. M., 1990. Engineering in an age of anxiety. *Issues Sci. Technol.* 6:37–43.

15

The Challenge of Global Warming

Dean Abrahamson

Introduction

The steadily increasing concentrations of greenhouse gases in the atmosphere are stark evidence that limits to the atmosphere's ability to assimilate wastes have been exceeded (Abrahamson 1989a). The first major international conference which considered policy responses to climatic change concluded:

> Humanity is conducting an unintended, uncontrolled, globally pervasive experiment whose ultimate consequences could be second only to nuclear war. . . . Stabilizing the atmospheric concentrations of carbon dioxide is an imperative goal. It is currently estimated to require reductions of more than 50 percent from present emission levels . . . Carbon dioxide emissions [should be reduced] by approximately 20 percent of 1988 levels by the year 2005 as an *initial* goal.*
>
> Government of Canada (1988)

The Earth has already experienced an average warming of approximately $0.7°$ Celsius over the past century. Greenhouse gases already in the atmosphere will increase global temperature by another degree. Releases certain to occur while policy responses are debated and implemented could easily add another couple of degrees. Greenhouse heating, once initiated, is irreversible in times of social, political, and economic relevance. Greenhouse heating, if present trends in greenhouse gas emissions are allowed to continue, could soon cause major dislocations in important economic systems and destroy the icons that have sustained those dedicated to preservation of environmental values.

Uncertainties remain about the degree of global heating that will result from increasing atmospheric burdens of greenhouse gases, about temperature-sensitive feedbacks, and about changes in other climate parameters. These uncertainties, however, are about detail, not about the general situation in which we find ourselves. The United States National Academies of Science and of Engineering and the Institute of Medicine submitted an unprecedented White Paper to then President-elect Bush in late 1988. It included the following statement:

---

* Emphasis added.

We believe that global environmental change may well be the most pressing international issue of the next century. . . . There is a growing perception that the future welfare of human society is to an unknown degree at risk. . . . *Our current scientific understanding amply justifies these concerns.**

National Academy of Science (1988)

Global Heating: The Issue

Carbon dioxide from burning of fossil fuels—coal, petroleum, and natural gas—was the only greenhouse gas generally associated with global warming prior to the early 1980s. Trends suggested that average global temperatures could rise by 1.5 to 4.5°C before the middle of the next century. Concerns regarding the implications of greenhouse heating abated somewhat as fossil fuel consumption growth rates fell sharply in response to government policies and increased energy prices during the late 1970s and early 1980s.

It had been long recognized that CO_2 was not the only greenhouse gas. However, until recently the global heating contribution from the other gases was uncertain. The other gases were examined systematically during the early 1980s. As a result, it became apparent that these gases together contributed at least as much greenhouse heating as did CO_2. Recognizing the importance of these other greenhouse gases doubled the anticipated increase in global temperature.

The 1980s have also seen continued improvement in atmospheric models (Firor 1989, Wetherald, this volume) and the formation of a scientific consensus regarding the importance and general characteristics of global climatic change. As the models became more sophisticated and included more detail, the projected heating from greenhouse gases crept upward. Contemporary models show a climate sensitivity of from nearly 3 to over 5°C for a doubling of atmospheric carbon dioxide or the equivalent in other greenhouse gases. The highest value is at least as likely as the lowest.

General circulation models of the atmosphere include the major geophysical feedbacks but not several recognized biological and chemical feedbacks that make the warming increase as a result of the warming itself. One such feedback is the increased rate of respiration with increasing global temperature, which could produce very large releases of carbon dioxide and of methane from soils and biota (Woodwell 1989). These additional feedbacks, most of which seem to be positive, could result in "a climate sensitivity as great as 8–10°C for an initial radiative forcing equivalent to doubling carbon dioxide" (Lashof 1989). Such a doubling will probably occur by 2030 unless efforts to limit greenhouse gas emissions meet with spectacular success (Schneider 1989).

---

* Emphasis added.

Greenhouse Heating: Policy

The politics of climatic change are also evolving rapidly. The landmark 1979 report to the United States Council on Environmental Quality by Woodwell et al. (1979) was, according to Pomerance (1989), among the first attempts to place the greenhouse effect on the policy agenda. The policy issue was initially framed as prevention versus adaptation. Would it be necessary for society to limit activities that produce greenhouse gases or could we simply adapt to a warming world (Abrahamson and Ciborowski 1988)? This debate could be sustained only while the magnitude and rate of global warming were thought to be small.

The gross inadequacy of a purely adaptive response began to be recognized by the mid-1980s, and a political consensus that it is necessary to slow, eventually halt, and possibly reverse global warming began to form. It has found its expression in statements by heads of state, in legislation, in committee and hearing reports, and in conference statements, most notably the 1987 Villach/Bellagio Conference (Jaeger 1988) and the 1988 Toronto meetings. Recognizing the potentially catastrophic impacts that could result from an average global warming of even a couple of degrees, the 1988 Toronto Conference called for the reduction in carbon dioxide emissions by 20% by the year 2005 as an initial step toward stabilization of the atmospheric concentration. A similar goal has been outlined in other governmental and nongovernmental contexts.

The burning of fossil fuels currently releases approximately 6 billion tons of carbon, in the form of CO_2, to the atmosphere. Deforestation releases another 1–3 billion tons (Houghton, this volume). The total releases of CO_2, and of methane from biota and soils as a result of the global warming experienced to date is not known, but has been estimated to be between 1 and 6 billion tons per year (Woodwell 1989).

Reducing *fossil fuel* emissions by 20% of 1988 levels will require a reduction to approximately the 1975 level of energy use. Unless it is possible to dramatically reduce the rate of deforestation, cutting *total* CO_2 emissions by 20% would require moving global fossil fuel use to the levels of the 1960s. Until the United States halts the destruction of her own old-growth forests, her efforts to force or entice an end to tropical deforestation cannot enjoy much credibility (Booth 1989).

The focus on reducing only CO_2 emissions may have the effect of drawing attention away from the other greenhouse gases. These gases—primarily methane, several chlorofluorocarbons, nitrous oxide, and tropospheric ozone—contribute as much to global heating as does CO_2. It is particularly important that attention be focused on the greenhouse potential as well as the ozone-depleting potential of the CFCs. Although the substitutes being considered have less impact on stratospheric ozone, some of them are powerful greenhouse gases (Shine 1988).

The details of greenhouse gas sources and the subtle chemical interactions between greenhouse gases in the atmosphere are important and provide much grist for scientific mills (Ramanathan et al. 1987). From a broad policy perspective, however, such detail can be distracting. What is important is that the past couple of years have witnessed the realization that global heating must be limited, that it is no longer credible to talk of adaptation as the only appropriate policy response, and that the technical means exist to take a major first step toward climate stabilization.

Reducing Carbon Dioxide Emissions

Sober analyses of governmental actions necessary to actually *achieve* reductions in greenhouse gas emissions are now needed. Happy talk about greenhouse gas reductions which are theoretically possible or about the ease with which societies will be able to adjust to a climatic change predicated upon the most optimistic scenario of global heating is not helpful. It is time for realistic representations of possible future global heating, of impacts of climatic change, and of governmental actions necessary to realize the means to reduce greenhouse gas emissions. How much must energy prices be increased? What energy efficiency regulations are needed? How can a halt to United States and tropical deforestation be achieved? Are there substitutes for industrial chemicals that are not themselves potent greenhouse gases? What actions will be necessary to forestall new commitments to fossil fuels, most importantly coal? What changes in the way we regulate utilities are needed to achieve energy conservation and a shift to renewable energy sources?

Reducing CO_2 emissions by 20% to 1975 levels will but slow, not halt, global heating (Schneider 1989). Stabilization of global climate is an imperative. Estimates have been made of what will be required to stabilize the concentrations of greenhouse gases recently by the United States Environmental Protection Agency (EPA) (Lashof and Tirpak 1989). The EPA analysis, presented with the usual caveats and qualifiers, shows, for example, that CO_2 emissions must be reduced by at least 50 and perhaps 80%.

There are several ways to reduce CO_2 buildup in the atmosphere: a shift from deforestation to reforestation, energy conservation, and switching from fossil to nonfossil energy sources. Carbon dioxide can be removed from the atmosphere and stored in trees. Between one and two million square kilometers of newly planted trees would remove one billion tons of CO_2 per year for 40–60 years until the forest reached maturity. A land area 10 to 20 times the size of the State of New York would be needed to absorb current United States CO_2 emissions and an equal area to compensate for the emissions of the other greenhouse gases (but see Houghton, this volume).

Reforestation can help only if new forests survive. Further analyses are needed to establish where and how new forests could survive in the face of the climatic change that now appears to be unavoidable, and what would be necessary to assure that there would be no harvesting beyond limits of sustainable yield. Forests in the mid- and high-latitudes may be particularly at risk from climatic change (Cook, this volume) and those in the tropics from the axe and the torch. Halting deforestation will also help to maintain genetic diversity, reduce erosion, stabilize local and regional climates, cleanse water and air, and preserve opportunities for future generations.

The vigorous utilization of techniques to increase the efficiency with which energy is used, but with a conventional mix of primary energy supplies, could achieve approximately a 10% reduction in fossil-fuel related greenhouse gas emissions by 2020 (Goldemberg et al. 1988). This could be accomplished even with conventional population growth projections, with energy services in developing countries increasing to the levels of Western Europe in the 1970s, and with an increase of 50–100% in industrial economies. The necessary technology is now available or in advanced stages of development and could be introduced at a conventional rate of capital turnover and expansion. The greenhouse gas emission reductions would not increase the economic cost of energy services over those of the present. Although necessary, increasing efficiency is not sufficient. Achieving the necessary reductions in greenhouse gas emissions will also require shifts in primary energy supply from fossil to nonfossil sources.

There is little hope for slowing climatic change if new commitments continue to be made to coal and the other hydrocarbons. Yet, conventional wisdom is that coal will surpass petroleum as the world's most utilized fuel between now and the middle of the next century, global coal use will triple, and international trade in steam coal will rise 10- to 15-fold (Douglas 1989). The threat posed by growth of coal utilization in China and India is often cited (Ehrlich, this volume) but these countries do not stand alone. Major United States institutions are committed to very large increases in coal utilization. So-called clean coal technology, the deployment of which would increase greenhouse gas emissions, is now slated to receive a public dole of over $500 million of federal funds during the next fiscal year. Continued subsidies of coal, the most environmentally noxious of the fossil fuels, and of destruction of old-growth forests are among the considerations which led to the observation ". . . the implications of the greenhouse phenomenon have not played the slightest role in long-term strategic planning by the [U.S.] government" (Wirth 1989).

Switching from coal and oil to natural gas has been proposed as a near-term measure to reduce greenhouse gas emissions, because burning natural gas produces considerably less CO_2 than does burning oil or coal. Carbon dioxide, however, is not the only greenhouse gas involved. Any appreciable release of natural gas through leakage during gas production, transmission, or distribution would offset the CO_2 advantage enjoyed by natural gas over the other fossil fuels because methane is more than ten times more effective a greenhouse gas as is carbon dioxide. In gas systems where more than 2 or 3% of natural gas is lost to the atmosphere, switching to natural gas would increase rather than decrease global warming (Abrahamson 1989b).

Replacing fossil-fuels with renewable energy systems, primarily solar, will be necessary in addition to energy conservation and replacing deforestation by reforestation (Beyea, this volume, Johansson et al. 1989). There are those who are attempting to use the global warming issue as the basis for a revival of nuclear power or who may soon assert that fusion will provide clean, safe, and abundant energy. Experiments that claim to demonstrate room temperature nuclear fusion have recently been announced. The next few years should clarify this exciting work. Even if fusion feasibility is demonstrated, it could not become a commercial reality within the time available to respond to the threat of global warming.

A reexamination of fission will reveal that its economic, safety, proliferation, diversion, public acceptance, and waste isolation problems are unlikely to be solved (Abrahamson and Johansson 1990). The nuclear weapons proliferation risk which would accompany an attempt to replace global fossil fuel with nuclear fission is staggering. Global commercial energy consumption to sustain the human enterprise now exceeds 10 TW-years (trillion watt-years) per year, 7–8 TW of which is derived from fossil fuels. Replacing the fossil fuel would require between 7,000 and 8,000 large nuclear power plants, each of which would produce approximately 1,000 kg of plutonium annually. Between 7 and 8 million kg of plutonium would therefore be produced per year and would be shipped hither and yon between the various facilities that constitute the nuclear power fuel cycle. Plutonium commercialization would create major hazards because of plutonium's incredible toxicity in addition to its potential use in weapons. Plutonium is the most toxic material ever considered for commerce: a millionth of a gram can cause lung cancer. A typical shipment would contain 250 kg—and there would be approximately 40,000 shipments annually. Approximately 10 kg of plutonium are needed to construct an atomic bomb.

Nuclear power clearly stands out as having risks comparable to those of large and rapid climatic change because of the risk of proliferation of nuclear weapons, the diversion of nuclear explosives by criminals and terrorists, and of accidents and sabotage at nuclear reactors or reprocessing plants. In the long run, there is no evidence that nuclear power is so necessary as to justify accepting these risks. In the short run, investments should be made where they can make the greatest impact on reducing greenhouse gas emissions. Nuclear power could eventually play a role in responding to global heating *only* if proliferation resistant fuel cycles and inherently safe reactors are developed, demonstrated, and achieve public and market acceptance. In the meantime there are other less problematic energy supply options.

Summary

Some may argue that I have not met standards of scientific objectivity, that global warming may not be as serious as has been represented, or that I have not adequately presented the uncertainties. As to objectivity, I am very much aware that the motto of the 1933 Chicago World's Fair—Science Finds, Industry Applies, Man Conforms—is yet the dominant paradigm of contemporary industrialized society.

I have not, as is fashionable, presented the most optimistic case of future climatic change. *If* we are extremely fortunate in that the most favorable outcomes of current climate models ultimately prove to be fact *and* the feedbacks not included in present models prove to cancel each other out, *and if* we pursue aggressive, effective, policies to reduce greenhouse gas emissions, global heating might be limited to 1 or 2°C more than the nearly 1°C warming already observed. Yet even this climatic change would have serious impacts. Hansen (1988), one of the most respected climatologists, has observed:

> In view of the facts that (1) even conservative projections of carbon dioxide and trace gas growth indicate an equivalent doubling of carbon dioxide by the second half of the next century, and (2) the warmest time in the past 100,000 years was only about one degree C warmer than today, we can confidently state that major greenhouse climate changes are a certainty.
>
> Hansen (1988).

Even the most optimistic scenario is bad news.

As to uncertainties, they provide a further compelling reason to slow and halt global climatic change as quickly as possible. If there were no uncertainties, we would at least be able to plan. The National Academy of Sciences (1987) has summarized: "We have little confidence in predictions about many details of the forecasts: local changes by city or state, exact shifts of desert regions or extent of monsoons, changes in river flows, or overall economic impacts." It is these so-called details that would have to be known for a planned response to climatic change, and there is little prospect that climate models will provide them in time.

It may seem that I have made the problem appear very difficult. If so, it is because it is very difficult. We are confronted with major and rapid climatic change, uncertainties about details needed for planning, the necessity to achieve major reductions in the use of the most important energy sources, the apparent inability to halt deforestation either in the United States or in the tropics, questions about the long-term efficacy of reforestation, the possibility that substitutes for the ozone-destroying industrial chemicals will themselves be greenhouse gases, and a society obsessed with short-term interests (see Wyman et al., this volume).

The Brundtland Report (World Commission on Environment and Development 1987) details the challenge of making room for a world population of 8 to 14 billion people within the next century and a several-fold increase in world economic activity. A world with doubled or tripled human population, with a severalfold increase in consumption, and with greenhouse gases, industrial pollutants, and other assaults on the environment proportional to those of today is not only virtually unimaginable, but impossible. We have no alternative but to constrain

consumption and to devise new means of production that can provide the necessary goods and services without causing irreversible biotic impoverishment.

Global climatic change is not simply another pollution issue to be resolved
through microeconomic analyses of marginal tradeoffs. It is not going to go
away by pie-in-the-sky descriptions of evolutionary changes that are theoretically
possible or by invocation of the invisible hand. It will not be resolved by placing
faith in some miraculous technical fix, or by hoping that heretofore unrecognized
natural processes will act to stabilize climate.

Global heating will change the way each of us lives and works. It will also
mean that ours is the last generation in which an individual can generate nearly
a ton of CO_2 from air travel to give a keynote speech about global warming!

References

Abrahamson, D. (ed.). 1989a. *The Challenge of Global Warming*. Island Press, Washington, DC.

Abrahamson, D. 1989b. *Relative Greenhouse Effect of Fossil Fuels and the Critical Contribution of Methane*. Mimeo. Humphrey Institute of Public Affairs, University of Minnesota, Minneapolis, MN.

Abrahamson, D. and P. Ciborowski (eds.). 1988. *The Greenhouse Effect: Policy Responses*. University of Minnesota Center for Urban and Regional Affairs, Minneapolis, MN.

Abrahamson, D. and T. B. Johansson. 1990. Elements of a greenhouse energy strategy. *Bull. Atom. Sci.*, in press.

Booth, W. 1989. New thinking on old growth. *Science* 244:141–143.

Douglas, J. 1989. Quickening the pace of clean coal technology. *Electric Power Research Institute Journal* 14:10–13.

Firor, J. 1989. Greenhouse effects and impacts on physical systems. In *The Challenge of Global Warming*. D. Abrahamson (ed.), pp. 113–122. Island Press, Washington, DC.

Goldemberg, J., T. B. Johansson, A. K. N. Reddy, and R. H. Williams. 1988. *Energy for a Sustainable World*. Wiley Eastern Ltd., New Delhi. A summary version with the same title was published by the World Resources Institute, Washington, DC.

Government of Canada. 1988. The changing atmosphere: implications for global security. In *The Challenge of Global Warming*, D. Abrahamson (ed.), pp. 44–62. Island Press, Washington, DC.

Hansen, J. (ed.) 1988. *Developing Policies for Responding to Climatic Change*, WMO/TD No. 255. World Meteorological Organization, Geneva.

Jaeger, J. 1988. Developing policies for responding to climate change. In *The Challenge of Global Warming*, D. Abrahamson (ed.). pp. 96–107. Island Press, Washington, DC.

Johansson, T. B., B. Bodlund and R. H. Williams (eds.). 1989. *Electricity: Efficient End-use and New Generation Technologies, and Their Planning Implications*. Lund University Press, Lund, Sweden.

Lashof, D. A. 1989. The dynamic greenhouse: Feedback processes that may influence future concentrations of atmospheric trace gases and climatic change. *Clim. Change* 14:213–242.

Lashof, D. and D. Tirpak. 1989. *Policy Options for Stabilizing Global Climate*, Draft. US Environmental Protection Agency, Washington, D.C.

National Academy of Sciences. 1987. *Current Issues in Atmospheric Change*. National Academy Press, Washington, DC.

National Academy of Sciences, National Academy of Engineering, and Institute of Medicine. 1988. *Global Environmental Change*, Washington, DC.

Pomerance, R. 1989. The dangers from climate warming: A public awakening. In *The Challenge of Global Warming*, D. Abrahamson (ed.), pp. 259–269. Island Press, Washington, DC.

Ramanathan, V., L. Callis, R. Cess, J. Hansen, I. Isaksen, W. Kuhn, A. Lacis, F. Luther, J. Mahlman, R. Reck, and M. Schlesinger. 1987. Climate-chemical interactions and effects of changing atmospheric trace gases. *Rev. Geophys.* 25:1441–1482.

Schneider, S. 1989. The greenhouse effect: Science and policy. *Science* 243:771–781.

Shine, K. P. 1988. The greenhouse effect, presented to the Ozone Depletion Conference, London, Nov. 28–29, 1988.

Wirth, D. A. 1989. Climate chaos. *Foreign Policy* 74:3–22.

Woodwell, G. M. 1989. Biotic causes and effects of the disruption of the global carbon cycle. In *The Challenge of Global Warming*, D. Abrahamson (ed.), pp. 71–81. Island Press, Washington, DC.

Woodwell, G. M., G. MacDonald, D. Keeling, and R. Reuelle. 1979. Energy and climate. Report to United States Council on Environmental Quality. U.S. Government Printing Office, Washington, DC.

World Commission on Environment and Development. 1987. *Our Common Future*. Oxford University Press, Oxford and New York.

16

Now What Do We Do?

Richard L. Wyman,
David W. Steadman,
Martin E. Sullivan, and
Marilyn F. Walters-Wyman

Introduction

This chapter, in part, results from a conversation during the conference between R. Houghton and R. Wyman. Houghton said "The conference has been very well attended, the audience is enthused and attentive, and it seems things are going well. There have been several conferences like this one recently, and we have been successful in getting the word out to several thousand people, but now what do we do?" The problem is that there are billions of people on earth, with different . socioeconomic, linguistic, religious, educational, and political backgrounds. How do we reach them all?

As stated by Brown et al. (1989), there is little or no precedent for action on the scale called for during the next decade. The environmental threats now facing the world have so much momentum that unless steps are taken now to reverse them, they will soon overwhelm our ability to respond. The effort must be concerted, rapid, and clearly directed.

The thoughts and analyses presented in this chapter developed after the conference. Several authors have suggested things that can be done in their own chapters; in addition, we thought it would be appropriate to bring them together here and to build upon them in the hope of finding a way to preserve our planet's life support system in all its diversity.

Perspectives from the Book

It is clear that the main problem facing humankind is too many human beings. Several authors suggest that a first environmental and social priority must be the stabilization of the world population. We also must reduce pollution by overdeveloped countries, which means reducing per capita consumption of nonessential commodities; we have to change our life styles. We need to recycle and to increase the efficiency with which we use energy in our automobiles, buildings, and appliances. The development of alternative energy sources, such as solar energy and photovoltaics, is another pressing need. We must help the developing countries establish sustainable societies that do not destroy natural systems and that do not add to greenhouse gases.

We require sound conservation practices now to give species a chance when the climate does change, and we do not have them. Reserves must be designed so that they are larger, interconnected, and contain diverse habitats. Climate models need to become even more sophisticated and they must be able to portray accurately the interactions and feedbacks within the atmosphere/ocean/land surface/ice-system. If model outputs are to be useful to resource managers they need to provide more information on regional, local, and seasonal variability.

Human Behavior, Education, and the Redistribution of Resources

Currently approximately 25% of the world's population is malnourished, and between 10 and 20 million people die each year of starvation, malnutrition, and malnutrition-related diseases. Much of this malnutrition is due to the unequal distribution of resources needed to produce food. The ability to solve many of the problems discussed in this book depends on educating the peoples of the world about the necessity of preserving their environment. A major part of this education must demonstrate that life would be better if families were limited to two or fewer children. Unfortunately these goals are very difficult to accomplish for at least two reasons. First, people who are chronically malnourished and/or starving do not make good students. Second, many people in the Third World must use their remaining natural resources, regardless of scarcity, just to stay alive. How do we overcome these obstacles?

The human animal possesses at least two fundamental behavioral tendencies that complicate any attempt at creating a world that will continue to support us. These are the tendencies to be territorial and to form hierarchically organized systems. Territoriality gives rise to the feeling that *we* are somehow different from *them*. We fight wars because our territory (including perhaps our ideals, goals, social values, and political and religious philosophies) is threatened. We dichotomize peoples of the planet into friend and foe, and resources then become *mine* and *theirs*. Thus we feel little genuine concern when *they* are starving or ruining their environment. Because their environment is our environment, this kind of thinking has to change.

The tendency to organize ourselves into hierarchically organized systems is another fundamental attribute of humans (and many other animals as well, Waal 1989). Our religious, political, military, and educational institutions are examples. Someone has to be the boss and someone else the worker. Quite naturally, this system often results in grossly unfair and unequal distribution of material wealth. This tendency may be at the root of sayings such as "striving to succeed," "climbing to the top," and "the struggle for power." Those that win in this game do so through the accumulation of material wealth. Those that do not win have little or nothing at all. The status-conscience, greed-ridden persona of the 1980s exemplify how our reward system for doing well in a hierarchy can go astray. We must recognize and control these basic tendencies in our behavior, for greed leads to consumption of natural products far beyond sustainable levels.

Our economic system and our nationalism must be flexible and responsive to the needs of all the world's people, not just to those who are fortunate enough to live within our borders. This is because we all need sufficient protein for normal development of neural systems and processes. How can it be that millions of people die in our world for lack of food and other basic needs, while at the same time in the United States we are producing millionaires at a record rate and grocery stores are stocked as never before?

Women and Children

On the average, some behavioral characteristics of male humans differ from those of females (Hrdy 1981). Males tend to be more aggressive, think about short-term success, and how to move up the hierarchy (Wilson 1978). Females tend to be more cooperative, at least among the extended family unit, are long-term thinkers, and show a tendency to be less hierarchically organized. In primitive societies, males are the hunters and females are the gatherers (Irons 1983), and this was probably similar to the social organization of humankind earlier in its history. These differences are reflected in how the sexes interact with their environment. Traditionally men go out and conquer their environment, whereas women have worked with theirs to insure its continued productivity. With the coming of the agricultural and then industrial revolutions, women have lost much of their personal interaction with the earth; they are no longer in control of what happens to it.

Historically, women and children have held a lower position in society than men, and in most cultures they still do. Because of that lower position they have suffered discrimination in income, prestige, and power, including physical abuse and the lack of adequate support structures. The only ones who suffer more in the world today are the children. Because of the likelihood that global climate change coupled with an exploding human population will reduce further the global average standard of living, those people in the poorest economic position and lowest in the hierarchy will bare the bulk of the suffering. These will be women and children.

The already grim realities women and children face will probably worsen considerably as the stresses on existing resources intensify. Food production and distribution are already inadequate, considering 40,000 children die daily from starvation, malnutrition, and malnutrition-related diseases. Per capita grain production has been declining since 1970 in Africa followed by Latin America in the 1980s (Brown et al. 1989). The United States failed to produce a surplus of grain in 1988 and 1989, and the global grain store is down to about 50 days supply (Brown et al. 1989).

Even in the United States and many other developed countries, existing conditions for women and children could stand improvement. Women have not attained equality in pay, insurance rates, employment, housing opportunities, or politics. Fourteen other industrial nations have lower infant mortality rates than the United States, yet the highest standard of living is enjoyed in the United States. The United States lags far behind many other industrialized countries in development and implementation of new birth control methods (Roberts 1990). Legislation affecting child care and education come in second to defense. As is the case virtually everywhere, men comprise the majority of politicians who enact legislation affecting women and children.

Because human overpopulation is the main problem, the solution to environmental decline depends, in part, on women taking charge of their lives, especially their reproductive responsibilities, an issue that affects all others. Individuals must overcome cultural, social, and religious training that prevent them from making environmentally realistic decisions about the number of children they will have. This is a tremendous challenge in many countries. In Zimbabwe, for example, men forbid women to practice contraception because they believe women that do will become promiscuous, contraceptives cause infertility, and users produce disabled offspring (Anonymous 1989).

Most Third World women want to limit the number of children they have. Marta Alma, a 27-year-old Peruvian woman, pregnant with her eighth child says, "I would have liked to have just two children, no more. I don't know what to do with them" (Anonymous 1989). Consider the African mother who represents 60% of the labor force, earns 10% of the total cash income, and grows 80% of the food, although she maybe the last to sit down to a meal. She rises earlier and goes to bed later than anyone else after working up to 18 hours. More children means more work. This could be deadly because her chance of dying during pregnancy is already a frightening 5%.

All governments need to provide funding for family planning, and yet the 1989 budget for international population assistance by the United States was the lowest since 1983 (Brown et al. 1989). The funding needs to address social, cultural, and economic issues that prevent the status of women from rising. We face a moral problem involving the way we view each other and the other life on earth. We suggest that if a different global perspective is to develop concerning the natural world, a change in our attitude, regardless of sex or age, must lead the way.

Education

Education holds our hope for the future. Environmental education should form the backbone of a new global morality. Every student on the Earth should learn to recognize the finite limits of our planet, that we have the ability to alter it's climate and to destroy it's life-support system. We must come to realize that our future can be made brighter only by limiting our family size and by carefully planned, conservative use of natural resources.

Education must also bring about changes in how we all perceive life on earth. To describe living things, we use terms such as resources, pests, game, crops, or harvestable surpluses; and we think that wildlife needs management. What really needs to be managed is the human impact on natural systems. As Vitek (1990) points out, the beliefs of most people in the industrialized world include (1) humans are superior to the rest of the natural world; (2) our moral obligations do not extend to the natural world; (3) nature is a machine, and science is our way of dissecting and controlling it; (4) the Earth has been given to us to populate, modify, subdue, and dominate; (5) land only has value if it is developed; and (6) economic well-being depends upon consumption and expansion. These beliefs have produced the problems we now face.

Environmental education in schools should begin at kindergarten and be integrated through the entire system until graduation. Courses dealing with only environmental issues and ecology should be a part of each year's curriculum. In college all students should be required to take two or more courses on ecology and man and the environment. At the graduate level, we need programs to produce professionals fluent in all aspects of conservation biology, policy, and planning.

We need to train foreign scientists, who will return to their home countries with the ability to create their own educational programs and influence the thinking of policy makers. We need professionals who can manage large nature preserves in the historical context of humans coexisting with other living things. Sustainable development of most of the natural world, while not the best option, is likely to be the only real way to exist on a planet expected to have 8 to 14 billion people.

National and International Politics

Considering the events that have occurred recently in Europe and elsewhere, the world may be entering a new era of international political understanding from which international environmental understanding should be a natural outgrowth. The Soviet Union's ambassador E. Shevardnadze (Report to U.N. General Assembly, 1989) stated "The biosphere recognizes no divisions into blocs, alliances, or systems." The leaders of the United States do not seem to know what to make of these recent and rapid changes. Brown et al. (1989) reports that "sadly rather than leading the way, the nation (United States) has dragged its feet over the last eight years on some key environmental issues." For instance, 21 nations signed the Protocol on the Reduction of Sulfur Emissions to limit acid rain damage, but the United States did not. Although 12 countries agreed to reduce nitrogen oxide emission by 30% over the next decade, the United States did not. While the Prime Ministers of Canada and Norway called for a cut of CO_2 emissions by 20%

by the year 2005, the United States was silent. At a time when the world needs family planning services, the United States withdrew funding from UNFPA. We have not taken advantage of potentially enormous economic and environmental opportunities to develop nonfossil energy sources to curb global warming (Fulkerson et al. 1989).

Even British Prime Minister Thatcher says the Cold War is over and we are now in a "new relationship much wider than the Cold War ever was." It is time for the United States to recognize that security can no longer be bought with military hardware (Brown et al. 1989). Many more countries are threatened by environmental deterioration than by external military aggression. Yet of the $14 billion spent yearly by the United States on foreign aid, one-third or $4.7 billion is for military purchases. Meanwhile, aid for population, energy, and environmental programs totals slightly more than $0.3 billion (Brown et al. 1989).

Clearly we need leaders with a vision of the future, a vision that weighs as heavily the consequences of our actions for our children's children as it does for ourselves.

Priorities in Conservation Research

This section summarizes broadly the most important priorities for research in conservation biology, and it draws heavily from the work of Soule and Kohm (1989). We present research priorities that will help us understand the processes that maintain biotic complexity and priorities that will allow us to protect the diversity which remains (Soule and Kohm 1989).

At the outset, it is clear that we need to know much more about how many species there are and where they are concentrated. We desperately need to inventory the world's biota so that we can identify important areas to protect now. At the same time, we must also recognize that many areas, even though they lack inventories, must be saved today because of imminent threats to their existence.

At the ecosystem level, we need to know what are the functional and spatial characteristics of ecosystems needed to sustain viable populations. How do we recognize keystone species and keystone processes? What are the impacts of global atmospheric and climatic changes? How can deteriorated ecosystems be rejuvenated? A start on answering these question has begun, but much work remains. We are particularly ignorant of processes in tropical ecosystems. Clearly an important approach is long-term studies of basic ecosystem processes, but this kind of research is currently difficult to get funded.

The next level of organization is the community, assuming there is a continuum of ecologic complexity. At this level of study, species interactions are the prime focus. Interactions of central interest are predation, competition, mutualism, diseases, and parasites. What are the important interactions and how do we determine them? Once these questions are answered our focus will shift to managing communities to preserve these keystone processes and interactions and controlling detrimental interactions. Also we will need to ascertain the impacts of invading species (both natural and introduced).

Populations of single species represent another lower level of the ecosystem. Understanding how populations are controlled is vital, because if we fail to save populations, we fail to save biodiversity (Soule and Kohm 1989). Are there general characteristics of rare versus common species? What makes them different and how are they similar? What limits a species to a particular geographic range? Why are some species more prone to range reduction as a result of the human activities, such as those discussed in this book? What can we do to ameliorate the conditions that cause range reductions? Introduced species are often implicated in the decline of native species, yet we are entering a time when humans will be introducing new organisms through bioengineering. How will these new species affect natural systems? Can they be used in biological control of pests without threatening existing species? Finally, natural dispersal represents a means to rejuvenate lost populations through immigration of individuals from populations that are still doing well. We need to be prepared to help in dispersal by providing extensive corridors of natural habitat, thereby perhaps eliminating the need to focus on the problems of individual species.

Genetic studies of populations offer an area of research that may be critical to saving species. Since evolution works through genetic variation, the loss of variation may mean that species will be unable to adapt to even slowly changing conditions. What is the minimum population size needed to maintain genetic diversity in the face of changing environmental conditions? How much inbreeding can species withstand before individuals lose viability? How can we prevent population bottlenecks in time or space that reduce genetic variation? Considering the great diversity of organisms on earth, there is no simple or single answer to any of these questions.

Many animals and plants already require human intervention to save them. Much work remains before we will be able to control propagation of many endangered species. Observations on the most basic aspects of reproductive behavior are lacking for many species. Cryopreservation of germplasm may save some species until their habitats can be restored, but we lack the knowledge and the resources. Research is needed on what constitutes a good release program. Given changing global conditions, we do not even know where to release an endangered species so that it will be safe in the future.

If we can save plant communities we will automatically save many of the associated species. For vast numbers of species we need to know more about the natural process of pollination, seed propagation and seed dispersal. Preservation of large tracts of relatively natural habitat will provide the setting for such research.

Fragmentation of habitats is one of the major threats facing species today and in the future. It affects the ability of populations to sustain themselves through loss of habitat (and hence smaller population size) and through isolation. Yet we know very little about how much habitat fragmentation most species can withstand. How does habitat fragmentation affect basic ecosystem processes, and how small can a fragment become before it's edge dominates these processes? What is the current rate of fragmentation of the world's ecosystems? We also need to know how fragmentation will interact with species to produce detrimental responses because of population size, genetics, diseases, and parasites.

Perhaps the most important thing we need to know is how to get human beings to live nonaggressively with natural diversity. We must confront the development-conservation polarity. How do different societies and cultures perceive the natural world and how can that perception be used and modified to develop sustainable economies without destroying biodiversity? Agriculture must be integrated with nature rather than dominating and supplanting it. Our economic system must change so that success is no longer measured by how much of nature we destroy. We are already the richest country on earth, so why should we strive for an always-growing economy? On a finite planet with limited natural resources (Fig. 16.1), environmental costs (e.g., habitat and species loss and degradation) must be incorporated into formulas used to calculate profit. In this way the profit motive can be used to help the environment.

What You Can Do as an Individual

Limit your family to two or fewer children. Many American couples can afford more than two children, but the planet cannot (Brown et al. 1989). If the United States would adopt a two children per family policy, it would make it easier for the U.N. Secretary General, the President of the World Bank, and other international leaders to espouse such a goal.

Be informed. Become familiar with the facts about environmental problems. Do not allow false or distorted publicity to confuse you. Be aware of the motives behind antienvironmental publicity and lobbies. Three recent climate stabilization bills before Congress faced stiff opposition from the auto, oil, and power industries (Brown et al. 1989), who obviously want you to buy their cars and use their oil and electricity, regardless of the environmental impact. This is the only way that they can make a profit in our current economic system.

Join and become active in as many environmental organizations as your time and finances permit. Support local nature preserves through volunteer work and financial contributions. They are the keepers of biodiversity near you.

In your home you can do many things to make a difference. Remember even small acts by individuals make a difference when multiplied by 5.3 billion. Repair leaky faucets, which can lose up to 100 l of water a day. Take brief showers or shallow baths. Don't wash your dishes, brush your teeth, or comb your hair with the water running. Use low volume toilets that are now available. Do not use

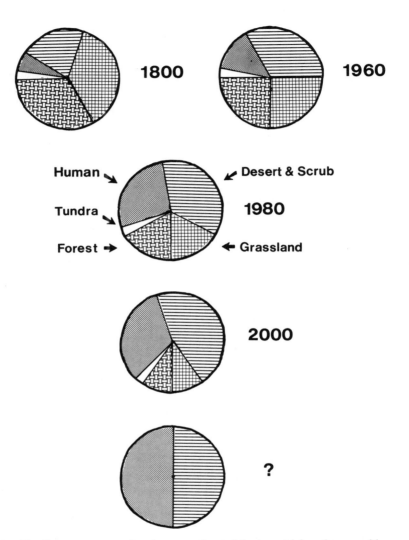

Fig. 16.1. Pie diagrams representing the proportions of the terrestrial earth covered by major ecosystem types for the past 200 years. Human means land dominated by human activity including agriculture. In 1800, grasslands and forests each represented approximately one-third of terrestrial ecosystems. By 1960 grasslands and forests each represented about one-quarter and by 1980 they each represented only about one-sixth of terrestrial systems. By the year 2000, they are projected to each represent only about one-eighth to one-tenth. If the world's human population is not stabilized, greenhouse gas emissions continue to grow, and natural habitats are increasingly destroyed; sometime in the next century natural habitats will disappear. We must work to prevent this scenario from occurring. Data from the Global 2000 Report to the President, Council on Environmental Quality and Department of State (1980).

your toilet as a disposal system for household items that can be disposed of without water.

Conserve energy by turning off unneeded lights and turning down your thermostat. Install energy efficient lights. Compact fluorescent bulbs are available and if used by the United States population could cut CO_2 emission by 10% per year. Separate your garbage and recycle it. The rule should be: Use it until it breaks, fix it, use it again until it cannot be fixed, and then recycle it. Do not buy unnecessary electric appliances like electric knives, can openers, and toothbrushes. These things not only waste energy when you use them, they require great quantities of energy and materials to manufacture. If you must build a home make it energy efficient and leave as much of the natural environment alone as you can, especially the trees and soil.

The average United States automobile emits it own weight in CO_2 each year, a staggering 200 million tons per year for the country. Do not drive when you can walk or ride a bike. It is healthier too. Form car pools when commuting or use mass transit. Support the development of mass transit in communities that lack it. Buy only as large a car as you need and be sure that your car has emission controls that work. Urge auto makers to make cars that last—planned obsolescence should be a crime. Drive sanely. Jack rabbit starts and screeching halts result in excessive fuel consumption and increased tire wear. Do not let your motor idle needlessly. Actively support the development of alternatives to the internal combustion engine. Combination solar power and gas-assisted engines can now get up to 40 km/l. A change from the current 4 km/l to 20 km/l for cars in the United States would result in a reduction of 150 million tons of CO_2 per year (Brown et al. 1989).

You can also help through the kinds of things you do around your home and yard. Whenever possible, plant native trees and shrubs to support indigenous wildlife. Compost organic waste like leaves, twigs, grass clippings, and left over vegetables. Start a garden. During World War II, Americans grew 40% of their own food in backyard gardens. Limit pesticide and herbicide use and eliminate it whenever possible. Use only 'safe' pesticides like those made from plant products, for example, rotenone, pyrethrums, and nicotine sulfate. Mulch your garden to reduce watering. Do not overfertilize. You can even eliminate fertilizers by using compost. Lawns are an especially noxious habit. We use as much fertilizers on our lawns as India uses to feed its people. We contaminate our lawns with herbicides and pesticides. Then we mow them and collect the grass into plastic bags and throw the bags into landfills. We might as well pump the oil used to make the fertilizer, pesticides, and plastic directly from the well into the landfill.

When shopping, take a cloth bag with you that can be reused for years. Do not buy small items packaged individually, especially if the packaging includes nonbiodegradable plastic. If you are given no choice, complain to the store manager. Buy merchandise packaged in recyclable containers. Do not buy disposable diapers. The plastic in them does not break down and they contain dioxin. Avoid aerosol cans, which are costly, dangerous to the ozone layer, and difficult to dispose. Buy things in bulk whenever you can. Make your own baby food— the baby food jar, lid, and label represent at least 36% of the cost. Never buy novelties, clothing, or accessories made from the skin or other parts of rare or endangered animals and plants. This includes furniture made from tropical hardwood trees. Avoid buying products from companies known to be environmentally insensitive.

In your community you should learn about zoning and planning actions and encourage environmental awareness in those activities. Protest unnecessary roads, highways, airports, shopping centers, and other land-clearing activities. Actively resist the development of dams, stream channels, and canals. They destroy natural environments. Support the development of local sewage processing facilities even if it means higher taxes. Encourage and financially support the development of local green belts and forest corridors. The mowed land along our nation's highways could support billions of trees. Fight the location of polluting industries in or near your town or city.

Speak out, pass the word along, and inform others. Become strident. Write or call your local, state, and national elected officials, give them details about environmental issues and ask them to take immediate action. When they fail to do so, tell them. If they do not respond appropriately, do not vote for them. In your local, state and federal elections, vote and work for candidates with an environmental conscience. Support politicians who favor family planning in this country and in other countries. Encourage and vote for politicians who believe in a sustainable future. Ask them, for example, to promote legislation that would make the development of photovoltaics a reality. This might include tax incentives and subsidies for entrepreneurs willing to develop these and other alternative energy strategies.

Uniting Environmental Organizations

Currently there are many environmental organizations and institutions that are working independently of one another. In many regards they are remaking the wheel with each new undertaking and activity. A mechanism needs to be found that can bring these organizations and institutions together. They all share many common goals and objectives, and their ability to communicate those goals and objectives to the public and to politicians would be strengthened greatly if they were represented as a united front.

Conclusion

"It is absurd to consider that all human activities are justifiable because humans are part of nature . . . (because) today our species is capable of wholesale elimination of biotas and ecosystems" (Soule and Kohm 1989). We are using our ability to destroy the life support system of the planet (Fig. 16.1) (Odum 1987).

The scope of the problems we face—overpopulation, global climate change, air and water pollution, deforestation, loss of biodiversity, sea level rise—makes it seem that there is nothing one person can do. This is not true. Human beings create the problems, human beings can solve them. We must start now. Time is running out.

References

Anonymous. 1989. Zimbabwe promotes male responsibility. *Popline* March–April:3.

Brown, L. R., C. Flavin, and S. Postel. 1989. No time to waste: A global environmental agenda for the Bush Administration. *World Watch* 2:10–19.

Fulkerson, W., D. B. Reister, A. M. Perry, A. T. Crane, D. E. Kash, and S. I. Auerbach. 1989. Global warming: An energy technology R & D challenge. *Science* 246:868–869.

Hrdy, S. B. 1981. *The Women that Never Evolved*. Harvard University Press, Cambridge, MA.

Irons, W. 1983. Human female reproductive strategies. In *Social Behavior of Female Vertebrates*, S. K. Wasser (ed.), pp. 169–213. Academic Press, New York.

Odum, E. P. 1989. *Ecology and our Endangered Life-Support System*. Sinauer. Sunderland, MA.

Roberts, L. 1990. U.S. lags on birth control development. *Science* 247:909.

Soule, M. E. and K. A. Kohm. 1989. *Research Priorities for Conservation Biology*. Island Press. Washington, DC.

United States Council on Environmental Quality and Department of State. 1980. *The Global 2000 Report to the President: Entering the Twenty-first Century* Vols. I–III. U.S. Government Printing Office, Washington, DC.

Vitek, W. 1989. Environmental education: A framework for the future. Testimony presented to the New York State Assembly and Senate Environmental Conservation Committees. Joint Hearings on Environmental Education. Dec. 11, 1989.

Waal, F. de-. 1989. *Chimpanzee Politics: Power and Sex among Apes*. The Johns Hopkins University Press, Baltimore, MD.

Wilson, E. O. 1978. *On Human Nature*. Harvard University Press. Cambridge, MA.

Index